GOOD $ENSE

BUDGET COURSE

Biblical Financial Principles for
Transforming Your Finances and Life

BUDGET COURSE

Biblical Financial Principles for Transforming Your Finances and Life

Leader's Guide

**Dick Towner
and John Tofilon**

With contributions from the
Good $ense Ministry team of
Willow Creek Community Church

GRAND RAPIDS, MICHIGAN 49530

Requests for information should be addressed to:
Willow Creek Association
67 E. Algonquin Road
Barrington, IL 60010

Zondervan
5300 Patterson SE
Grand Rapids, MI 49530

ISBN: 0-744-13727-6

Cover design by Rick Devon, Adam Beasley

Interior design by Ann Gjeldum

Produced with the assistance of the Livingstone Corporation. Project staff includes: Ashley Taylor, Christopher D. Hudson, Carol Barnstable, and Paige Drygas.

Printed in the United States of America

03 04 05 06 07/ /10 9 8 7 6 5 4 3 2

DEDICATION

Dick Towner

To Pop and Gram Wernicke who raised me and modeled for me a simple and frugal lifestyle. While their lifestyle was shaped in part by income circumstances, it was lived with contentment, making it easy for me to later accept the biblical truth that a person's life does not consist in the abundance of their possessions.

To my incredibly gifted and incredibly loving wife, Sibyl, who helped me to understand that frugality for its own sake simply leads to sinful hoarding, but that the true end result of frugality is liberality. Thank you, dear Sibyl, for modeling this for me and for helping me to experience the joy of giving.

And finally, to the body of believers known as College Hill Presbyterian Church in Cincinnati, Ohio. Not only did you baptize me as a child, nurture me as a teenager, marry me as a young adult, mature my faith, ordain me as an elder, and allow me to serve as part of the ministerial team for fourteen years, but you encouraged and provided the platform for the development of the vast majority of what is contained within these pages. My gratitude is beyond expression.

John Tofilon

There is nothing like getting involved in what God is doing, especially when the tug of the Holy Spirit turns into a lifelong calling. This project is dedicated to the following people whose influence has enabled me to fulfill that calling.

To Bruce Saarela, for giving me the opportunity over twenty years ago to develop my skills and passion by designing and teaching budget seminars. To Kent Carlson, for making "the ask" ten years later to get back in the game. To Dick Towner, for leaving the door wide open for me to be creative, sometimes at the cost of his sanity. To Bill Hybels, for challenging me to lean into my calling. To my wife,

Charlotte, for thirty years of being my support; and to our three children—David, Christopher, and Kaitlin—for enduring my budget mantras. To the Lord for showing me the need, giving me the vision, and sustaining me through it all.

Finally, this project is dedicated to you, the reader and course participant. I hope and pray this course helps you on your journey to becoming the person God wants you to be.

CONTENTS

Foreword 9

Acknowledgments 11

Preface 13

How to Use the Leader's Guide 15

1. The Financial Dilemma 25

2. Earning, Giving, and Saving 67

3. Saving and Debt 109

4. Spending 159

5. Balancing the Spending Plan 203

6. Record Keeping and Commitment 223

Appendix 271

FOREWORD

In school they tell us we're being equipped to earn it. Then for the rest of our lives—for about fifty or sixty hours a week—we're busy making it. We invest countless hours in thought and discussion deciding how to deal with it. We walk around shopping malls for hours on end determining how we're going to spend it. We're caught up more often than we'd like to admit worrying we won't have enough of it. We dream and scheme to figure out ways to acquire more of it.

Arguments over it are a leading cause for marital disintegration. Despair over losing it has even led to suicide. Passion for it causes much of society's crime. The absence of it causes many of society's nightmares. Some view it the root of all evil, while others think of it as the means for great good.

One thing is clear: We cannot afford to ignore the reality of the importance of *money.*

Over the years at Willow Creek Community Church we've been committed to tackling every important issue that faces the people who attend—from nutrition to sexuality, from building character to deepening relationships, from discovering and adoring the identity of God to preparing for death and eternity. One topic, however, that we've learned we must address regularly and directly is the subject that Christians wrestle with almost every day—the issue of how we handle personal finances.

Thankfully, there's no shortage of information on this crucial matter in the Bible, and it provides the basis for the materials you're about to dive into. More than two thousand Scripture passages touch on the theme of money. Jesus spoke about it frequently. About two-thirds of Jesus' parables make reference to our use of financial resources. He once warned that "where your treasure is, there your heart will be also." He talked often about these matters because he understood what was at stake. He knew that, left to our own devices, this area would quickly become a source of pain and frustration—and sometimes bondage. Worse, he saw how easily our hearts would be led astray from pure devotion to God into areas of worry and even obsession over possessions. He wanted to protect us from these pitfalls and to show us the liberty that comes from following him fully in every area of life, including this one.

So get ready to join the ranks of thousands of people from our church and other churches who have received tangible help in this area through Good $ense. This vital ministry has been refined and proven over many years by my friend and trusted co-laborer, Dick Towner, along with his Good $ense Ministry team. I'm confident you'll find fresh avenues to increased financial freedom and, along the way, grow a more grateful spirit and generous heart.

And as you and others from your congregation experience this, your church will be liberated so it can reflect more and more of that giving spirit and heart to the community around you, making it a magnet to people who are desperately looking for the kind of freedom, life, and love they see in you.

Bill Hybels
Founding and Senior Pastor
Willow Creek Community Church

ACKNOWLEDGMENTS

There are literally hundreds of people at Willow Creek Community Church and the Willow Creek Association whose expertise, support, wide array of contributions and encouragement were crucial throughout the development and completion of this project. Though space limitations prohibit naming all of them, their ranks include the following:

- The early group of volunteers and staff member George Lindholm who responded to God's vision in 1985 and began the Good $ense Ministry. Their leadership ranks included Warren Beach, Bill and Loretta Gaunt, John Frederick, Chuck Keenon, Jim Kinney, and Carl Tielsch. Stalwarts of the early counseling team included Bill and Joann Allen, Bob Baker, Candy Borst, Barry Gardner, Don and Zona Hackman, Dan Hollerick, Charlie Maxwell, Elizabeth Maring, Tom Stevens, Cyndy Sutherland, and Carol White. Staff assistance in the early years also came from Bruce Bugbee and Ken Fillipini.
- Current Good $ense volunteers, especially the following who have played an active role in the development of the materials: Russ Haan, Jerry Wiseman, Steve Sherbondy, Jenifer Nordeen-Lugar, Dan Rotter and Sue Drake. Thank you for your creativity and passion and the many contributions you made. Thanks, too, to the volunteer Good $ense Ministry Board, not only for your wise counsel and direction over the years, but even more for the deep bonds of friendship and mutual call to ministry we have shared.
- Norm Vander Wel and Jon Kopke, two friends of the heart who, though not connected with Willow Creek, provided insight and creativity and encouragement that was exceedingly helpful.
- Jim Riley, who followed me as director of the Good $ense Ministry at Willow Creek Community Church, and has been a true companion of the heart in seeking to help folks understand and implement biblical principles of stewardship in their lives. Thank you, Jim, for your commitment to this project and for your deep friendship.

- Wendy Seidman and her team—Bridget Purdome, Sue Drake, and Rebecca Adler. Their expertise in instructional design makes these materials effective in training and equipping people. Thanks to each of you not only for sharing your expertise but for taking the core values of this project into your own hearts.
- Christine M. Anderson, who managed the project, interjected her insights and wisdom at all the right times, provided encouragement when it was most needed, and exhibited amazing patience as we worked and reworked and reworked the material.
- Bob Gustafson, Steve Pederson, and Sharon Sherbondy for their expertise and enthusiasm in creating video segments that not only teach and train but also touch the heart.
- Bill Hybels, senior pastor. Early in his ministry Bill recognized and affirmed the vital connection between a biblical understanding of material possessions and ones spiritual well being. Over the years, his commitment to regular, passionate teaching on this topic has been an invaluable support and encouragement to the Good $ense Ministry . . . and a significant contribution to its effectiveness.
- Jim Mellado, Sharon Swing, and the entire Willow Creek Association Leadership Team for catching the vision for this project and for their support and encouragement as we worked to realize that vision.
- Joe Sherman and the publishing and marketing team at the Willow Creek Association for providing the resources to produce this curriculum and for believing it can make a difference is so many lives.
- Several donors whose faith in this project and generous financial contributions not only provided initial funding but were also a great encouragement to me personally.

PREFACE

We applaud you for teaching the *Good $ense Budget Course.* There is a tremendous need for churches today to educate and assist people with managing their resources in God-honoring ways. Your willingness to teach this course is a vital part of making this happen. To counter the persuasive and pervasive messages of our materialistic culture, people must hear God's truth and be trained and equipped to apply these truths to their lives. As the teacher of the *Good $ense Budget Course,* it is your privilege and your challenge to allow God to use you in this way.

There are many excellent reasons to teach this course. It may be you are motivated to teach because you have considerable expertise in money management and have handled your own finances in wise and God-honoring ways. Perhaps you desire to help free people from the crushing stress and anxiety caused by consumer debt; to help heal the wounded self-esteem and shattered confidence resulting from poor financial decisions; or to help strengthen marriages weakened by conflict over money. All of these are wonderful motivations for undertaking the challenge of teaching the *Good $ense Budget Course.*

But there is another vitally important reason for teaching this course. God can use your teaching to remove major stumbling blocks to spiritual growth and development in the lives of those you teach. There is a direct correlation between a person's relationship to money and stuff, and their relationship to God. The Bible clearly states we cannot serve both God and money (Matthew 6:24). Money can steal our hearts from God (Matthew 6:21). Concern over things of the world and the deceitfulness of riches can choke out God's Word in our lives (Matthew 13:22). Scripture is clear: money can become a rival god in our lives if we don't handle it in God-honoring ways. However, when money is no longer a rival god; when money no longer controls a person but the person controls money; and when the deceitfulness of riches is exposed and can no longer choke out God's Word, individuals are freed up to relate to God and to serve God in profoundly new and deeper ways. And you get to be a part of God's liberating work!

Nearly thirty years of teaching the Biblical Financial Principles contained in the *Good $ense Budget Course* have convinced us of its power to be used by God to change lives. And that is the ultimate purpose of this course—to change people from the inside out regarding their relationship to money and stuff.

Everything you need to effectively teach the course is provided. However, these materials alone cannot bring about life change and spiritual transformation. It will take the power of the Holy Spirit working through you for that to happen. In addition to thoroughly studying the content and practicing your presentation, we urge you to also prepare yourself spiritually. Reflect on the biblical texts and let them speak to you personally. Spend time in prayer and ask others to pray that God will speak through you. Consult the Recommended Resources list in the Appendix and do additional reading. If you can consult only one additional resource, we strongly recommend Randy Alcorn's *Money, Possessions and Eternity.*

One final word of encouragement. Don't be discouraged if fewer people than you hoped attend the course the first time it is offered. While some churches have been overwhelmed at the initial positive response, this is not always the case. People are often cautious about this very delicate and sensitive subject. However, the experience of nearly two decades of Good $ense Ministry at Willow Creek Community Church have proven that once the course is presented and lives are changed, word spreads and enthusiasm for the course grows. Inevitably, attendance at subsequent course offerings increases. When you speak with people about the course and promote it to your congregation, be sure to point out that it is for those at all points along the financial continuum, not just for those in financial difficulty.

Thank you for stepping forward to undertake this very important task. Our prayer is that God will use you in a special and powerful way.

Dick Towner and John Tofilon

HOW TO USE THE LEADER'S GUIDE

This Leader's Guide has been prepared to help you present this course in the most effective manner possible. These introductory pages provide ideas for presenting the sessions and list the materials and equipment required.

Group Size

The *Good $ense Budget Course* works with any size group:

- Small groups of less than 10
- Large groups of 10 to 100 people or more.

Although directions for the various group activities throughout this course have been written for medium to large sized groups, the instructions are easily transferred into small group situations. Small groups provide an excellent forum for presenting the *Good $ense Budget Course* because members of the group know each other, can encourage each other, and are there to hold each other accountable to apply the principles and skills they learn.

Format Options

The *Good $ense Budget Course* can be presented successfully in a number of delivery formats:

- **One-day workshop**
  There are six, 50-minute sessions in this course which total approximately five hours of content. In a one-day format, you would also need to allow time for lunch—45 to 60 minutes—and breaks. Short breaks of 5 to 10 minutes are recommended following Sessions 1 and 4; longer breaks of 15 to 20 minutes are recommended following Sessions 2 and 5. You may wish to use the following as a suggested schedule:

9:00 –	9:50 A.M.	Session 1: *The Financial Dilemma*
9:50 –	10:00 A.M.	*Break*
10:00 –	10:50 A.M.	Session 2: *Earning, Giving, and Saving*
10:50 –	11:10 A.M.	*Break*

11:10 – 12:00 NOON	Session 3: *Saving and Debt*
12:00 – 1:00 P.M.	*Lunch*
1:00 – 1:50 P.M.	Session 4: *Spending*
1:50 – 2:00 P.M.	*Break*
2:00 – 2:50 P.M.	Session 5: *Balancing the Spending Plan*
2:50 – 3:10 P.M.	*Break*
3:10 – 4:00 P.M.	Session 6: *Record Keeping and Commitment*

Rather than dispersing for lunch, consider providing a simple meal so participants can relax and spend time with each other. In addition to promoting camaraderie and interaction, this is also a great way to make sure you stick to the schedule.

Although the amount of time shown for each session is 50 minutes, we encourage you to allow more time. You may find that you will need additional time for the activities. The time allotted is intended to keep you and the participants moving quickly through the material. The 50 minutes does not include any extra time needed by some participants to complete the exercises, nor does it include any time for answering questions. To present a session in 50 minutes, it is necessary to maintain a brisk pace and strictly observe the times indicated in the Leader's Guide.

- **Six sessions of 50 minutes each**
  Teaching the sessions over six weeks gives participants time to absorb the material and put into practice what they have learned each week. If you teach the course over six weeks, plan on at least one hour for each session. This way you will be able to allow extra time for completing activities and answering questions.

- **Two sessions of 3 hours and 30 minutes each**
  By teaching Sessions 1, 2, and 3 together, and then teaching Sessions 4, 5, and 6 together, you can effectively present the course in two sessions. If you present the course in this format, allow at least one hour for each session with a 10-minute break after the first session and a 20-minute break after the second session.

- **One-, two-, or three-day retreats**
  In a retreat format you have flexibility to present the material to accommodate your schedule.

Participant Pre-work

Prior to attending the *Good $ense Budget Course,* participants are asked to complete the pre-work portion of the Participant's Guide. The pre-work is *strongly* encouraged and makes the course more valuable and productive for the participant.

Participant Activity

In this course, the deepest learning occurs when participants are working—in individual or group activities—not when the instructor is working (lecturing or presenting the content). The participant clearly gains new insights and knowledge from the lecture/content, and it is an invaluable part of the course; however, for participants to be transformed by that new information, they need time to process it.

The *Good $ense Budget Course* provides two primary ways for participants to process what they learn. These include individual, and small group activities. For example:

- Individual activity—giving participants time to work on their Spending Plans so they can wrestle with the numbers and determine actions steps they want to take
- Group activity—giving participants time to process with others the insights and ideas they just learned

How This Leader's Guide Is Organized

Each of the five sessions is divided into the following parts:

Session Snapshot

Provides a brief summary of the content to be discussed in the session and the overall context into which the session fits.

Objectives

Describes what participants are to accomplish and learn in that session.

Outline

Provides an overview of the content and sequence to be covered in the session.

Session Introduction, Discovery, and Summary

Describes the actual "teaching" part of the session containing the content to be presented, which is keyed to the visual aids to be used in the session. This material is presented in two columns as shown in the following example:

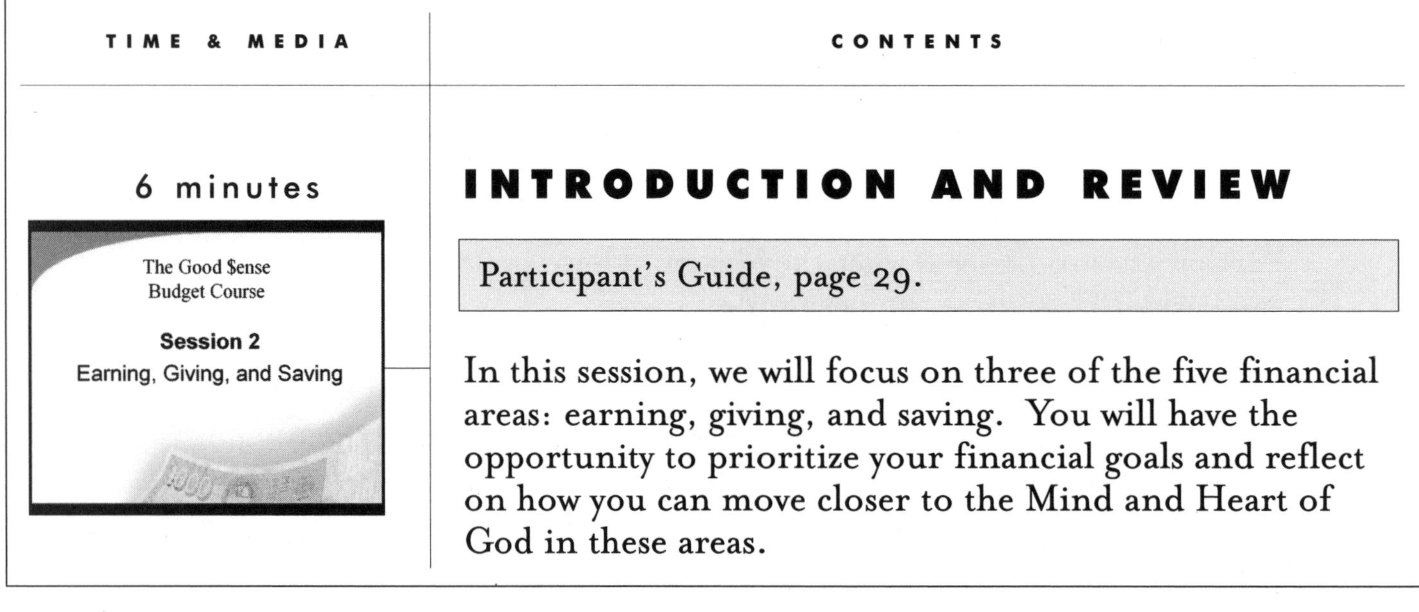

TIME & MEDIA	CONTENTS
6 minutes	**INTRODUCTION AND REVIEW**
The Good $ense Budget Course Session 2 Earning, Giving, and Saving	Participant's Guide, page 29. In this session, we will focus on three of the five financial areas: earning, giving, and saving. You will have the opportunity to prioritize your financial goals and reflect on how you can move closer to the Mind and Heart of God in these areas.

The Time and Media Column

The TIME notations indicate suggested times for each content block. Note: These times include just the CONTENTS portion of each session. They do not allow for any question-and-answer time, nor extra time participants may need to complete activities.

The MEDIA graphics indicate when video and PowerPoint slides (or overhead transparencies, if you're using that option) should be presented.

Included on the *Good $ense Budget Course* CD-ROM are two folders. If your facility is equipped with the computer equipment required to use PowerPoint software, the folder named "Sessions for Viewing" contains files for a four-color, electronic presentation.

If you will be using a standard overhead projector and transparencies, the folder "Sessions for Printing" contains files for black-and-white transparencies. To make overhead transparencies, you may use one of two methods.

1. Print out the files on your computer printer, using the appropriate type of transparency for your particular printer.

2. First print the files on white paper. Place a sufficient number of overhead transparency sheets (the kind specifically made for copiers) in the paper tray of a photocopier, and then run the printout through the copier. Your local full-service copy center should be equipped to make transparencies if you do not have access to the necessary equipment.

The Contents Column

The CONTENTS column is a detailed guide to the course material. If you had to, you could read this column start to finish, word-for-word, and the material would be presented completely and in the correct order. However, the more effective way is for you to use this information as a resource as you prepare to present the six sessions.

We recommend that you personalize this material by using your own words and illustrations. You might want to highlight key words and phrases so you'll be able to teach without having to read it word-for-word. If you prefer to write down your own material, there is space provided under the NOTES area (see "Notes" on page 29). Practice each session—including PowerPoint and video—at least once before presenting it to make sure you are comfortable with the material and are able to keep to the time you have allotted for the session. Also, be sure to have all visual aids organized and ready to use.

The CONTENTS column includes the following key elements:

1. The instructor narrative is shown in this standard typeface.

> No matter what the specific cultural myth is that influences us most, all of us are influenced by our culture and by this powerful stuff called money.

2. Statements the instructor should read *verbatim* are set off with an arrow. It is important to read these texts word-for-word because they appear in the Participant's Guide. Sometimes more than one paragraph is indented following an arrow. Every indented paragraph following an arrow should be read verbatim.

> Throughout this course we will contrast what the culture says about money with what the Bible says about money.
>
> We're also going to develop personal Spending Plans that will empower each one of us to achieve our financial goals.

3. Words shown in ALL CAPITAL LETTERS are words participants need to fill in the blanks found on the corresponding pages in their Participant's Guides.

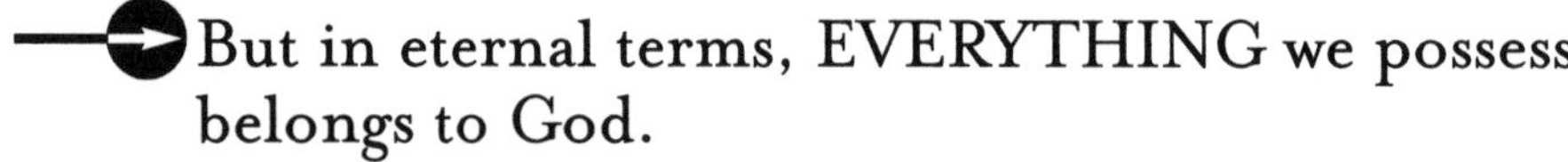

> But in eternal terms, EVERYTHING we possess belongs to God.

4. If you are using PowerPoint slides (rather than transparencies) the slides corresponding to content appear in the TIME & MEDIA column as show in the example below. When a slide has multiple points and "builds," the following symbol ▶ appears as a prompt to advance to the next point:

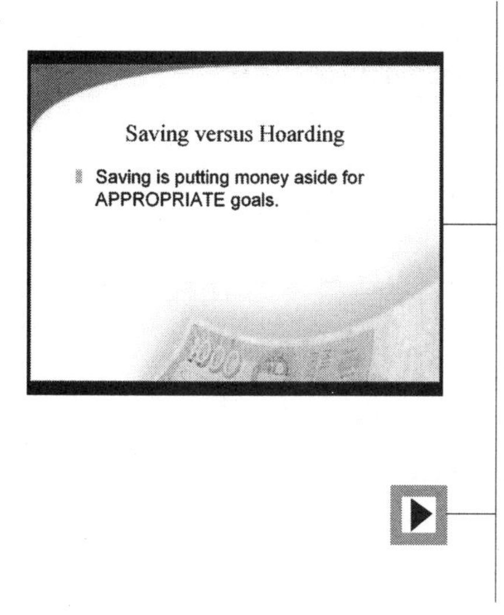
Saving versus Hoarding
Saving is putting money aside for APPROPRIATE goals.

▶

These Scriptures teach that it is wise to save for unexpected hardship, but also that it is foolish to stockpile beyond our needs.

→ So, what's the difference between saving and hoarding?

Saving is putting money aside for APPROPRIATE goals like retirement, education, etc.

Hoarding is continuing to put money aside after our goals are reached.

5. Directions to the instructor are shown in a contrasting typeface and enclosed in a shaded box. These directions are *not to be spoken* by the instructor.

> Call the group back together after 11 minutes.
>
> Who is influenced most by the first myth: "Things bring happiness"? Raise your hand.

6. A variety of activities are included throughout the course to help participants learn by talking to each other or working on their own. These include individual and small group activities.

Notes
Provides space to write your own words and illustrations to customize your presentation and replace portions of the instructor narrative.

Participant's Guide Pages
Allows you to view the page(s) participants are seeing as you talk without having to hold two books at the same time. It also helps you immediately know where the participants are in their books when someone asks.

Master Materials List

To present the *Good $ense Budget Course,* the following materials and supplies are needed:

- Leader's Guide
- Participant's Guides
- Name tags and markers
- Computer and projection equipment with CD-ROM disk if using PowerPoint slides. Be sure to test all components together before each class. Or, overhead projector, screen, transparencies, and pens if using overheads. Before each class, check to be sure transparencies are in the correct order, the projector works, and there are spare bulbs and pens.
- *Good $ense Budget Course* video cassette
- Video player and monitor—set up and ready to play—as well as all necessary cords and cables
- Extra calculators
- Optional: tape or CD player for music. Use this before and after sessions, as well as during breaks, to create a welcoming and relaxed atmosphere.

Facility Setup

To create a comfortable and relaxed atmosphere, we recommend using round tables. As shown in the example on the next page, seat four to six people at each table, leaving an open space at the front so no one has their back to the instructor.

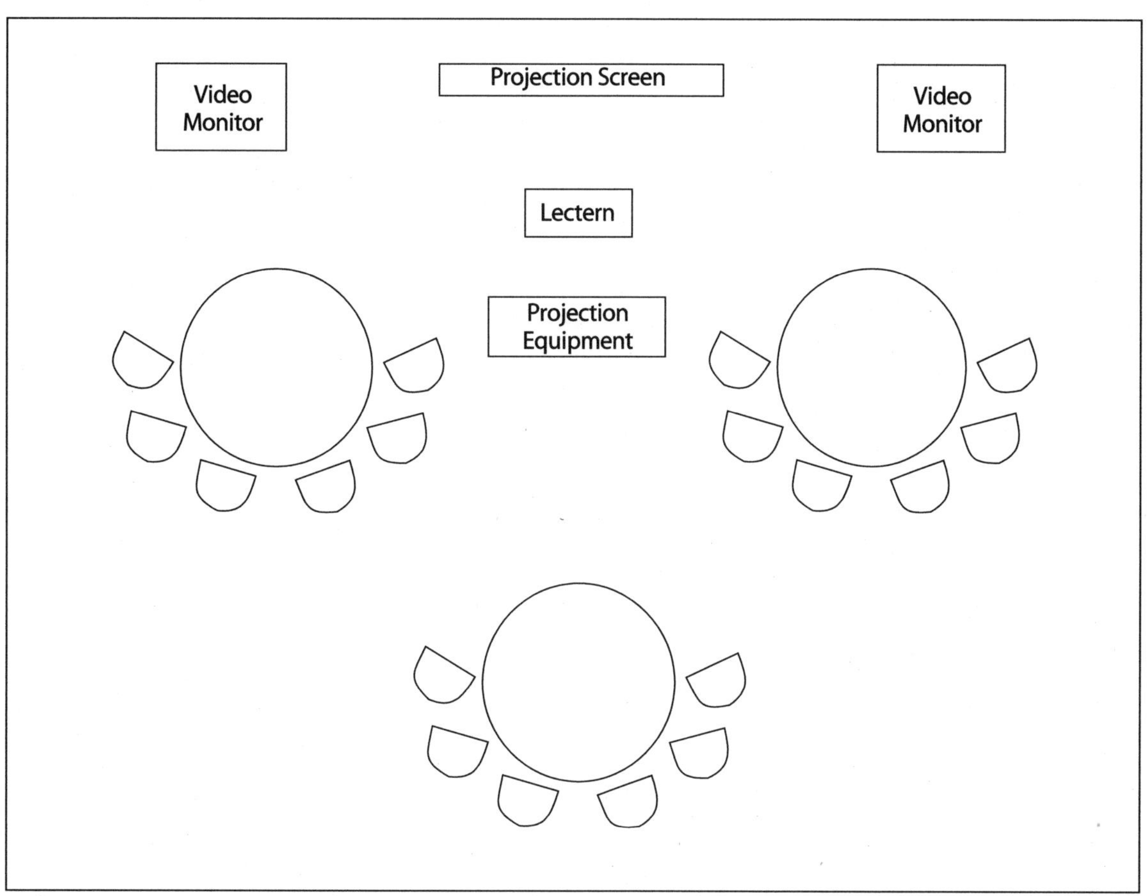
Video Monitor
Projection Screen
Video Monitor
Lectern
Projection Equipment

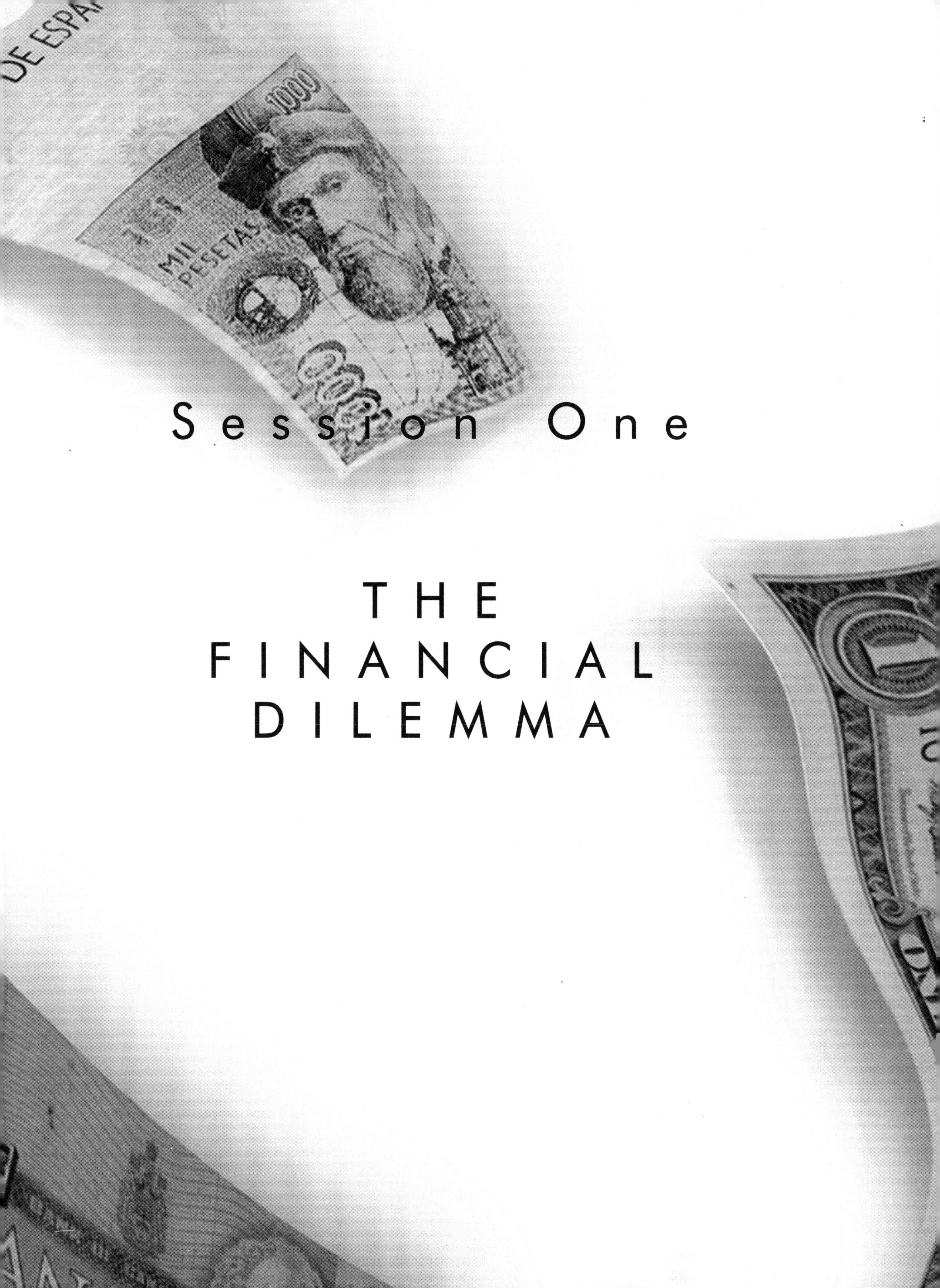

Session One

THE FINANCIAL DILEMMA

SESSION SNAPSHOT

OBJECTIVES

In this session, participants will:

1. Discover three prominent cultural myths about money.
2. Identify which cultural myth influences them most.
3. Reflect on how being a "trustee" versus an "owner" affects them.
4. Discover what a Spending Plan is and what its benefits are.

OUTLINE

I. Introduction and Welcome

II. Discovery

A. The Pull of the Culture
1. Video: *The Pull of the Culture*
2. Group Activity: *The Pull of the Culture*
3. Course Overview

B. The Mind and Heart of God
1. Three Truths
2. Video: *The Pearl of Great Price*
3. Group Activity: *The Pearl of Great Price*

C. The Pull of the Culture vs. the Mind and Heart of God
1. The Financial Dilemma
2. Five Financial Areas

D. The Spending Plan
1. What Is a Spending Plan?
2. The Benefits of a Spending Plan

III. Session Summary

THE FINANCIAL DILEMMA

TIME & MEDIA | **CONTENTS**

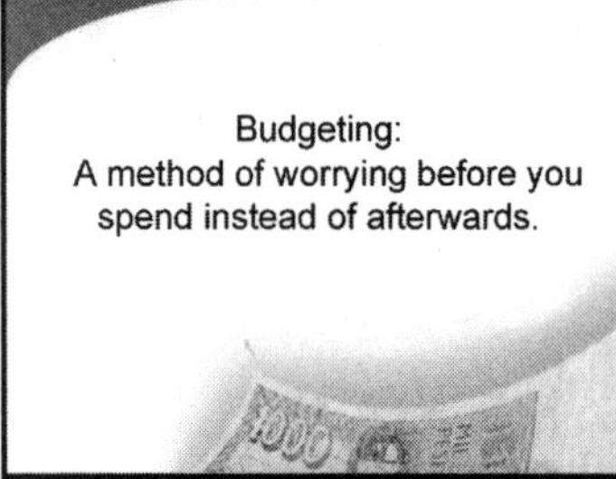

Budgeting:
A method of worrying before you spend instead of afterwards.

PowerPoint: *Financial Quotes*

Approximately 10 minutes prior to the beginning of the course, begin showing the *Financial Quotes* PowerPoint presentation.

Approximately 2 minutes prior to starting, ask participants to introduce themselves to those at their tables and share how long they have been attending the church.

INTRODUCTION AND WELCOME

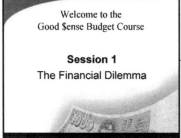

Welcome to the
Good $ense Budget Course

Session 1
The Financial Dilemma

1 minute

1. Call the group together.
2. Welcome participants to the *Good $ense Budget Course.*
3. Introduce yourself.

DISCOVERY (47 minutes)

Participant's Guide, page 16.

Welcome to the *Good $ense Budget Course.* Congratulations! You've taken a big step by being here.

→ Even though budgeting may be difficult, I firmly believe you can do it!

God believes you can do it too.

NOTES

Introduction and Welcome

You can do it!

> Philippians 4:13: "*I can do everything through him who gives me strength.*"

"Money is a powerful thing!"

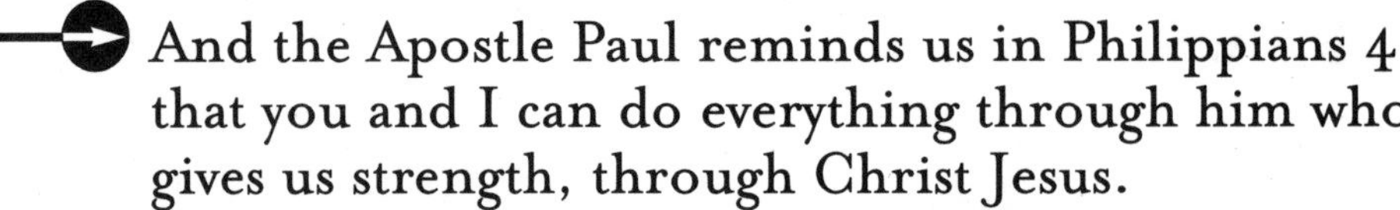

And the Apostle Paul reminds us in Philippians 4 that you and I can do everything through him who gives us strength, through Christ Jesus.

Optional Activity
Invite participants to affirm each other by asking them to: "Turn to the person next to you and say, 'You can do it!'"

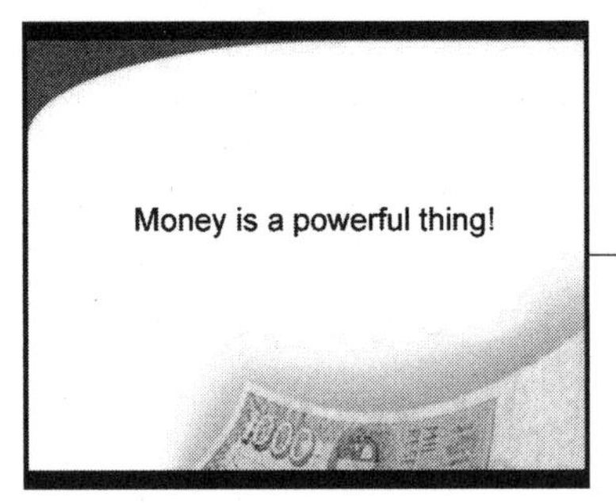
Money is a powerful thing!

There is a song entitled, "Money Is a Powerful Thing." The chorus goes like this: "Money is a powerful thing. It's more than green paper or a means of exchange. Money's got a powerful pull. It sits in your bank account and works on your soul. Money, money, money is a powerful thing."

The words to that song are so true. Money *is* a powerful thing. Because it's so powerful and works on our souls, many of us find it challenging to handle it well.

Most of us are here because we want our financial lives to be in order, and because we want to understand and experience the reality of genuine financial freedom. It's a journey and all of us are at different places. Some of us are just beginning and others of us are well on our way.

2 minutes

The Pull of the Culture

Participant's Guide, page 17.

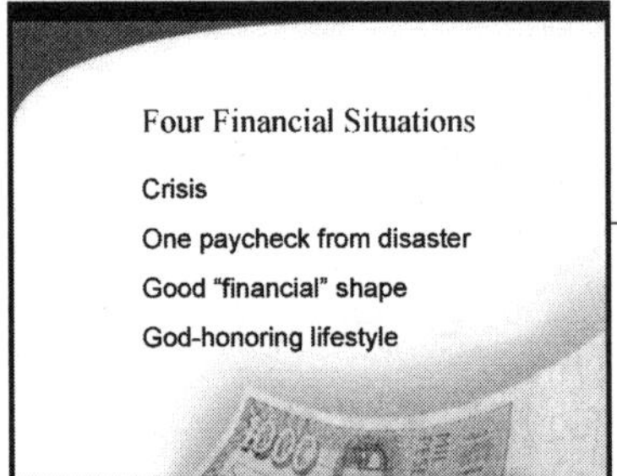
Four Financial Situations
Crisis
One paycheck from disaster
Good "financial" shape
God-honoring lifestyle

The reality is that most of us find ourselves in one of four financial situations:

- Crisis
- One paycheck from disaster
- Good "financial" shape
- God-honoring lifestyle

Let's take a closer look at each one.

NOTES

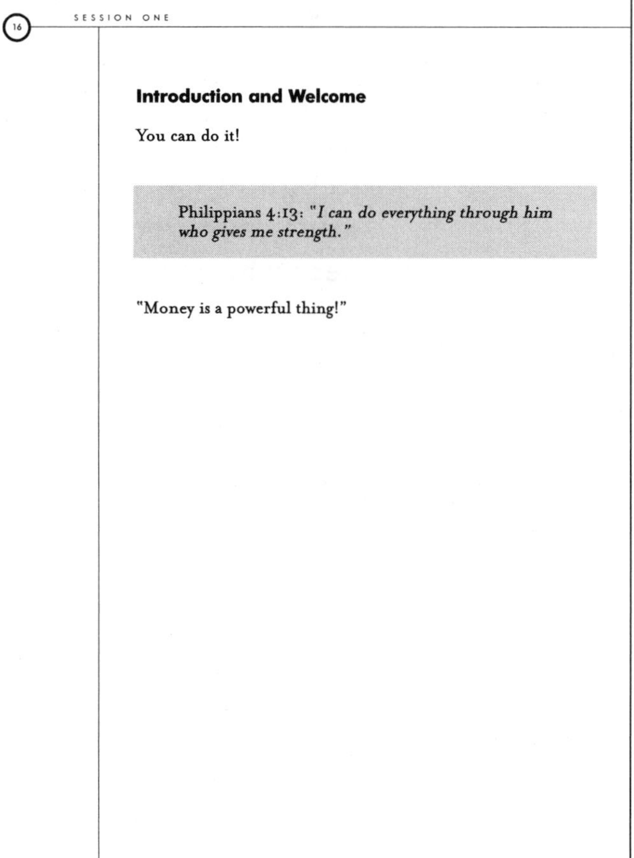

16 SESSION ONE
Introduction and Welcome
You can do it!
Philippians 4:13: "I can do everything through him who gives me strength."
"Money is a powerful thing!"

SESSION ONE 17

The Pull of the Culture

Most of us find ourselves in one of four financial situations:

- Crisis
- One paycheck from disaster
- Good "financial" shape
- God-honoring lifestyle

Money is the chief rival god.

If we don't control our money, it will control us:

- where we live
- where we work
- who we have as friends
- how we use our time

Crisis

Some of us are experiencing serious financial problems. You're in crisis. Coming here to face your financial problems shows tremendous courage. You've taken a big step, and we'll do our best to make this a safe and solution-filled experience. There is hope for everyone here who is in crisis.

One Paycheck from Disaster

Others of us may not be experiencing any immediate crisis and, from a distance, things appear to be good. But the reality is that we're tired of living from paycheck to paycheck and being just one paycheck from disaster. If this describes you, you are tired of your debt being too high and your savings being too low. This course will help you get a firm grip on your finances and develop a God-honoring financial lifestyle that will pull you back from the edge of disaster.

Good "Financial" Shape

A third group of us is in pretty good shape . . . financially. If this describes you, you're not in consumer debt, you save on a regular basis, and you invest wisely. From a purely financial standpoint, you're a good money manager, but you may not be fully honoring God with your financial resources. You're here seeking to fully understand the vision of leading a financial lifestyle from a Christian perspective. We hope to help you achieve that goal in this course.

God-honoring Lifestyle

If you're in the fourth group, you've already applied biblical principles and are handling your finances in a God-honoring way. Our hope for you is that this course will affirm your actions and bring you to an even deeper understanding of God's call in your life.

NOTES

The Pull of the Culture

Most of us find ourselves in one of four financial situations:

- Crisis
- One paycheck from disaster
- Good "financial" shape
- God-honoring lifestyle

Money is the chief rival god.

If we don't control our money, it will control us:

- where we live
- where we work
- who we have as friends
- how we use our time

If you have spiritual seekers in your group, you may want to say the following at this time:

"As you see, we're at different places financially. We're also at different points spiritually. Some of us have already made a commitment to follow Christ, while others of us are still exploring Christianity. Although we'll spend our time discussing finances from a Christian perspective, this course will also help each of us see God and his desires for us spiritually in new and deeper ways.

"As we've already said, even though we don't all share . . ."

Even though we don't all share the same starting point, we all have money. Some of us have a little more, some a little less, but we all have it. And money is a powerful thing! Some say it has a spiritual force or power all its own—that it wants to control us and reign on the throne of our lives.

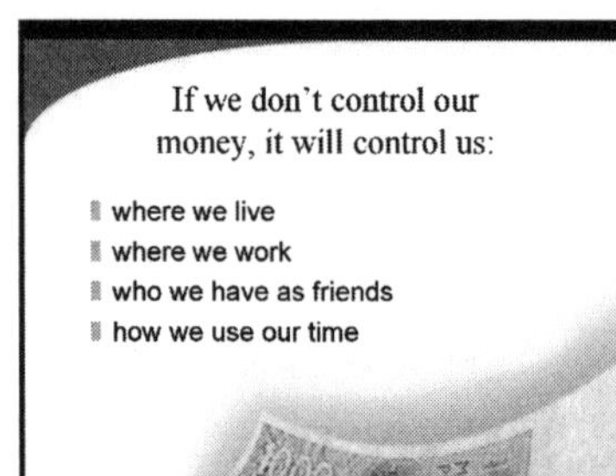
If we don't control our money, it will control us:
where we live
where we work
who we have as friends
how we use our time

For many of us, money is the chief rival god.

The fact is, if we don't control our money, it will control us. Money will end up making the key decisions in our lives: where we live, where we work, who we have as friends, and how we use our time. Money is a powerful thing.

Moreover, money's power is fueled by cultural myths that impact the way we view and use money. To get a clearer understanding of how our culture impacts our thoughts and actions about money, we're going to watch a video that shows this in more depth. Use the space provided on page 18 to write any notes.

NOTES

The Pull of the Culture

Most of us find ourselves in one of four financial situations:

- Crisis
- One paycheck from disaster
- Good "financial" shape
- God-honoring lifestyle

Money is the chief rival god.

If we don't control our money, it will control us:

- where we live
- where we work
- who we have as friends
- how we use our time

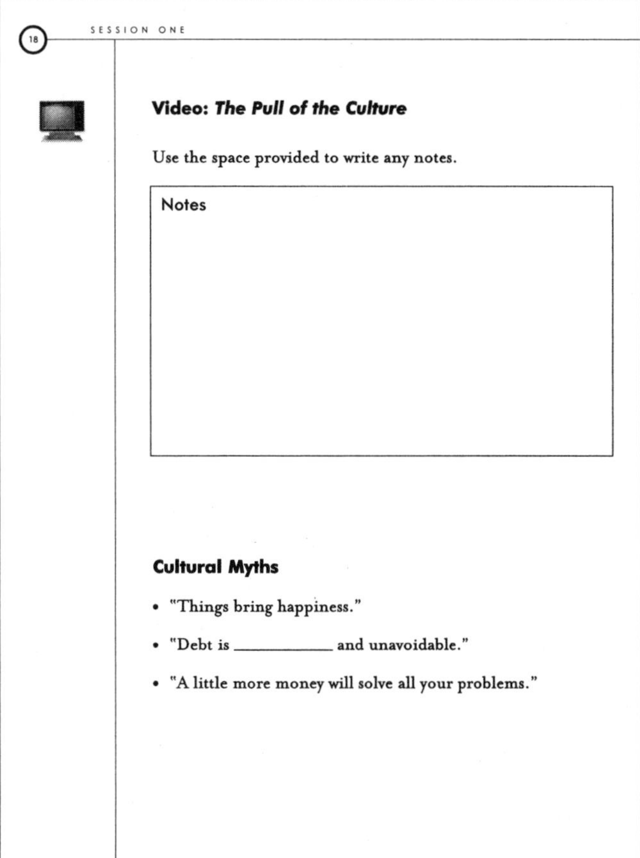
18 SESSION ONE
Video: *The Pull of the Culture*
Use the space provided to write any notes.
Notes
Cultural Myths
• "Things bring happiness."
• "Debt is ___________ and unavoidable."
• "A little more money will solve all your problems."

13 minutes

Video: *The Pull of the Culture* (12 minutes)

Participant's Guide, page 18.

View video: *The Pull of the Culture.*

Wrap-up (1 minute)
What are some comments or insights you have from watching the video?

Solicit three or four comments from the group. Be sure to repeat their answers so everyone hears the response.

Possible responses:
- Things don't bring happiness but we act like they do.
- I hadn't thought about how culture pulls at me like that before.
- Most of us really do have more things than we need.

Cultural Myths
- "Things bring happiness."
- "Debt is EXPECTED and unavoidable."
- "A little more money will solve all your problems."

As the video showed, the three most powerful cultural myths about money are:

- "Things bring happiness."
- "Debt is EXPECTED and unavoidable."
- "A little more money will solve all your problems."

Now let's talk about each of these in more depth.

10 minutes

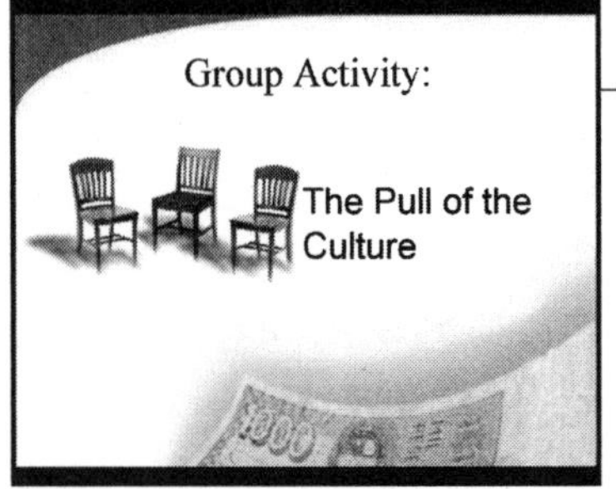
Group Activity:
The Pull of the Culture

Group Activity: *The Pull of the Culture*

Participant's Guide, page 19.

Objectives
1. For participants to meet each other.
2. For participants to identify the cultural myth that influences them most.

NOTES

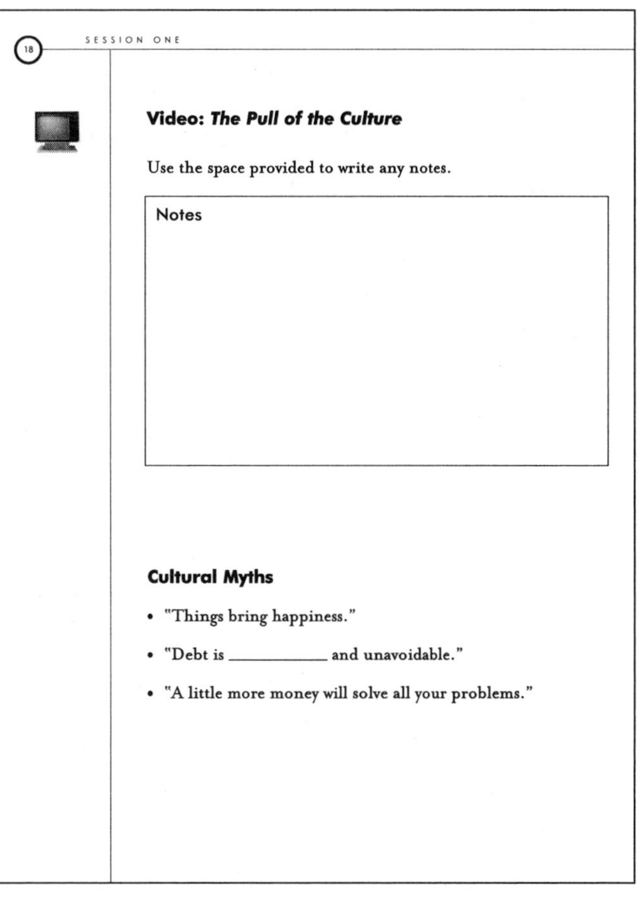

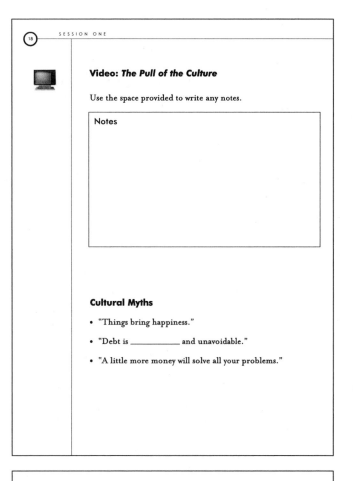

Video: *The Pull of the Culture*

Use the space provided to write any notes.

Notes

Cultural Myths

- "Things bring happiness."
- "Debt is __________ and unavoidable."
- "A little more money will solve all your problems."

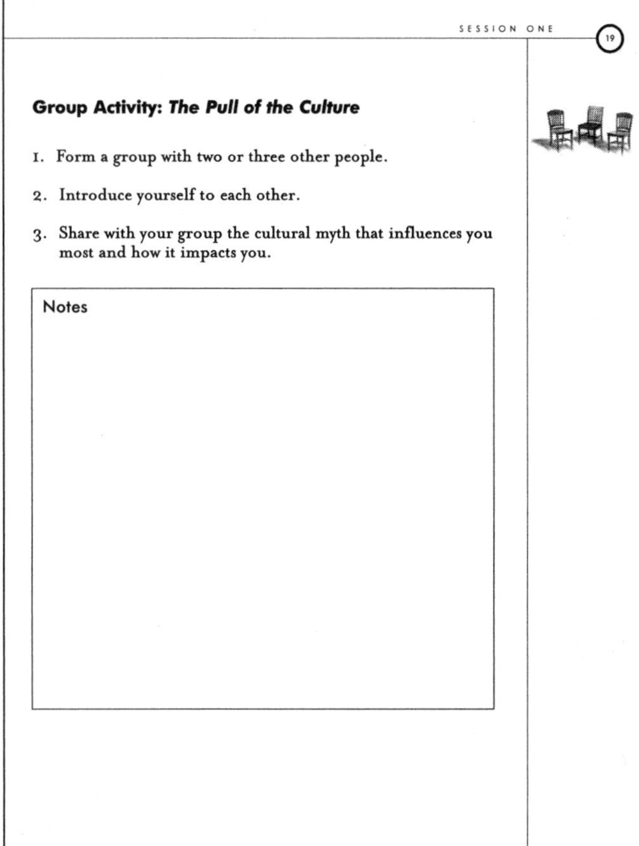

Group Activity: *The Pull of the Culture*

1. Form a group with two or three other people.
2. Introduce yourself to each other.
3. Share with your group the cultural myth that influences you most and how it impacts you.

Notes

Directions

1. Form a group with two or three other people.
2. Introduce yourself to each other.
3. Share with your group the cultural myth that influences you most and how it impacts you.

People sometimes find it difficult to discuss their thoughts and feelings about money. One of the best things you can do to help participants feel comfortable is to model vulnerability by first answering questions like this yourself. For example, share with the group the cultural myth that influences you and how it impacts your life. ("The cultural myth I'm most influenced by is 'things bring happiness.' It impacts me by making me want to go shopping if I'm having a hard day.")

By doing this throughout the course you will set the tone of vulnerability for the group.

Any questions on the directions? You have 9 minutes to complete this exercise.

Call the group back together after 9 minutes.

Who is influenced most by the first myth: "Things bring happiness"? Raise your hand.

Pause.

Who is influenced most by the second myth: "Debt is expected and unavoidable"? Raise your hand.

Pause.

Who is influenced most by the third myth: "A little more money would solve all my problems"? Raise your hand.

Pause.

NOTES

Group Activity: *The Pull of the Culture*

1. Form a group with two or three other people.
2. Introduce yourself to each other.
3. Share with your group the cultural myth that influences you most and how it impacts you.

Notes

No matter what the specific cultural myth is that influences us most, all of us are influenced by our culture and by this powerful stuff called money.

Turn to page 20.

1 minute

Course Overview

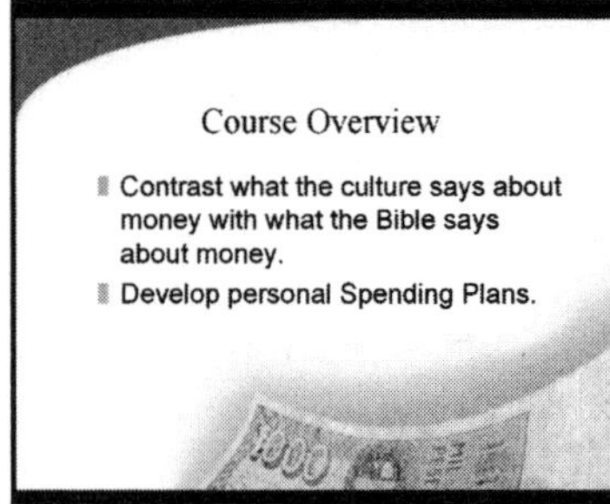

Participant's Guide, page 20.

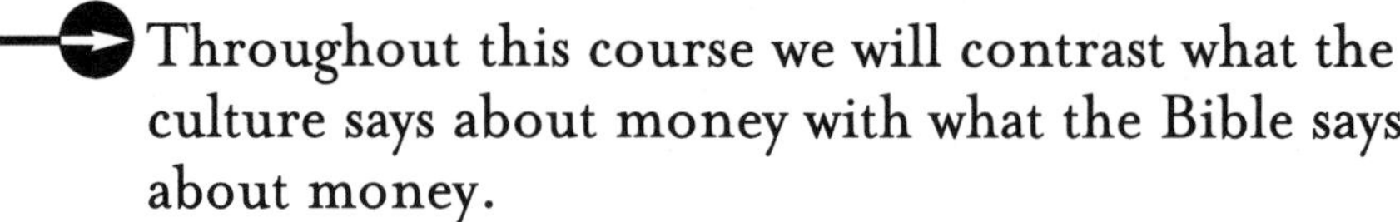

Throughout this course we will contrast what the culture says about money with what the Bible says about money.

We're also going to develop personal Spending Plans that will empower each one of us to achieve our financial goals.

Since this course is about finances, obviously it deals with such things as numbers, budgets, and debt reduction. But it's about so much more than that. For some of us it's about overcoming lifelong habits and coming to grips with the deeper causes of destructive behavior. For others it's about dealing with envy and greed. For all of us, it's about resisting the incredibly strong pull of a culture in which possession has become an obsession.

But this course is also about experiencing freedom in place of bondage, about peace in place of anxiety, and about improving our relationships—with others, with God, and even with ourselves.

This course is about spiritual growth and development. Many of us tend to compartmentalize and consider our financial and spiritual lives separately. But Scripture clearly states that our spiritual lives and our financial lives are interwoven and can't be separated.

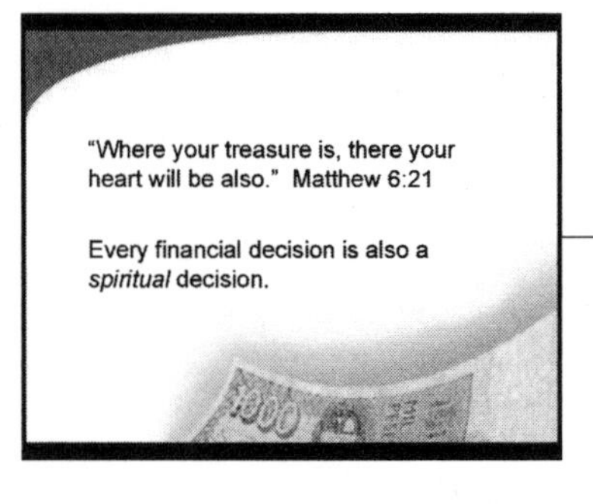

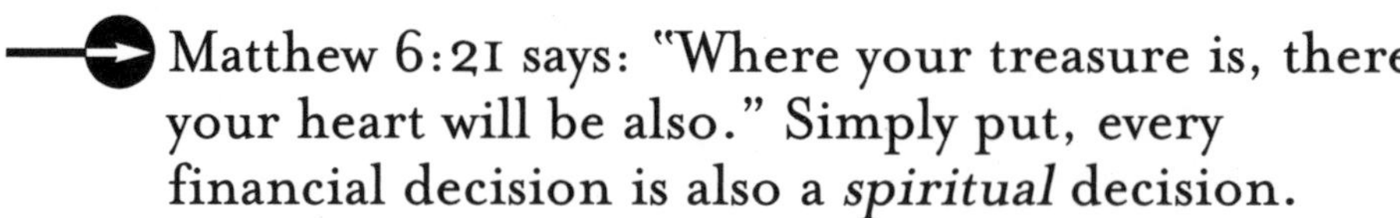

Matthew 6:21 says: "Where your treasure is, there your heart will be also." Simply put, every financial decision is also a *spiritual* decision.

NOTES

Course Overview

- Contrast what the culture says about money with what the Bible says about money.
- Develop personal Spending Plans.

Matthew 6:21: *"Where your treasure is, there your heart will be also."*

Every financial decision is also a *spiritual* decision.

Dealing with these kinds of heart issues requires the presence of the Holy Spirit to lead, empower, and guide us. So let's pray for that right now.

You may wish to substitute your own prayer below.

Dear Father, help us to do the task that is before us and to be encouraged because your strength and guidance are sufficient. Be with us in a special way. Help me speak with clarity, and help each person here to listen with understanding. May you be honored. In Christ we pray, amen.

So how do we guard against being controlled by money? By acknowledging and submitting ourselves to a more powerful force—the Mind and Heart of God.

While our culture is hard at work trying to influence and control our financial behavior, God is quietly encouraging us to not be conformed to this world but to be transformed by the renewing of our minds. One of the best ways to renew our minds is to understand what the Bible says about money and our relationship to it.

2 minutes

The Mind and Heart of God

Participant's Guide, page 21.

On page 143 in your Appendix is a list of Scripture verses that deal specifically with how we are to view and use money. Don't turn there now, but after this session I'd encourage you to reflect on them.

The Mind and Heart of God
God created everything.
God owns everything.
We are trustees.

Three Truths

For now, let's talk about the core truths they represent. These truths can be summarized in three statements:

- God created everything.
- God owns everything.
- We are trustees.

NOTES

The Mind and Heart of God

Three Truths:

- God created everything (Genesis 1:1).

- God owns everything.

> Psalm 50: *"Every animal of the forest is mine, and the cattle on a thousand hills . . . for the world is mine and all that is in it."*
>
> Psalm 24:1: *"The earth is the LORD's and everything in it, the world, and all who live in it."*

- We are trustees.

> 1 Corinthians 4:2: *"Now it is required that those who have been given a trust must prove faithful."*

  - A trustee has no rights, only responsibilities.

  - In eternal terms, ____________________ we possess belongs to God.

Let's take a closer look at each core truth.

God created everything. Genesis 1:1 says that in the beginning there was nothing, and God created.

He created every grain of sand on the earth and every star in the galaxies. Sometimes, it's easy to lose sight of that fact, because we live and work in environments humans have created. But the truth is that first there was nothing, and then there was everything. God created.

God owns everything.

God did not create everything and then go off somewhere else in infinity and turn his back on his creation. Scripture makes it clear that God continues to be involved in creation and has retained ownership of all he created.

In Psalm 50 God declares, "Every animal of the forest is mine, and the cattle on a thousand hills . . . for the world is mine, and all that is in it." And Psalm 24:1 says, "The earth is the LORD's, and everything in it, the world, and all who live in it."

We are trustees.

God created and retained ownership. He then *entrusted* to each of us, who are created in his image, a portion of his creation. Thus, we are trustees, trustees for God of whatever we have been given.

First Corinthians 4:2 says, "Now it is required that those who have been given a trust must prove faithful."

In order to prove faithful, it is important to understand the role of a trustee.

NOTES

The Mind and Heart of God

Three Truths:

- God created everything (Genesis 1:1).

- God owns everything.

> Psalm 50: *"Every animal of the forest is mine, and the cattle on a thousand hills . . . for the world is mine and all that is in it."*
>
> Psalm 24:1: *"The earth is the LORD's and everything in it, the world, and all who live in it."*

- We are trustees.

> 1 Corinthians 4:2: *"Now it is required that those who have been given a trust must prove faithful."*

  - A trustee has no rights, only responsibilities.

  - In eternal terms, ____________________ we possess belongs to God.

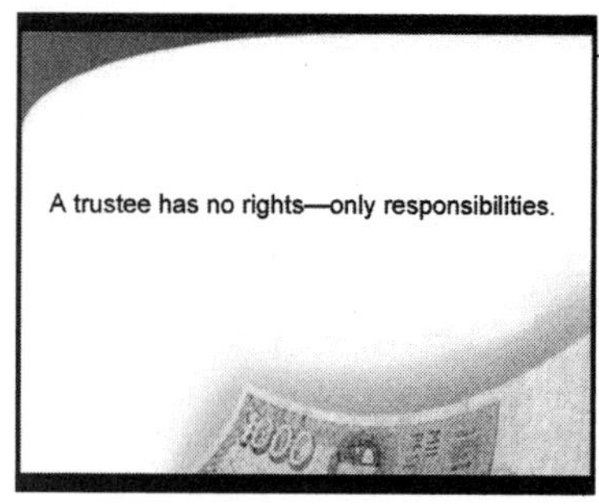
A trustee has no rights—only responsibilities.

A trustee has no rights, only responsibilities—the responsibility to care for what belongs to someone else.

For example, if you were incapacitated and I were made trustee of your estate, I would have no rights to your assets, only the responsibility of handling them wisely on your behalf. If I were to violate that trust and manage your affairs in my best interests instead of yours, I could be hauled into court to stand before a judge and explain why I had violated that trust.

The importance of our role as trustees can't be over-emphasized. All other Biblical Financial Principles flow out of this understanding. You and I may have titles to our cars and deeds to our houses and, in earthly terms, we own them.

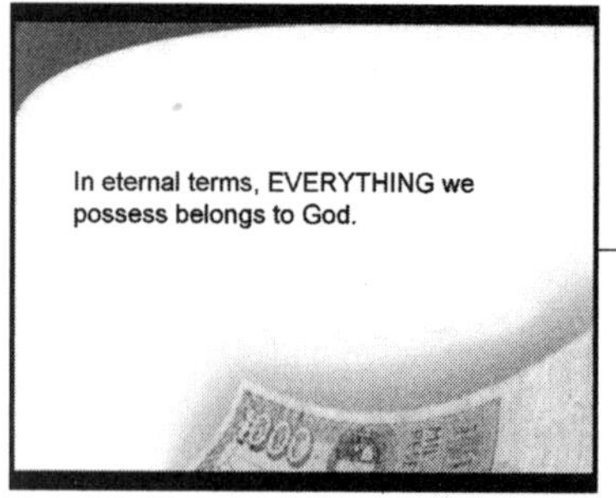
In eternal terms, EVERYTHING we possess belongs to God.

But in eternal terms, EVERYTHING we possess belongs to God.

To get an even clearer picture of how important this concept is, we're going to watch a video based on the parable of the pearl of great price in Matthew 13. In this parable Jesus describes the Kingdom of Heaven as a precious pearl for which a merchant sold all he owned in order to buy it. The video has been created with illustrations rather than live actors and it's set in the 1940s.

Turn to page 22.

5 minutes

Video: *The Pearl of Great Price* (5 minutes)

Participant's Guide, page 22.

View video: *The Pearl of Great Price.*

That's how we need to look at our possessions—that we are trustees, not owners. Because this idea of trusteeship is so critical, we're going to spend some time discussing it.

NOTES

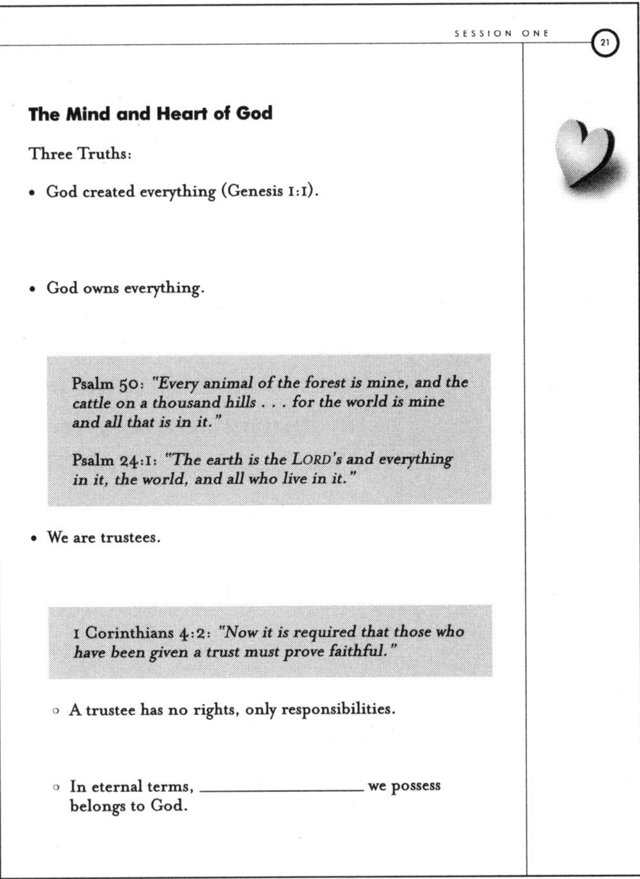

SESSION ONE 21

The Mind and Heart of God

Three Truths:

- God created everything (Genesis 1:1).

- God owns everything.

> Psalm 50: *"Every animal of the forest is mine, and the cattle on a thousand hills . . . for the world is mine and all that is in it."*
>
> Psalm 24:1: *"The earth is the LORD's and everything in it, the world, and all who live in it."*

- We are trustees.

> 1 Corinthians 4:2: *"Now it is required that those who have been given a trust must prove faithful."*

  - A trustee has no rights, only responsibilities.
  - In eternal terms, ______________ we possess belongs to God.

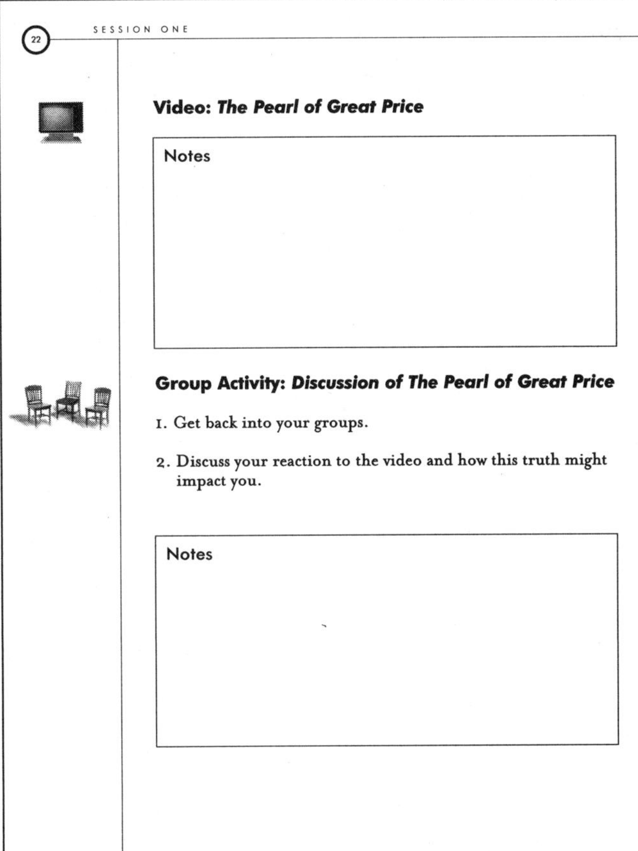

22 SESSION ONE

Video: *The Pearl of Great Price*

Notes

Group Activity: *Discussion of The Pearl of Great Price*

1. Get back into your groups.
2. Discuss your reaction to the video and how this truth might impact you.

Notes

9 minutes

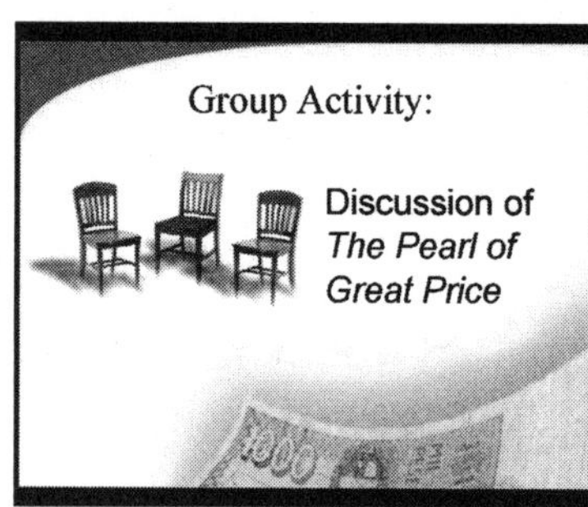
Group Activity:
Discussion of
The Pearl of
Great Price

Group Activity: Discussion of *The Pearl of Great Price*

Objective
For participants to begin to value the concept of being a trustee versus an owner.

Directions

1. Get back into your groups.
2. Discuss your reaction to this video and how this truth might impact you.

I'll give you 8 minutes to discuss this.

Call the group back together after 8 minutes.

Wrap-up (1 minute)
What are some of the reactions and insights you discussed?

Solicit two or three comments from the group. Be sure to repeat their answers so everyone hears the response.

Possible responses:

- It feels strange to think that God is the true owner of something I value deeply.
- It is making me look at my possessions differently.
- It's hard to really understand all the implications of this.

1 minute

There is an even deeper point to make here. The reality is that even our families belong to God.

Those of us who are parents need to understand that our children are not our really "our" children. They are God's children entrusted to us to raise and nurture according to Scripture.

NOTES

Video: *The Pearl of Great Price*

Notes

Group Activity: *Discussion of The Pearl of Great Price*

1. Get back into your groups.
2. Discuss your reaction to the video and how this truth might impact you.

Notes

In fact, we do not even own ourselves. We belong to God first of all because he created us. And, for those of us who have accepted Christ, we belong to God a second time because he saved us. Everything, including our very being, belongs to God.

We are trustees, not owners.

As a trustee, each of us will stand before God someday and answer the question: "What did you do with the things I entrusted to you?"

Obviously, this question applies to more than just financial matters, but our financial decisions will be a key part of the answer. I believe we all share the hope that God's response to our answer will be, "Well done, good and faithful servant, good and faithful trustee."

I want to take a moment now to pray and seal this important, life-changing point in our hearts.

You may wish to substitute your own prayer below.

Gracious Heavenly Father, we take this moment to acknowledge that we came into this world with nothing and we will leave it with nothing. All that we temporarily possess, even life itself, comes from and belongs to you. It is simply entrusted to us. We pray that this truth will touch our hearts and be reflected in our daily lives. Open our minds in the remainder of this course that we might learn to be ever wiser and more faithful trustees. In Jesus' name we pray, amen.

Now that we understand what being a *trustee* of God's resources really means, let's take a look at two forces that are at work in our daily lives.

NOTES

Video: *The Pearl of Great Price*

Notes

Group Activity: *Discussion of The Pearl of Great Price*

1. Get back into your groups.
2. Discuss your reaction to the video and how this truth might impact you.

Notes

3 minutes

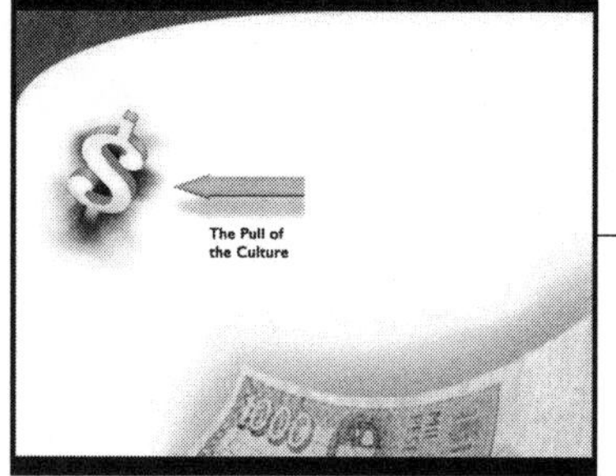

The Pull of the Culture vs. the Mind and Heart of God

Participant's Guide, page 23.

On one side we have the Pull of the Culture.

On the other side we have the Mind and Heart of God.

And there we are in the middle of these two forces.

Let's examine this financial dilemma from a biblical standpoint.

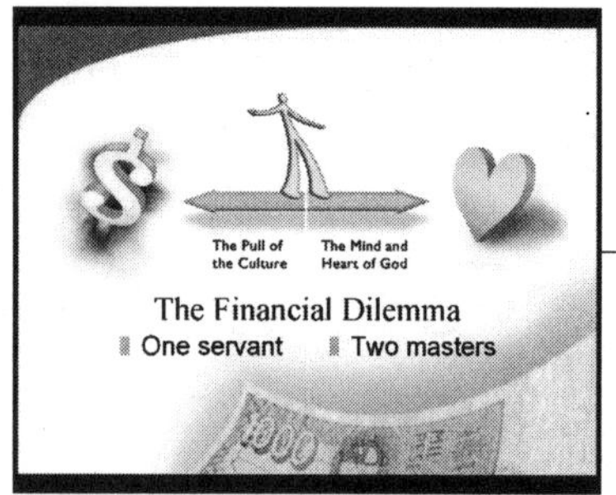

The Financial Dilemma

The financial dilemma is that there is one servant and two masters.

Matthew 6:24 says, "No one can serve two masters. For you will hate one and love the other, or be devoted to one and despise the other. You cannot serve both God and money" (NLT).

One master is money, which beckons us through the Pull of the Culture. It shouts that we will find financial freedom, fulfillment, contentment, and peace only by acquiring more things. The Pull of the Culture pleads, "Wear me, buy me, drink me, drive me, and I'll make you happy and successful and shower you with relationships."

The other master, God, doesn't shout or plead. He shares his mind and heart in an ever-quiet voice, and simply invites us to be faithful to him. Financial freedom is the byproduct of that faithfulness.

Matthew 6:33 says, "Seek first his kingdom and his righteousness, and all these things will be given to you as well."

This includes the promise of true financial freedom.

NOTES

The Pull of the Culture vs. the Mind and Heart of God

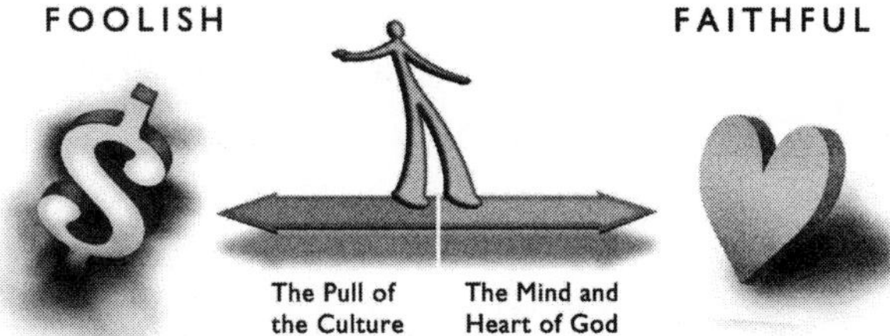

The Financial Dilemma

- One servant
- Two masters

Matthew 6:24 (NLT): *"No one can serve two masters. For you will hate one and love the other, or be devoted to one and despise the other. You cannot serve both God and money."*

Matthew 6:33: *"Seek first his kingdom and his righteousness, and all these things will be given to you as well."*

Matthew 25: *". . . good and faithful servants."*

Luke 12:21 (NLT): *"Yes, a person is a fool to store up earthly wealth but not have a rich relationship with God."*

Two Great Truths:

- God holds us ____________________ for how we manage the money and possessions entrusted to us.
- We will be found either faithful or foolish.

 ***Key Question: Will God consider my financial decisions to be faithful or foolish?***

The Bible makes it clear that one servant can't serve two masters. We need to make a choice, and the Bible is clear about where each choice will lead.

In Matthew 25 Jesus tells the parable of the talents. It is the story of a master who entrusts his property to three servants before leaving on a journey. When the master returns, he settles accounts with the servants.

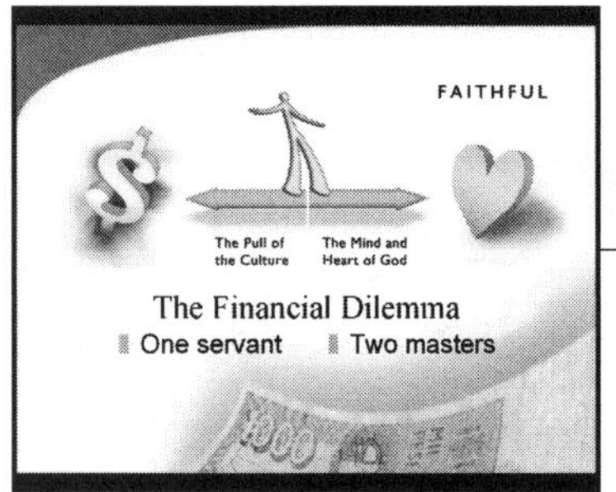

Two of the three used their resources wisely and were commended by the master as "good and *faithful*" servants.

In Luke 12 Jesus tells the parable of the rich fool. It is the story of a wealthy farmer who hoarded his goods and built even bigger barns to store his excess. God called him a "fool" and said that his life would be taken from him that night. Jesus concludes the story with these words:

"Yes, a person is a fool to store up earthly wealth but not have a rich relationship with God."

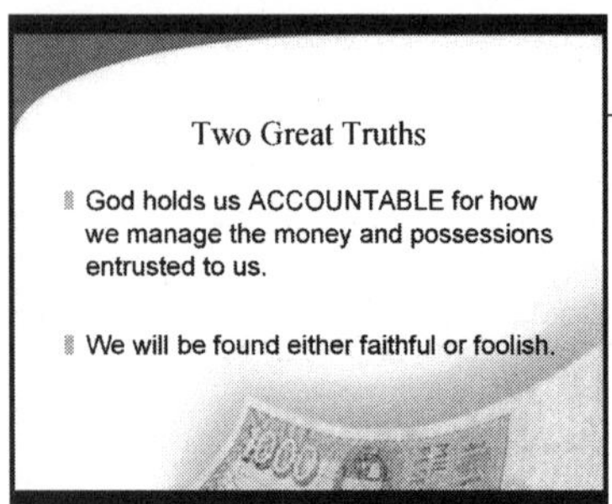

These parables shed light on two great truths:

- God holds us ACCOUNTABLE for how we manage the money and possessions entrusted to us.
- We will be found either faithful or foolish.

Every day we make financial decisions . . . and our financial decisions are spiritual decisions.

What are some of the financial decisions you make each day?

NOTES

The Pull of the Culture vs. the Mind and Heart of God

FOOLISH FAITHFUL

The Pull of the Culture

The Mind and Heart of God

The Financial Dilemma

- One servant
- Two masters

Matthew 6:24 (NLT): *"No one can serve two masters. For you will hate one and love the other, or be devoted to one and despise the other. You cannot serve both God and money."*

Matthew 6:33: *"Seek first his kingdom and his righteousness, and all these things will be given to you as well."*

Matthew 25: *". . . good and faithful servants."*

Luke 12:21 (NLT): *"Yes, a person is a fool to store up earthly wealth but not have a rich relationship with God."*

Two Great Truths:

- God holds us ____________________ for how we manage the money and possessions entrusted to us.
- We will be found either faithful or foolish.

Key Question: Will God consider my financial decisions to be faithful or foolish?

Solicit four or five comments from the group. Be sure to repeat their answers so everyone hears the response.

Possible responses:
- Should I buy lunch or bring it from home?
- Should I buy a cup of coffee?
- Should I play the lottery?
- Should I call now on my cell phone or wait until I can use a regular phone?
- Should I give to the church even though I'm in debt?

Every day we struggle with the Pull of the Culture.

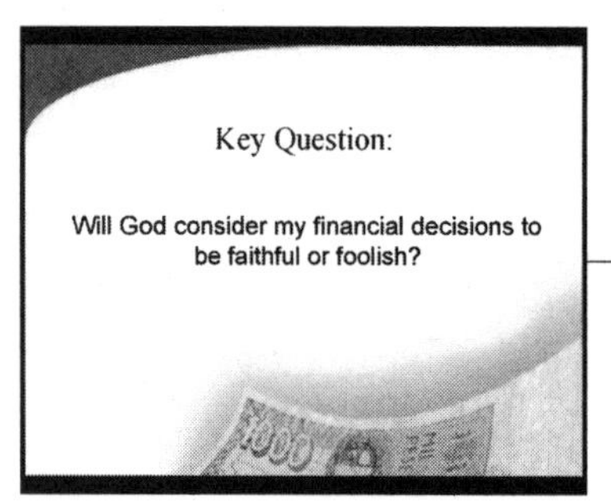

A key question to ask as we make these decisions is this: "Will God consider my financial decisions to be faithful or foolish?"

Turn to page 24.

Five Financial Areas

Participant's Guide, page 24.

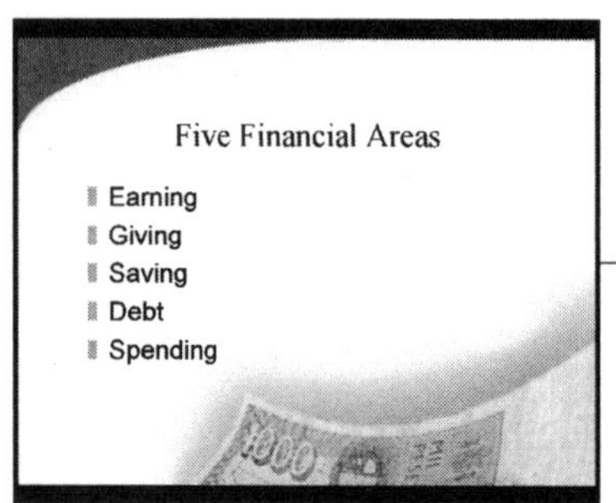

We're going to explore what financial faithfulness and financial foolishness look like in five key areas:

- Earning
- Giving
- Saving
- Debt
- Spending

These areas represent the usual way in which we get money—earning—and the four things we can do with it once we have it: We can give it away, save it, pay debt with it, or spend it.

NOTES

The Pull of the Culture vs. the Mind and Heart of God

The Financial Dilemma

- One servant
- Two masters

Matthew 6:24 (NLT): *"No one can serve two masters. For you will hate one and love the other, or be devoted to one and despise the other. You cannot serve both God and money."*

Matthew 6:33: *"Seek first his kingdom and his righteousness, and all these things will be given to you as well."*

Matthew 25: *". . . good and faithful servants."*

Luke 12:21 (NLT): *"Yes, a person is a fool to store up earthly wealth but not have a rich relationship with God."*

Two Great Truths:

- God holds us ________________ for how we manage the money and possessions entrusted to us.
- We will be found either faithful or foolish.

Key Question: Will God consider my financial decisions to be faithful or foolish?

Five Financial Areas

- Earning
- Giving
- Saving
- Debt
- Spending

When we choose to be faithful in these five financial areas, Scripture indicates that we become a:

- Diligent Earner
- ________________ Giver
- Wise Saver
- ________________ Debtor
- Prudent Consumer

Genuine financial freedom is:

The ________________ we experience as we faithfully manage our financial resources according to God's purposes and principles.

Being financially faithful leads to being financially free!

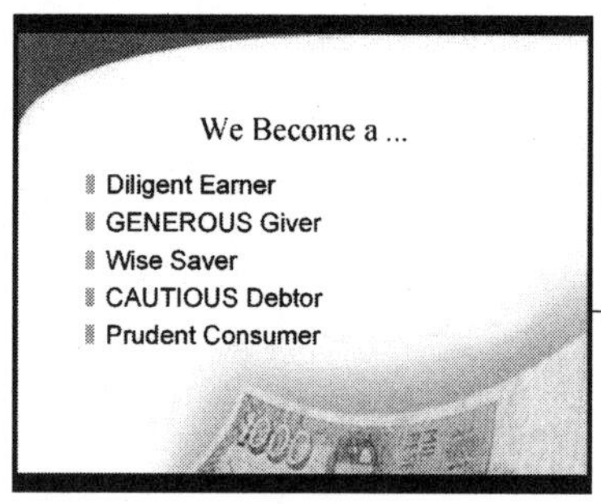

When we choose to be faithful in these five financial areas, Scripture indicates that we become a:

- Diligent Earner
- GENEROUS Giver
- Wise Saver
- CAUTIOUS Debtor
- Prudent Consumer

By becoming these things, we become free of anxiety about money and achieve genuine financial freedom.

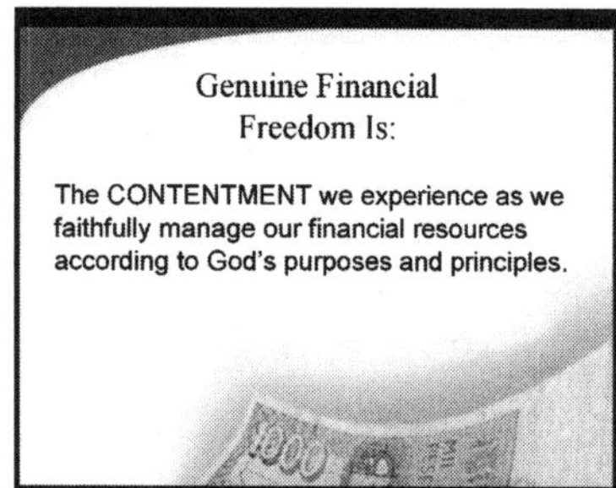

Genuine financial freedom is the CONTENTMENT we experience as we faithfully manage our financial resources according to God's purposes and principles.

As we grow in our understanding of the Mind and Heart of God and become more faithful in every financial decision, we will experience this freedom.

Being financially faithful leads to being financially free!

2 minutes

The Spending Plan

Participant's Guide, page 25.

We now have a framework to assess our progress toward the Mind and Heart of God. The next thing we need is a practical tool to help guide us.

That practical tool is a budget. We stated before that money is a powerful thing.

What Is a Spending Plan?

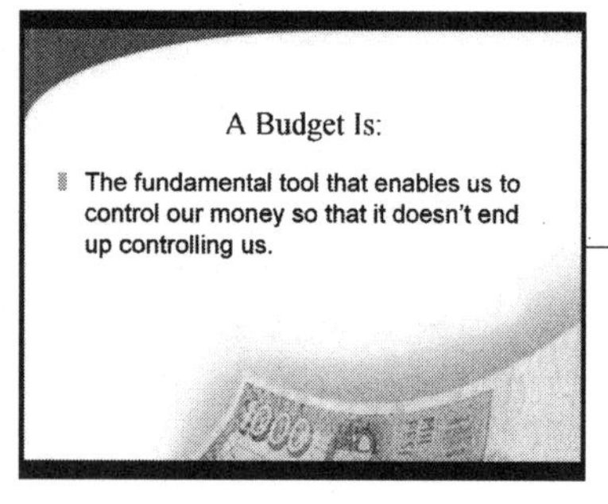

A budget is the fundamental tool that enables us to control our money so that it doesn't end up controlling us.

NOTES

Five Financial Areas

- Earning
- Giving
- Saving
- Debt
- Spending

When we choose to be faithful in these five financial areas, Scripture indicates that we become a:

- Diligent Earner
- ________________ Giver
- Wise Saver
- ________________ Debtor
- Prudent Consumer

Genuine financial freedom is:

The __________________ we experience as we faithfully manage our financial resources according to God's purposes and principles.

Being financially faithful leads to being financially free!

The Spending Plan

What Is a Spending Plan?

A budget is . . .

- The fundamental tool that enables us to control our money so that it doesn't end up controlling us.
- A Spending Plan for how we will allocate our financial resources.

A Spending Plan is:

- A way to reach our financial ___________ and live out our values and priorities.

A Spending Plan:

- Produces __________________.

  There is no true freedom without limits.

- Sets safe limits financially.

Since it is so important, we need to be clear on what a budget is.

A budget is a plan—a Spending Plan—for how we will allocate our financial resources.

Why do we have plans? We have plans to achieve something, to reach a goal, and our goals are based on our values and priorities.

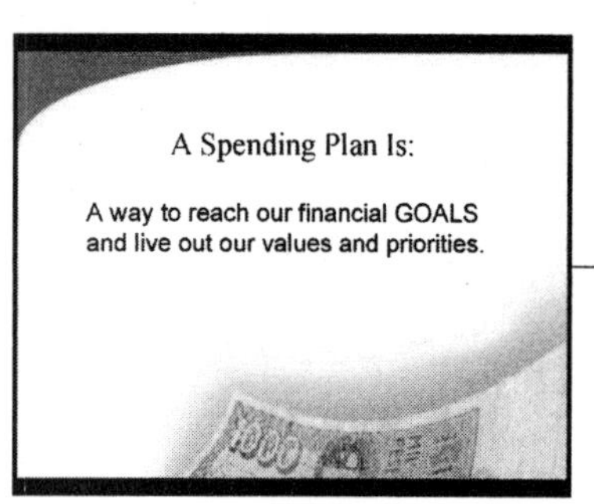

A Spending Plan is a way to reach our financial GOALS and live out our values and priorities.

From here on, we will substitute the term "Spending Plan" for the word "budget," since those words more aptly describe what it is.

In your pre-work, you were asked to fill out a goal sheet—we will look at this in the next session. The Spending Plan is the way you'll reach those goals. Being clear on your goals is important because they will serve as motivation to you as you develop and carry out your Spending Plan.

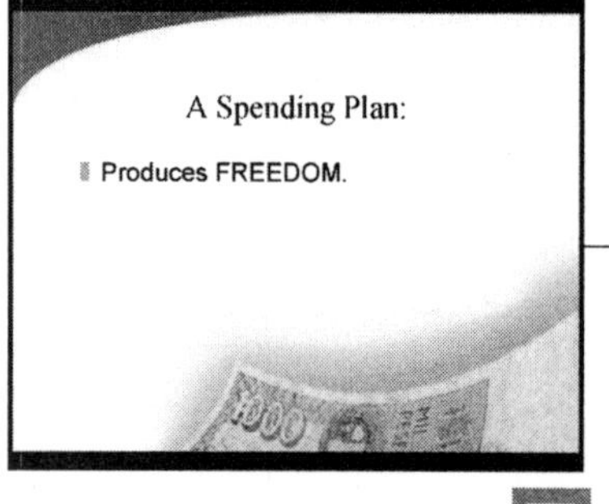

A key point to understand is that a Spending Plan is not restrictive or confining but produces FREEDOM. A foundational principle of life is that there is no true freedom without limits. A Spending Plan sets safe limits financially.

Let me give you a word picture. Imagine you're on a beautiful beach. A hundred yards or so out in the water, someone has set out some ropes and buoys. Beyond the ropes and buoys are dangerous undertows and shark activity. Within the boundaries, you can swim and play in safety and complete freedom.

Can you go beyond the buoys? Of course you can. It's pretty easy to swim beneath the rope and venture out. Is it smart to go beyond the buoys? No, because you're likely to get sucked down by the undertow or eaten alive by sharks.

NOTES

The Spending Plan

What Is a Spending Plan?

A budget is . . .

- The fundamental tool that enables us to control our money so that it doesn't end up controlling us.
- A Spending Plan for how we will allocate our financial resources.

A Spending Plan is:

- A way to reach our financial ____________ and live out our values and priorities.

A Spending Plan:

- Produces ____________________.

There is no true freedom without limits.

- Sets safe limits financially.

Now, think about a Spending Plan. It sets safe boundaries for how we use our money. By spending within its limits, we can safely and freely enjoy our resources.

What happens when we spend beyond those limits? We get sucked down by the undertow of debt and eaten alive by a whole series of financial sharks that want a piece of us!

Turn to page 26.

The Benefits of a Spending Plan

Participant's Guide, page 26.

With that understanding, let's take a closer look at the benefits of a Spending Plan.

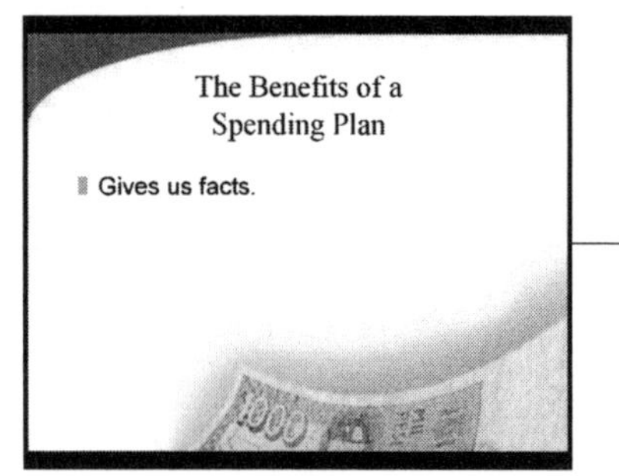

First, it gives us the facts about how we're doing.

It removes the guesswork and the anxiety we feel when we don't really know what the true situation is. The Bible teaches that it is the truth that sets us free. A spending plan allows us to discuss our finances and make decisions based on fact rather than emotion.

Secondly, it avoids WASTE.

Without a Spending Plan we *will* spend more money. We all want to be good stewards and not waste God's resources. We also want to hear God say, "Well done, good and faithful servant—good and faithful trustee."

Thirdly, it keeps our VALUES and priorities in check.

A Spending Plan reflects what is really important to us. Without it, we can easily fall into spending patterns that conflict with our financial goals or are not God honoring. Following a Spending Plan ensures that our walk will be consistent with our talk.

NOTES

The Spending Plan

What Is a Spending Plan?

A budget is . . .

- The fundamental tool that enables us to control our money so that it doesn't end up controlling us.
- A Spending Plan for how we will allocate our financial resources.

A Spending Plan is:

- A way to reach our financial __________ and live out our values and priorities.

A Spending Plan:

- Produces __________________.

There is no true freedom without limits.

- Sets safe limits financially.

The Benefits of a Spending Plan

❑ Gives us facts.

❑ Avoids ___________.

❑ Keeps our ___________ and priorities in check.

❑ Leads to financial freedom.

A Spending Plan is for *everyone*—not just those in financial difficulty.

Finally, it leads to financial freedom.

A Spending Plan enables us to spend with confidence and freedom because it establishes safe limits. It allows our families to experience that freedom as well.

For these reasons a Spending Plan is for *everyone*—not just those in financial difficulty.

Let me pause here. Which benefit do you think would most impact you? Place a check by it.

Pause. Wait until most participants are done before moving on.

On page 145 is a Spending Plan worksheet. Notice that it looks exactly like the "What I Spend" pre-work sheet except for the title. In your pre-work the "What I Spend" sheet was used to record what you currently spend. Your goal is to convert the "What I Spend" sheet to a personal Spending Plan that reflects your goals—to move from "what it is" to "what I want it to be."

Go ahead now and remove the Spending Plan worksheet from your Participant's Guide.

Pause. Wait until most participants are done before moving on.

1 minute

SESSION SUMMARY

Participant's Guide, page 27.

In this session, we've learned about the dilemma we face in choosing between the Pull of the Culture and the Mind and Heart of God. We now have a framework and a practical tool—the Spending Plan worksheet—that will help us become financially faithful and financially free.

NOTES

The Benefits of a Spending Plan

- ❑ Gives us facts.
- ❑ Avoids ____________.
- ❑ Keeps our ____________ and priorities in check.
- ❑ Leads to financial freedom.

A Spending Plan is for *everyone*—not just those in financial difficulty.

SESSION SUMMARY

Course Goal

Commit to and begin developing a biblically-based Spending Plan.

Course Objectives

- Become aware of the Pull of the Culture
- Understand Biblical Financial Principles
- Develop a first draft of a Spending Plan
- Select a record-keeping system
- Commit to implementing the Spending Plan and record-keeping system

Course Sessions

- Session 1: The Financial Dilemma
- Session 2: Earning, Giving, and Saving
- Session 3: Saving and Debt
- Session 4: Spending
- Session 5: Balancing the Spending Plan
- Session 6: Record Keeping and Commitment

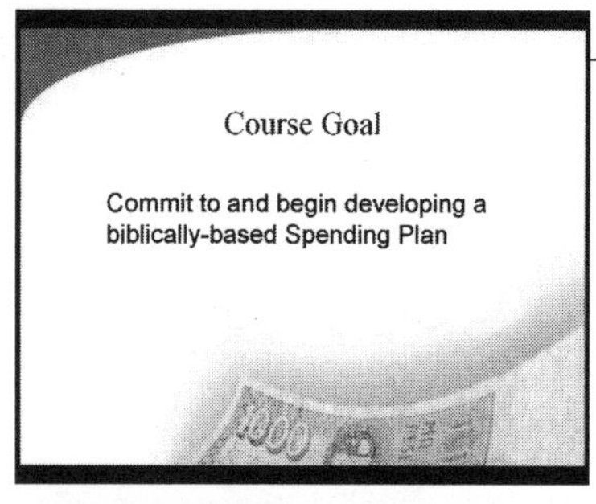

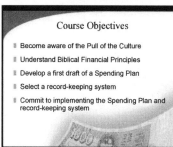

The goal of this course is for each of us to commit to and begin developing a biblically-based Spending Plan.

Course Objectives

- Become aware of the Pull of the Culture
- Understand Biblical Financial Principles
- Develop a first draft of a Spending Plan
- Select a record-keeping system
- Commit to implementing the Spending Plan and record-keeping system

Our objectives are for everyone to:

- Become aware of the Pull of the Culture
- Understand Biblical Financial Principles that should guide us
- Develop a first draft of a Spending Plan
- Select a record-keeping system, and
- Commit to implementing a Spending Plan and record-keeping system.

We'll accomplish our goal and objectives through six sessions.

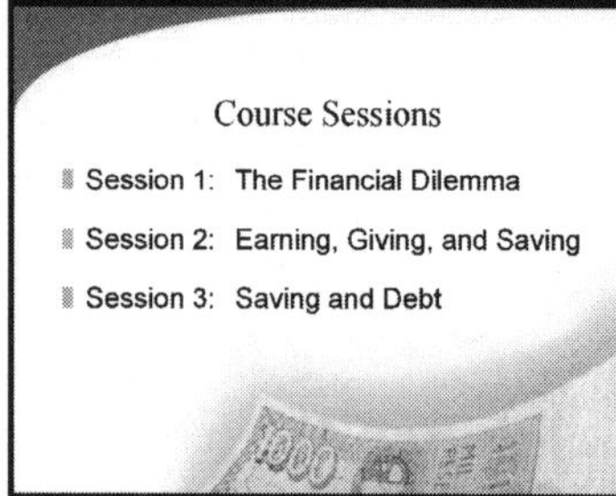

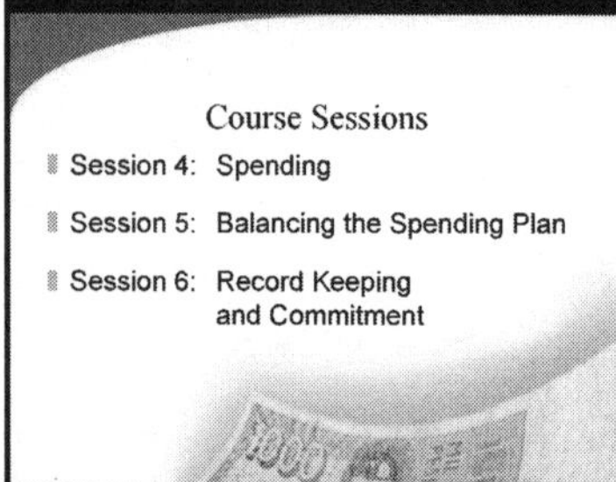

In session one, we've already covered the Financial Dilemma. In session two we'll cover Earning, Giving and Saving. In session three we'll finish Saving and discuss Debt. In session four we'll cover Spending, and in session five we'll Balance the Spending Plan. During this session' we'll also give you extended time to work on your Spending Plan. Finally, in session six we'll cover Record Keeping and Commitment.

As we go through each session, you'll refer back to your pre-work so you can set new goals for your Spending Plan based on the insights you receive.

At the end of this course, you will leave with an initial draft of a Spending Plan in your hand, the knowledge in your head to implement it, and the commitment in your heart to follow through with it.

Break.

Session Two

EARNING, GIVING AND SAVING

SESSION SNAPSHOT

OBJECTIVES

In this session, participants will:

1. Prioritize their financial goals.
2. Reflect on how they can become closer to the Mind and Heart of God as earners, givers, and savers.
3. Complete the Spending Plan worksheet categories for income and giving.

OUTLINE

I. Introduction and Review
Individual Activity: *Goals to Achieve this Year*

II. Discovery

A. Earning
1. The Pull of the Culture vs. the Mind and Heart of God
2. Practical Tips on Earning
3. Individual Activity: *Spending Plan Application*

B. Giving
1. Video: *The Offering*
2. The Pull of the Culture vs. The Mind and Heart of God
3. Individual Activity: *The Generous Giver*
4. Practical Tips on Giving
5. Individual Activity: *Spending Plan Application*

C. Saving
1. The Pull of the Culture vs. the Mind and Heart of God
2. Group Activity: *Your Money Tendency*

III. Session Summary

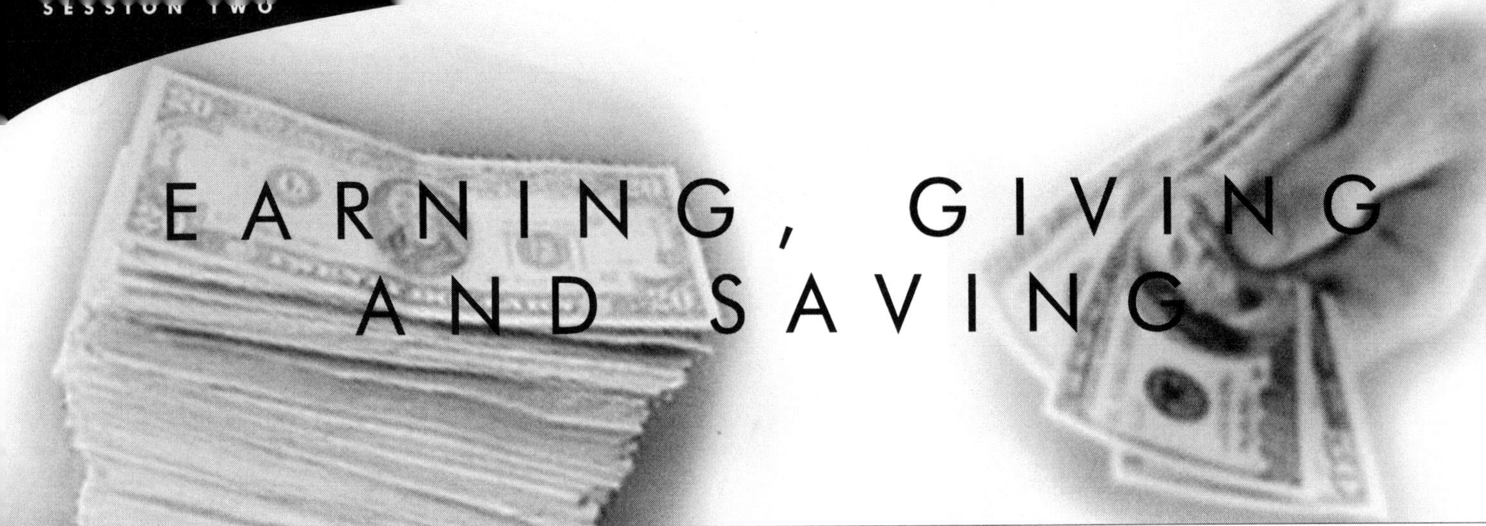

EARNING, GIVING AND SAVING

TIME & MEDIA | CONTENTS

6 minutes

The Good $ense Budget Course

Session 2

Earning, Giving, and Saving

INTRODUCTION AND REVIEW

Participant's Guide, page 29.

In this session, we will focus on three of the five financial areas: earning, giving, and saving. You will have the opportunity to prioritize your financial goals and reflect on how you can move closer to the Mind and Heart of God in these areas.

You will also complete your Spending Plan worksheet for income and giving. Since your Spending Plan is based on your goals, let's begin this session by taking a few minutes to review the goal sheet you filled out in your pre-work.

Go ahead and get that sheet out. It's called "Goals to Achieve this Year." And then turn to page 30 in your Participant's Guide.

Pause until most participants have located their sheet.

Individual Activity: *Goals to Achieve this Year*

Participant's Guide, page 30.

Objective
For participants to review and prioritize their goals.

NOTES

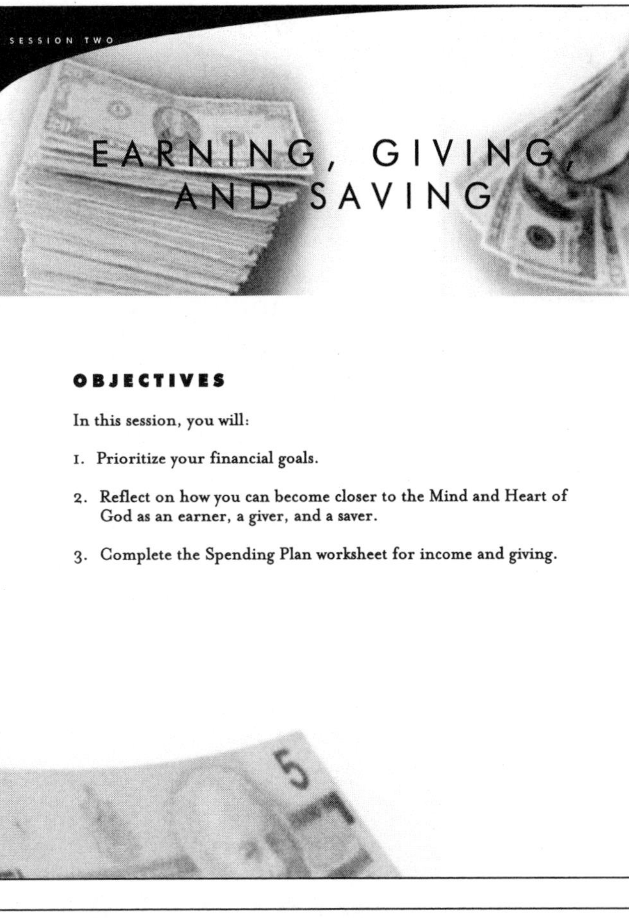

OBJECTIVES

In this session, you will:

1. Prioritize your financial goals.
2. Reflect on how you can become closer to the Mind and Heart of God as an earner, a giver, and a saver.
3. Complete the Spending Plan worksheet for income and giving.

Individual Activity: *Goals to Achieve This Year*

In light of what we covered in the previous session, review your pre-work sheet to determine if you want to keep your goals the same or make any changes. If you were not able to complete this portion of the pre-work, do so now.

Prioritize your goals, and list the top three in the space provided:

Goal 1: ____________________

Goal 2: ____________________

Goal 3: ____________________

Directions

1. In light of what we covered in the previous session, review your pre-work sheet to determine if you want to keep your goals the same or make any changes. If you were not able to complete this portion of the pre-work, do so now.
2. Prioritize your goals, and list the top three in the space provided.

You'll have 5 minutes to complete this.

Call the group back together after 5 minutes.

As we go through the course, we'll walk through each category on the Spending Plan worksheet. Now that you've been able to review and prioritize your goals, you'll be able to develop a Spending Plan that will reflect those goals.

DISCOVERY (44 minutes)

Earning

Participant's Guide, page 31.

In this session, we are going to talk about the first area of our financial lives—earning. Earning is about more than just finances. It's about who you *are* and who you are *becoming* as an earner. It's about the tension we face as earners between choosing to follow the Pull of the Culture or seeking the Mind and Heart of God.

Let's start by looking at the Pull of the Culture.

NOTES

Individual Activity: *Goals to Achieve This Year*

In light of what we covered in the previous session, review your pre-work sheet to determine if you want to keep your goals the same or make any changes. If you were not able to complete this portion of the pre-work, do so now.

Prioritize your goals, and list the top three in the space provided:

Goal 1: ____________________

Goal 2: ____________________

Goal 3: ____________________

Earning

The Pull of the Culture vs. the Mind and Heart of God

FOOLISH FAITHFUL

The Pull of the Culture The Mind and Heart of God

The Pull of the Culture on the earner says:

- "Your value is measured by your __________ and your paycheck."
- "A little more money will solve all your problems."

The Mind and Heart of God counters:

- Our value is not measured by what we do but by who we are—beloved sons and daughters of God.
- We are called to join him in the ongoing management of his creation.
- Work is a __________, not a curse.

2 minutes

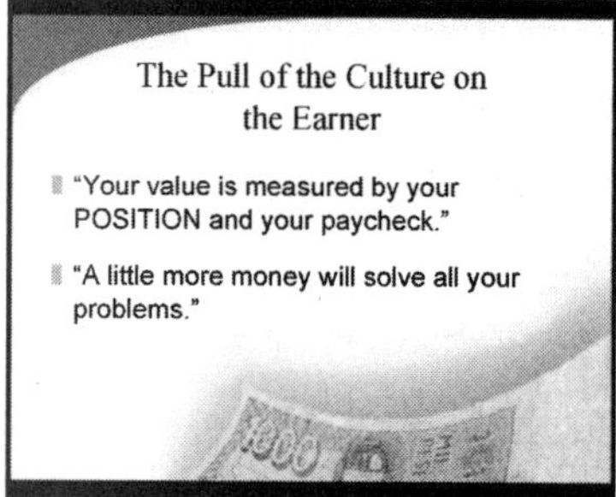

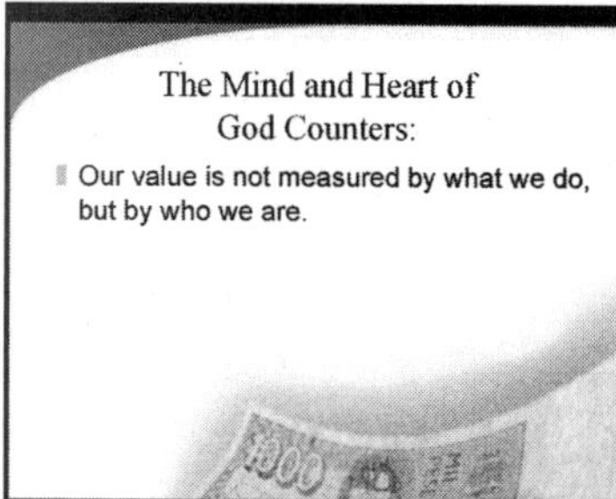

The Pull of the Culture vs. the Mind and Heart of God

The Pull of the Culture on the earner says, "Your value is measured by your POSITION and your paycheck."

It drives us to earn more and deceives us with the lie, "A little more money will solve all your problems."

The Mind and Heart of God counters these cultural myths with the message that our value is not measured by what we do but by who we are . . . beloved sons and daughters of God.

Scripture also makes it clear that work is a blessing.

Genesis 1 states that, after creating man and woman in his own image, God blessed them and called them to join him in the ongoing management of his creation.

By that act, God established that work is a BLESSING, not a curse, and that all work has dignity.

Turn to page 32.

The Diligent Earner

Participant's Guide, page 32.

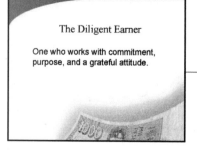

The Bible characterizes the God-honoring earner as "diligent."

The diligent earner is one who works with commitment, purpose, and a grateful attitude.

Let's talk about this further.

NOTES

Earning

The Pull of the Culture vs. the Mind and Heart of God

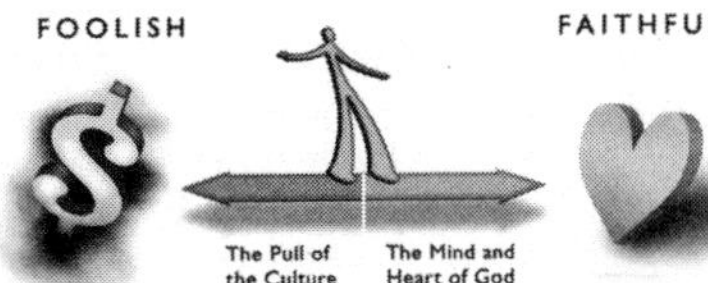

The Pull of the Culture on the earner says:

- "Your value is measured by your __________ and your paycheck."
- "A little more money will solve all your problems."

The Mind and Heart of God counters:

- Our value is not measured by what we do but by who we are—beloved sons and daughters of God.
- We are called to join him in the ongoing management of his creation.
- Work is a __________, not a curse.

The Diligent Earner is:

One who works with commitment, purpose, and a grateful attitude.

- Be diligent.

> Colossians 3:23 (NLT): *"Work hard and cheerfully at whatever you do."*

- Be ____________________.

> Colossians 3:23 (NLT): *"[Work] as though you were working for the Lord rather than for people."*

  - Serve God.
  - Provide for ourselves and those dependent on us.

> 1 Timothy 5:8 (NLT): *"Those who won't care for their own relatives . . . have denied what we believe."*

- Be ____________________.

> Deuteronomy 8:17-18: *"You may say to yourself, 'My power and the strength of my hands have produced this wealth for me.' Remember the LORD your God, for it is he who gives you the ability to produce wealth."*

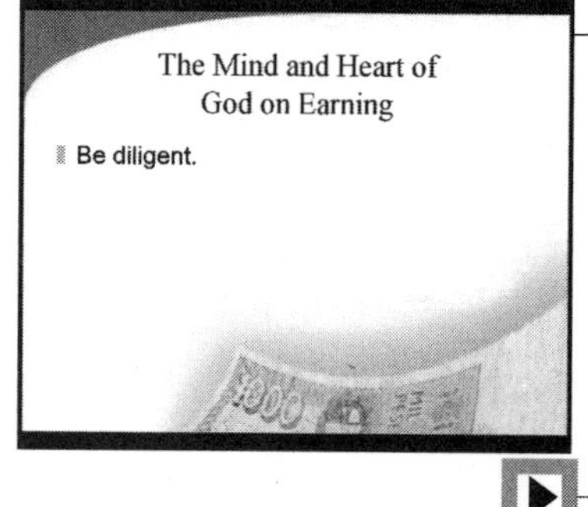

The Mind and Heart of
God on Earning
Be diligent.

Colossians 3:23 commands us to be diligent: "Work hard and cheerfully at whatever you do" (NLT).

This same verse also calls us to be PURPOSEFUL. We are to work "as though you were working for the Lord rather than people" (NLT). When we work we have the opportunity to serve God.

First Timothy 5:8 further clarifies a key purpose of work by calling us to provide for ourselves and those dependent on us. This verse says that "those who won't care for their own relatives . . . have denied what we believe" (NLT).

Finally, we are to be GRATEFUL. Deuteronomy 8:17–18 reminds us that even our ability to earn is a gift from God: "You may say to yourself, 'My power and the strength of my hands have produced this wealth for me.' Remember the LORD your God, for it is he who gives you the ability to produce wealth."

2 minutes

Practical Tips on Earning

Participant's Guide, page 33.

Keeping these points in mind, let's look at the earning/income section of the Spending Plan worksheet.

Net Take-home Pay

Notice under Salary #1 and #2, we ask you to put down your *net* take-home pay.

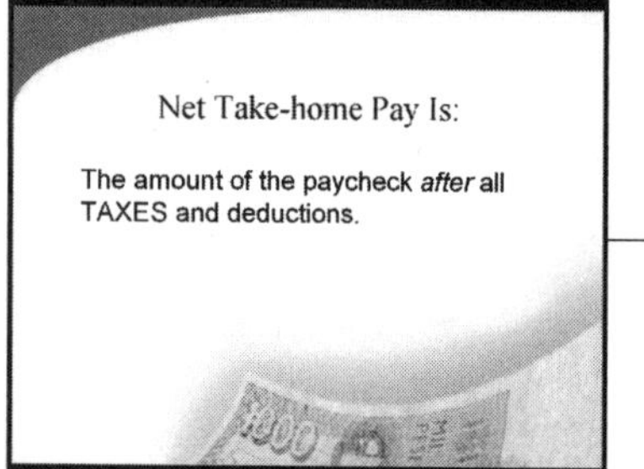

What we mean by that is:

the amount of the paycheck *after* all TAXES and deductions.

That's an easy figure to write down for those of you whose paycheck stays the same.

NOTES

The Diligent Earner is:

One who works with commitment, purpose, and a grateful attitude.

- Be diligent.

> Colossians 3:23 (NLT): *"Work hard and cheerfully at whatever you do."*

- Be ______________________.

> Colossians 3:23 (NLT): *"[Work] as though you were working for the Lord rather than for people."*

  - Serve God.
  - Provide for ourselves and those dependent on us.

> 1 Timothy 5:8 (NLT): *"Those who won't care for their own relatives . . . have denied what we believe."*

- Be ______________________.

> Deuteronomy 8:17-18: *"You may say to yourself, 'My power and the strength of my hands have produced this wealth for me.' Remember the LORD your God, for it is he who gives you the ability to produce wealth."*

Practical Tips on Earning

Net take-home pay is:

The amount of the paycheck *after* all ___________ and deductions.

Variable Income:

Take a ______________________ estimate of your after-tax annual income (based on your income of the past few years) and divide by twelve.

Example: $30,000 ÷ 12 = $2,500 per month*

Two-Income Strategy:

Cover all the basics—all ongoing necessary expenses—with one income. For example:

- Giving
- Savings
- Housing
- Food
- Clothing
- Transportation
- Basic household
- Basic entertainment

*See page 107 in the Appendix for more information.

But some of you have *variable* incomes because you are self-employed or your income is based on commissions. How many of you have variable incomes? Raise your hand.

Pause.

Variable Incomes

Take a CONSERVATIVE estimate of your after-tax annual income—based on your income of the past few years—and divide by twelve.

Example:
$30,000/12 = $2,500 per month

For those of you in this situation:

Take a CONSERVATIVE estimate of your after-tax annual income—based on your income of the past few years—and divide by twelve.

For example, a $30,000 estimate of after-tax annual income divided by twelve months results in an estimated average monthly income of $2,500 per month.

In months when income exceeds $2,500, the excess goes into short-term savings to be drawn on in months when income is less than $2,500.

If you would like more information on variable incomes and how to arrive at a conservative estimate, see page 107 in the Appendix during the next activity.

Two Incomes

Notice on your Spending Plan worksheet that there is room for more than one income.

How many of you are from two-income families? Raise your hand.

Pause.

Let's take a minute to talk about a strategy for living on two incomes.

NOTES

Practical Tips on Earning

Net take-home pay is:

The amount of the paycheck *after* all __________ and deductions.

Variable Income:

Take a ____________________ estimate of your after-tax annual income (based on your income of the past few years) and divide by twelve.

Example: $30,000 ÷ 12 = $2,500 per month*

Two-Income Strategy:

Cover all the basics—all ongoing necessary expenses—with one income. For example:

- Giving
- Savings
- Housing
- Food
- Clothing
- Transportation
- Basic household
- Basic entertainment

*See page 107 in the Appendix for more information.

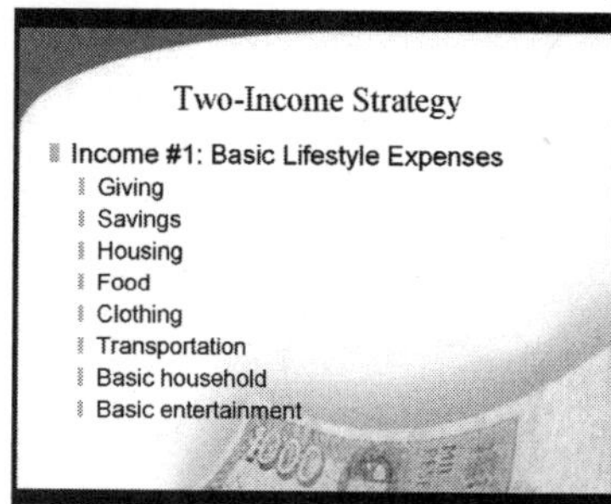

The principle is to cover all the basics—all ongoing necessary expenses—with one income. For example, that would include:

- Giving
- Savings
- Housing
- Food
- Clothing
- Transportation
- Basic household
- Basic entertainment

Turn to page 34.

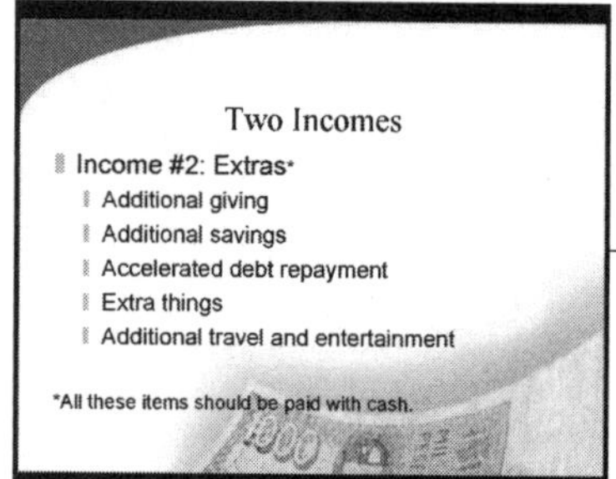

Participant's Guide, page 34.

The second income should be used only for "extras." For example,

- Additional giving
- Additional savings
- Accelerated debt repayment
- Additional travel and entertainment
- Other non-essentials

All these items should be paid with cash so you don't have any ongoing payments.

Thus, if the second income stops for any reason, your basic needs can still be met.

If your present situation makes it impossible to meet basic expenses with one income, then put a significant amount of that second income into savings so that there is money in reserve in case that second income is lost.

Another practical tip on earning has to do with your raises.

NOTES

Practical Tips on Earning

Net take-home pay is:

The amount of the paycheck *after* all __________ and deductions.

Variable Income:

Take a ____________________ estimate of your after-tax annual income (based on your income of the past few years) and divide by twelve.

Example: $30,000 ÷ 12 = $2,500 per month*

Two-Income Strategy:

Cover all the basics—all ongoing necessary expenses—with one income. For example:

- Giving
- Savings
- Housing
- Food
- Clothing
- Transportation
- Basic household
- Basic entertainment

*See page 107 in the Appendix for more information.

The second income should be used only for "extras":

- Additional giving
- Additional savings
- Accelerated debt repayment
- Additional travel and entertainment
- Other non-essentials

All these items should be paid with cash.

If your present situation makes it impossible to meet basic expenses with one income, then put a significant amount of that second income into savings so that there is money in reserve in case that second income is lost.

Question: What happens to your raises?

(See page 108 in the Appendix.)

Deciding ____________________ how you'll use raises is a key strategy in reaching your financial goals.

Individual Activity: *Spending Plan Application*

Fill in the Income category on the Spending Plan worksheet.

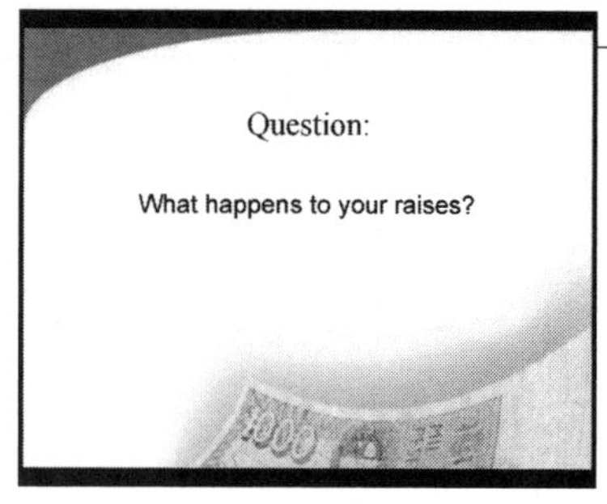
Question:
What happens to your raises?

The question is: What happens to your raises?

Some might answer that 10 percent of the raise goes to God's work in the world and 10 percent goes to savings. That's excellent! But even these folks would have to acknowledge that the other 80 percent of their raise just seems to disappear into some black hole. Spending somehow expands to use all the available funds, and three or four months later, most of us can't tell where our raise went.

And yet, even a modest raise on a modest salary can add up to a significant amount of additional income in just a few years. An example of this appears in your Appendix on page 108.

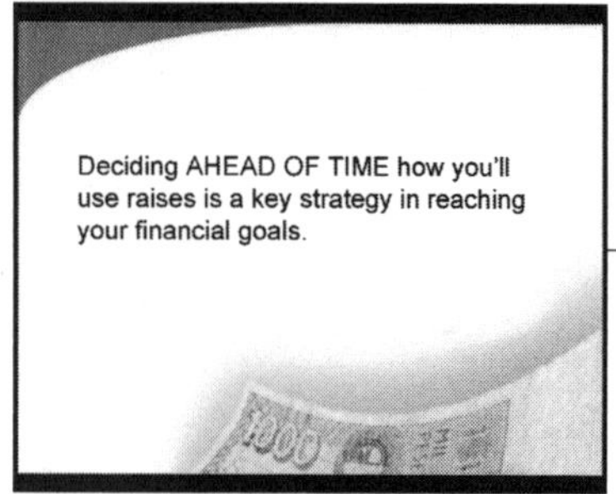
Deciding AHEAD OF TIME how you'll use raises is a key strategy in reaching your financial goals.

Whatever your financial goals are, deciding AHEAD OF TIME how you'll use raises is a key strategy in reaching your financial goals.

5 minutes

Individual Activity: *Spending Plan Application*

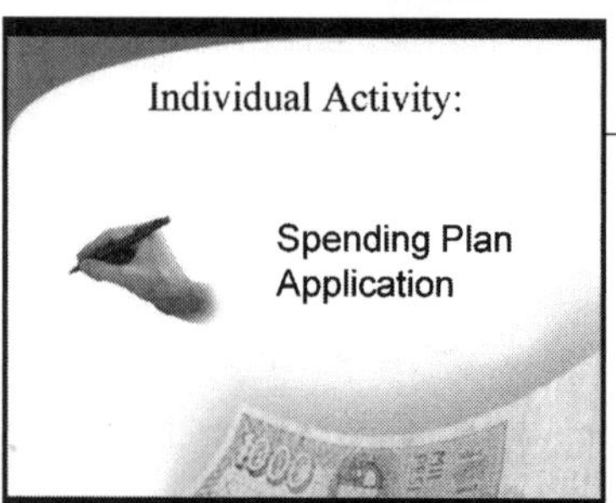
Individual Activity:
Spending Plan Application

Objective
For participants to document their current income on the Spending Plan worksheet.

Directions
Fill in the income category on the Spending Plan worksheet. You'll have 5 minutes.

Call the group back together after 5 minutes.

Congratulations. You have completed the first section of your Spending Plan worksheet. Now, let's look at the next section on your Spending Plan.

7 minutes

Giving

Participant's Guide, page 35.

NOTES

The second income should be used only for "extras":

- Additional giving
- Additional savings
- Accelerated debt repayment
- Additional travel and entertainment
- Other non-essentials

All these items should be paid with cash.

If your present situation makes it impossible to meet basic expenses with one income, then put a significant amount of that second income into savings so that there is money in reserve in case that second income is lost.

Question: What happens to your raises?

(See page 108 in the Appendix.)

Deciding ______________________ how you'll use raises is a key strategy in reaching your financial goals.

Individual Activity: *Spending Plan Application*

Fill in the Income category on the Spending Plan worksheet.

The second area of our financial lives is giving. But just as it was for earning, giving is about more than just finances. It's about who you *are* and who you are *becoming* as a giver.

We're going to begin by watching a video that shows a variety of viewpoints about giving.

Video: *The Offering* (6 minutes)

View video: *The Offering*.

There are lots of emotions surrounding the topic of giving. Some of us may feel like our personal needs are more urgent than those of the body of Christ. Some of us may be guilt ridden, and others may feel pride about how much they are giving.

The key question is: How can we become like the fourth character in the drama and view giving as a grateful response to God's ownership of *all* we have?

Let's begin by looking at what our culture says about giving.

4 minutes

The Pull of the Culture vs. the Mind and Heart of God

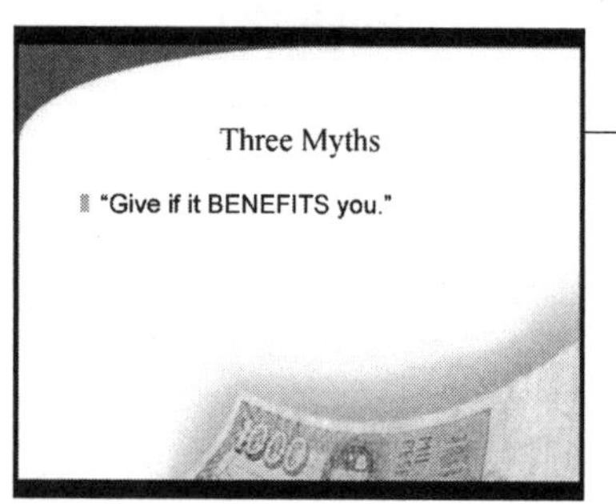

The Pull of the Culture uses three myths to pull the giver away from the Mind and Heart of God.

→ First, "Give if it BENEFITS you."

Our culture tends to promote giving in the context of its benefits to the individual: "Give as a tax benefit. Give if it makes you feel good. Give if it results in popularity or position or power."

→ Next, "Give if there is anything left over."

NOTES

Giving

Video: *The Offering*

Notes

The Pull of the Culture vs. the Mind and Heart of God

FOOLISH

FAITHFUL

The Pull of the Culture

The Mind and Heart of God

Three Myths:

- "Give if it ______________ you."
- "Give if there is anything left over."
- "Give out of a sense of duty."

For the vast majority of people, giving comes last. During the 1980s and 1990s—the most prosperous period in U.S. history—although giving increased in absolute dollars, it decreased as a percentage of income. At its core, our culture promotes giving as something you do with whatever is left over.

Finally, "Give out of a sense of duty."

Our culture tells us that we have a duty to give something. But, for the most part, giving out of duty is only a token gesture rather than truly generous giving from the heart.

In each case, the culture pulls us toward a self-centered mindset rather than one consistent with the Mind and Heart of God.

Let's look at the Mind and Heart of God on giving.

Turn to page 36.

The Generous Giver

Participant's Guide, page 36.

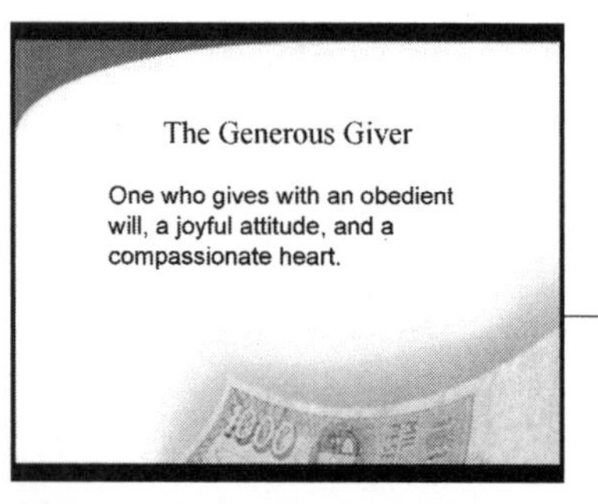
The Generous Giver
One who gives with an obedient will, a joyful attitude, and a compassionate heart.

The Bible characterizes the God-honoring giver as "generous."

The generous giver is one who gives with an obedient will, a joyful attitude, and a compassionate heart.

We Are Made to Give

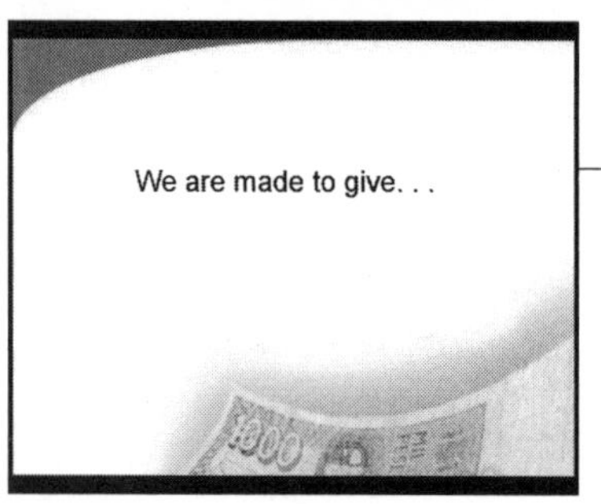
We are made to give. . .

In the Mind and Heart of God, we are made to give.

NOTES

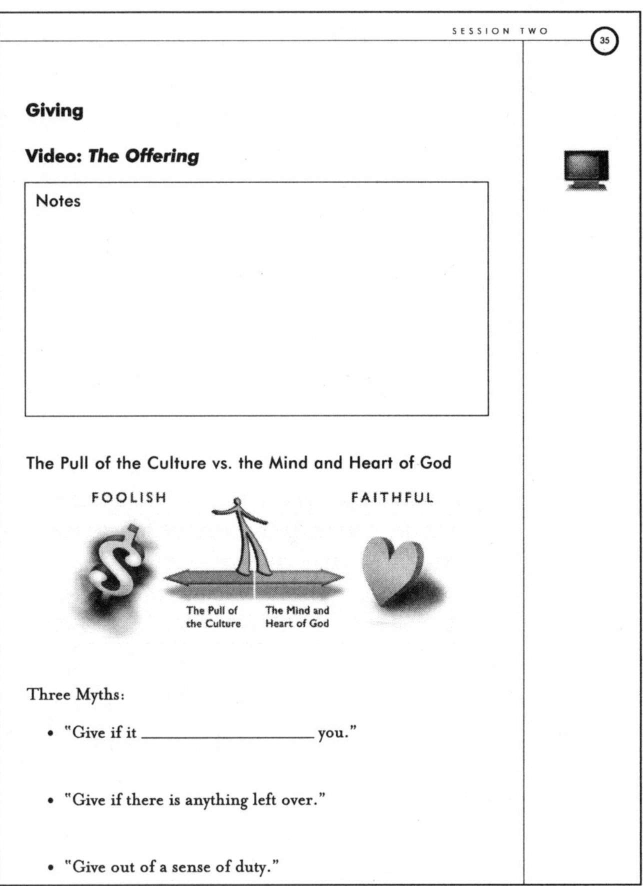

SESSION TWO 35

Giving

Video: *The Offering*

Notes

The Pull of the Culture vs. the Mind and Heart of God

FOOLISH FAITHFUL

The Pull of the Culture — The Mind and Heart of God

Three Myths:

- "Give if it ________________ you."
- "Give if there is anything left over."
- "Give out of a sense of duty."

36 SESSION TWO

The Generous Giver is:

One who gives with an obedient will, a joyful attitude, and a compassionate heart.

- We are made to give.
- Why God wants us to give:
  - As a response to God's ____________________.

    James 1:17 (NLT): *"Whatever is good and perfect comes to us from God above."*

  - To focus on him as our source of security

    Matthew 6:19–20a (NLT): *"Don't store up treasures here on earth, where they can be eaten by moths, and get rusty, and where thieves break in and steal. Store your treasures in heaven."*

    Matthew 6:32b–33 (NLT): *"Your heavenly Father already knows all your needs, and he will give you all you need from day to day if you live for him and make the kingdom of God your primary concern."*

  - To help achieve economic justice
  - To bless others and to be blessed
  - To break the __________ of money

We are made to be channels, not reservoirs. A body of water without an outlet becomes stagnant. A life without an outlet for some of its resources becomes stagnant. Giving is the channel for God's heart to flow through us—a heart of love, generosity, and compassion. When we give, we become more of who God wants us to be. Created in his image, we are not complete or fully satisfied unless we share a portion of what we have with others. Simply put, giving changes lives.

God Wants Us to Give

Let's take a look at what the Bible says about why God wants us to give.

First of all, giving is a response to God's GOODNESS. James 1:17 says "Whatever is good and perfect comes to us from God above" (NLT).

Our giving is simply a way to say, "Thank you, I'm grateful."

Second, God wants us to focus on him as our source of security. In Matthew 6, Jesus issues this warning to his followers: "Don't store up treasures here on earth, where they can be eaten by moths, and get rusty, and where thieves break in and steal. Store your treasures in heaven" (NLT).

In other words, don't base your security on riches that just one economic downturn could quickly destroy, but base your security on things of God that will last forever.

In this same chapter of Matthew Jesus goes on to say, "Your heavenly Father already knows all your needs, and he will give you all you need from day to day if you live for him and make the kingdom of God your primary concern" (Matthew 6:32b–33 NLT).

NOTES

The Generous Giver is:

One who gives with an obedient will, a joyful attitude, and a compassionate heart.

- We are made to give.
- Why God wants us to give:
    - As a response to God's ______________________.

James 1:17 (NLT): *"Whatever is good and perfect comes to us from God above."*

- To focus on him as our source of security

Matthew 6:19–20a (NLT): *"Don't store up treasures here on earth, where they can be eaten by moths, and get rusty, and where thieves break in and steal. Store your treasures in heaven."*

Matthew 6:32b–33 (NLT): *"Your heavenly Father already knows all your needs, and he will give you all you need from day to day if you live for him and make the kingdom of God your primary concern."*

- To help achieve economic justice
- To bless others and to be blessed
- To break the ____________ of money

We are to trust God for our ultimate provision.

Third, God wants to use us to help achieve economic justice in the world.

Throughout Scripture, material blessing has been linked to obedience, particularly in reference to justice and compassion for the poor. If God has blessed us beyond our needs, chances are it's not for the purpose of raising our standard of living but for the purpose of raising our standard of *giving*. We are called to love. We can give without loving, but we cannot love without giving.

Fourth, God wants us to give to bless others and to be blessed.

The relationship between giving and blessing goes all the way back to God's original covenant with Abraham. In Genesis 12:2-3 God tells Abraham that he is being blessed in part so that he can be a blessing to others. It *is* more blessed to give than to receive. We *do* reap what we sow. We miss that joy and blessing in our own lives when we hold on to what we have with clenched fists rather than sharing freely with others.

A final and very important reason for giving is that it breaks the HOLD money can otherwise have on us.

Earlier we pointed out that money is a very powerful thing. It wants to have our allegiance, to capture our hearts, to *control* us! But the unnatural act of giving it away rather than using it for other purposes breaks the hold money might otherwise have over us. This is a very crucial point and perhaps a key reason for the Bible's strong emphasis on giving. Here's a true story that illustrates this point.

If you have a personal story or know of someone whose experience demonstrates how a God-honoring giver broke the hold money had on them, you may wish to replace the following story with your own.

NOTES

The Generous Giver is:

One who gives with an obedient will, a joyful attitude, and a compassionate heart.

- We are made to give.
- Why God wants us to give:
  - As a response to God's ______________________.

James 1:17 (NLT): "*Whatever is good and perfect comes to us from God above.*"

  - To focus on him as our source of security

Matthew 6:19–20a (NLT): "*Don't store up treasures here on earth, where they can be eaten by moths, and get rusty, and where thieves break in and steal. Store your treasures in heaven.*"

Matthew 6:32b–33 (NLT): "*Your heavenly Father already knows all your needs, and he will give you all you need from day to day if you live for him and make the kingdom of God your primary concern.*"

  - To help achieve economic justice
  - To bless others and to be blessed
  - To break the ___________ of money

For weeks, Elizabeth had been looking forward to purchasing a very expensive dining room set. She had the money to do so, but for some reason she couldn't escape the nagging feeling that this was not the best use of her resources. Finally, after weeks of wrestling over what to do, she sat down and wrote two checks to Christian ministries that equaled the cost of the dining room set.

While this act was undoubtedly pleasing to God and gave Elizabeth the feeling she had done the right thing, the surprising thing was what happened afterward. Within twenty-four hours, she had lost all desire for the dining room set. In fact, she could not believe she had ever wanted it! She already had a wonderful dining room set, and the purchase of a new one now seemed entirely foolish. Her mindset had been completely changed.

The point of the story is that the act of giving broke the hold that money—in this case, the stuff it could buy—had on Elizabeth. Giving does something in our lives that nothing else can do. Don't miss its joy and blessing.

Now we're going to take some time to reflect on giving.

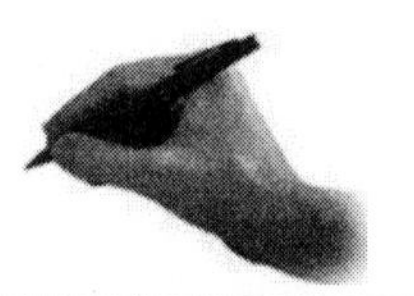

Individual Activity:
The Generous Giver

Individual Activity: *The Generous Giver*

Participant's Guide, page 37.

Objective
For participants to identify how God wants them to grow in the area of giving.

Directions

1. After thinking through the Mind and Heart of God on giving, in what way is God nudging you?
2. Is there an action step he wants you to take? If so, write it in the space provided.

I'll give you 5 minutes to complete this.

Call the group back together after 5 minutes.

NOTES

The Generous Giver is:

One who gives with an obedient will, a joyful attitude, and a compassionate heart.

- We are made to give.
- Why God wants us to give:
  - As a response to God's ____________________.

James 1:17 (NLT): "*Whatever is good and perfect comes to us from God above.*"

  - To focus on him as our source of security

Matthew 6:19–20a (NLT): "*Don't store up treasures here on earth, where they can be eaten by moths, and get rusty, and where thieves break in and steal. Store your treasures in heaven.*"

Matthew 6:32b–33 (NLT): "*Your heavenly Father already knows all your needs, and he will give you all you need from day to day if you live for him and make the kingdom of God your primary concern.*"

  - To help achieve economic justice
  - To bless others and to be blessed
  - To break the __________ of money

Individual Activity: *The Generous Giver*

1. After thinking through the Mind and Heart of God on giving, in what way is God nudging you?

2. Is there an action step he wants you to take? If so, write it in the space provided.

Many of us desire to be closer to the Mind and Heart of God as givers, but because of personal circumstances, we find it very difficult. Let's talk about how we can get started and begin to build giving into our Spending Plan worksheets.

Turn to page 38.

2 minutes

Practical Tips on Giving

Participant's Guide, page 38.

→ Although generous giving is ultimately a matter of the heart, the biblical benchmark for giving is the tithe.

Generally, the tithe is defined as 10 percent. For our purposes in this course, we won't stress percentages. If we did, some of you would say, "You don't have any idea what my personal circumstances are. To give 10 percent would be an unbelievable, overwhelming hardship."

If you are a Christ-follower, however, it should be your desire to reach the goal of the tithe. To do so, we stress two things.

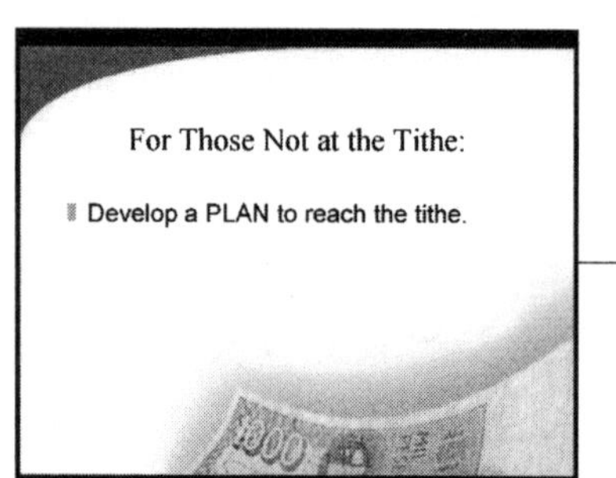
For Those Not at the Tithe:
Develop a PLAN to reach the tithe.

→ For those not at the tithe: first, you need to develop a PLAN to reach the tithe.

Goals require plans. Later, we'll talk about some action steps that can free up money. And, if giving more to God's work is a priority for you, you'll find ways to do that.

→ Second, begin by giving SOMETHING.

It may not be very much, but start with at least something, regardless of your circumstances.

NOTES

Practical Tips on Giving

The biblical benchmark for giving is the tithe.

For those not at the tithe:

- Develop a ____________________ to reach the tithe.
- Begin by giving ______________________.

For those at the tithe:

> The tithe is a wonderful goal to aspire to; it's a terrible place to stop.

Key Question: How much of *God's* money do I need to live on?

Individual Activity: *Spending Plan Application*

1. Refer back to page 30 where your goals are listed, and page 37 where your action step for giving is written. Consider your current financial situation and what you are becoming as a giver.
2. Set a short-term goal for giving, and fill in the giving line on your Spending Plan worksheet.

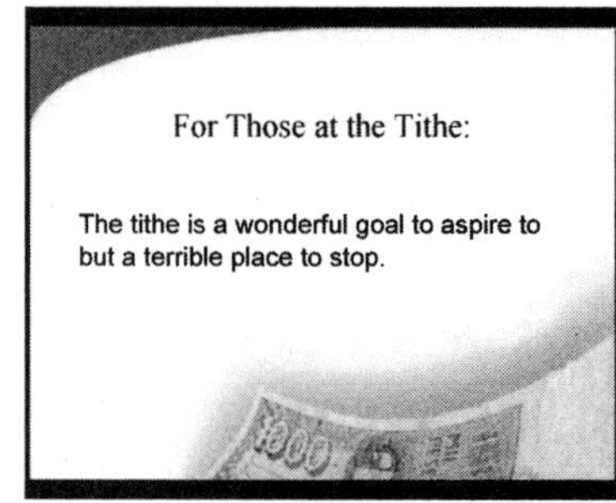
For Those at the Tithe:
The tithe is a wonderful goal to aspire to but a terrible place to stop.

Another reason we've chosen not to emphasize a specific percentage is that some of you might be inclined to say, "Right on! I'm already at 10 percent. I'm doing my fair share and everybody else ought to be there, too."

➔ For those at the tithe, we affirm your commitment, but while the tithe is a wonderful goal to aspire to, it's a terrible place to stop.

For example, a family of four earning $25,000 a year and giving $2,500 to God's work in the world may be approaching sacrificial giving. On the other hand, a family of four earning $250,000 a year and giving $25,000 to God's work in the world is not even close to giving with a generous heart.

Season-of-life issues are also a factor. For example, a couple may be in a season of life when their children are raised and on their own. Their house is paid for, and they have all the basic possessions they need. They have a pension plan that will provide money for retirement. They are at a stage in life in which income is going up and expenses are dropping. In all probability, to give only 10 percent wouldn't be God honoring.

Once again, generous giving is ultimately an issue of the heart. The question that flows out of a loving, obedient heart is not, "How much of *my* money should I give to God's work in the world?"

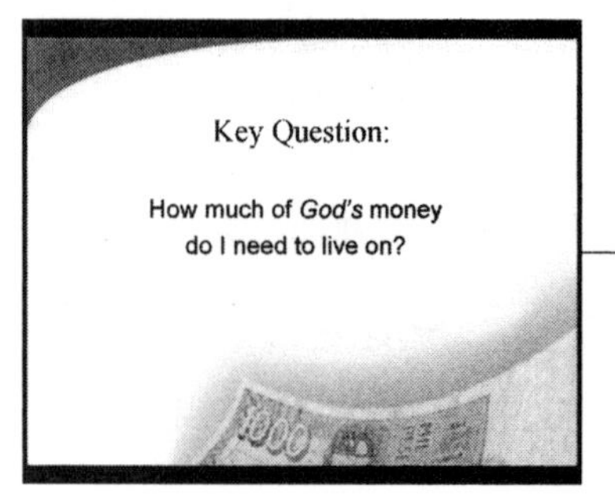
Key Question:
How much of *God's* money do I need to live on?

➔ Rather, the question is, "How much of *God's* money do I need to live on?"

We do need a portion of God's money to provide for our needs, our family's needs, and to plan appropriately for the future, but the rest is all to be available for God's purposes.

Now let's look at how we can incorporate giving into our Spending Plan worksheets.

NOTES

38 SESSION TWO

Practical Tips on Giving

The biblical benchmark for giving is the tithe.

For those not at the tithe:

- Develop a ________________ to reach the tithe.
- Begin by giving ________________.

For those at the tithe:

The tithe is a wonderful goal to aspire to; it's a terrible place to stop.

Key Question: How much of God's money do I need to live on?

Individual Activity: *Spending Plan Application*

1. Refer back to page 30 where your goals are listed, and page 37 where your action step for giving is written. Consider your current financial situation and what you are becoming as a giver.
2. Set a short-term goal for giving, and fill in the giving line on your Spending Plan worksheet.

5 minutes

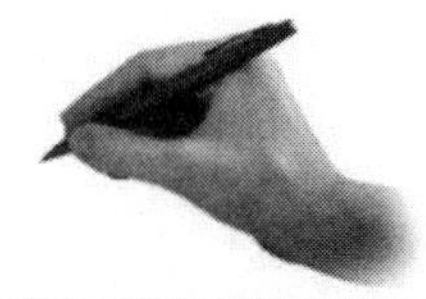

Individual Activity:
Spending Plan Application

Individual Activity: *Spending Plan Application*

Objective
For participants to set short-term goals for giving.

Directions

1. Refer back to page 30 where your goals are listed, and page 37 where your action step for giving is written. Consider your current financial situation and what you are becoming as a giver.
2. Set a short-term goal for giving, and fill in the giving line on your Spending Plan worksheet.

You have 5 minutes to do this.

Call the group back together after 5 minutes.

Saving

Participant's Guide, page 39.

FOOLISH
Saving
FAITHFUL
The Pull of the Culture
The Mind and Heart of God

The third area of our financial lives is saving. As in previous sections, the key question is, Who are you becoming as a saver? Are you becoming more faithful or more foolish? Just as we suggested you begin your Spending Plan by giving to God, we suggest that your next step be giving to yourself—which is saving.

3 minutes

The Pull of the Culture vs. the Mind and Heart of God

The Pull of the Culture says, "Eat, drink, and be merry, for tomorrow you die."

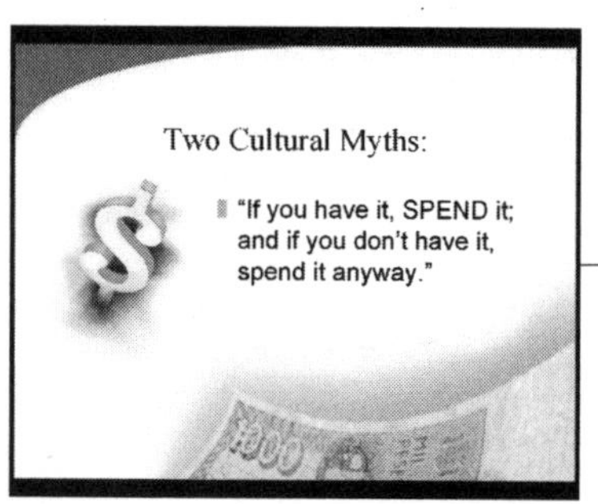
Two Cultural Myths:
"If you have it, SPEND it; and if you don't have it, spend it anyway."

Embodied in this attitude are two additional cultural myths about saving.

First, "If you have it, SPEND it; and if you don't have it, spend it anyway."

NOTES

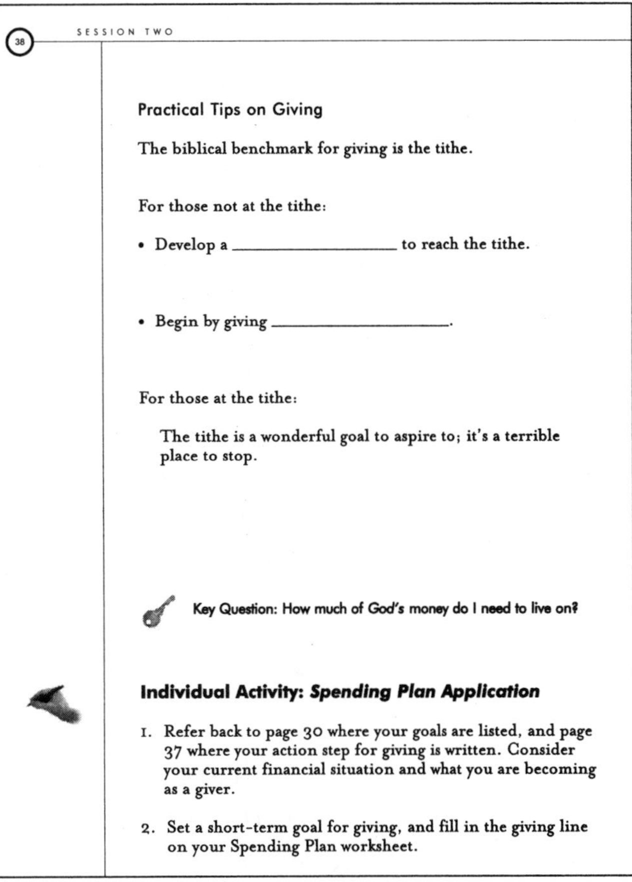

Practical Tips on Giving

The biblical benchmark for giving is the tithe.

For those not at the tithe:

- Develop a ________________ to reach the tithe.
- Begin by giving ________________.

For those at the tithe:

The tithe is a wonderful goal to aspire to; it's a terrible place to stop.

Key Question: How much of *God's* money do I need to live on?

Individual Activity: *Spending Plan Application*

1. Refer back to page 30 where your goals are listed, and page 37 where your action step for giving is written. Consider your current financial situation and what you are becoming as a giver.
2. Set a short-term goal for giving, and fill in the giving line on your Spending Plan worksheet.

Saving

The Pull of the Culture vs. the Mind and Heart of God

Two Cultural Myths:

- "If you have it, ____________ it; and if you don't have it, spend it anyway."
- "It is futile to save."

The culture not only discourages saving, it encourages spending—even to the point of debt. Many of us have bought into this way of thinking. A consequence of insufficient savings is an inability to meet financial emergencies. For example, the United States has one of the lowest savings rates of all developed nations. In the years 1997 to 2000, over 4 million bankruptcies occurred during one of the most prosperous periods in U. S. history.

> The bankruptcy statistic above was reported in *USA Today* (November 24, 2000). You may wish to update this statistic by checking the website for the Administrative Office of the U.S. Courts, www.uscourts.gov.

Second, "It is futile to save."

The culture further discourages saving by promoting a short-term, immediate gratification mentality and diminishing the value of planning ahead. The culture tells us, "You work hard for your money. Enjoy it—while you can! Besides, establishing good savings takes too long and, in the end, you won't have enough anyway. It's futile to save."

Turn to page 40.

The Wise Saver

> Participant's Guide, page 40.

In contrast, the Bible characterizes the God-honoring saver as "wise."

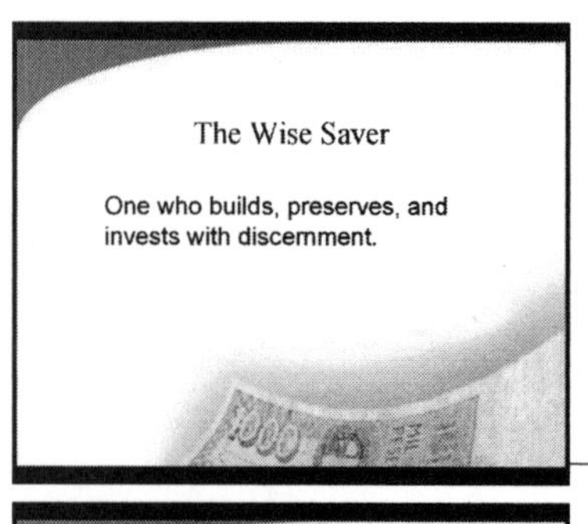

The wise saver is one who builds, preserves, and invests with discernment.

The Mind and Heart of God on saving is:

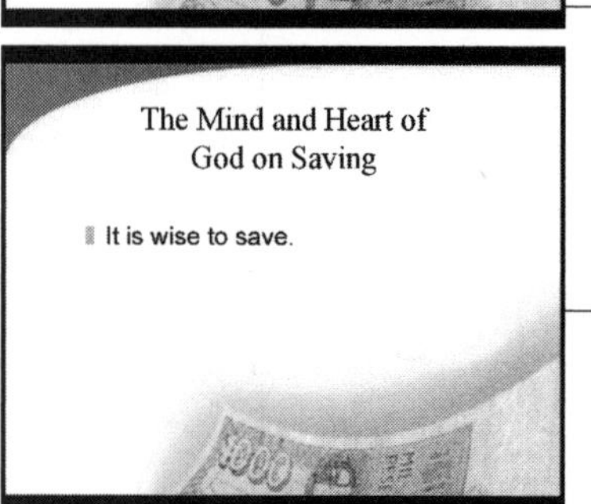

First, it is wise to save. Proverbs 21:20 says, "In the house of the wise are stores of choice food and oil . . . but [the] foolish . . . devour all [they have]."

NOTES

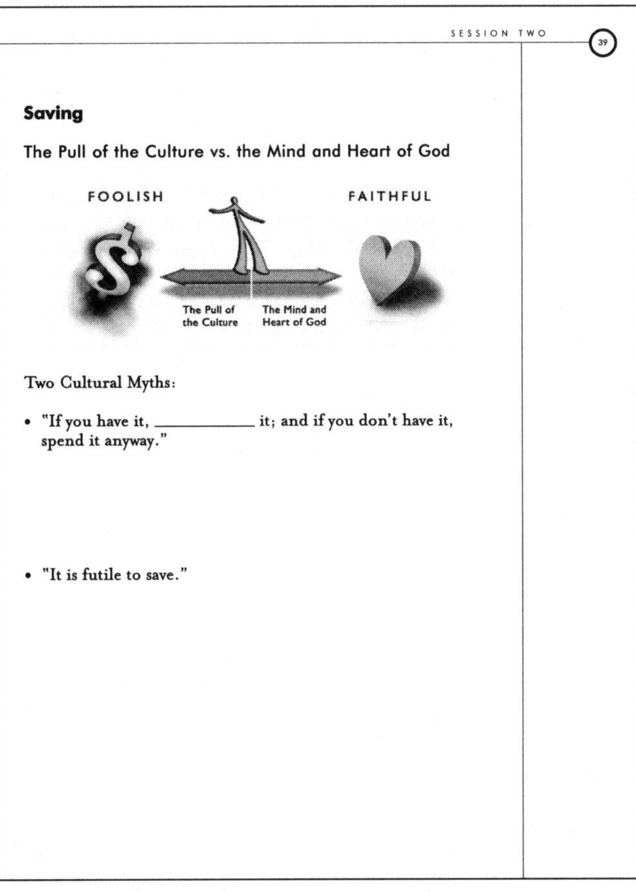

Saving

The Pull of the Culture vs. the Mind and Heart of God

Two Cultural Myths:

- "If you have it, __________ it; and if you don't have it, spend it anyway."

- "It is futile to save."

The Wise Saver is:

One who builds, preserves, and invests with discernment.

The Mind and Heart of God on saving is:

- It is wise to save.

> Proverbs 21:20: *"In the house of the wise are stores of choice food and oil, but a foolish man devours all he has."*

- It is sinful to hoard. (Luke 12:16–21)

What's the difference between saving and hoarding?

- Saving is putting money aside for __________ goals.
- Hoarding is continuing to put money aside after our goals are reached.

How can we avoid hoarding?

- Understand our __________

- Answer the question, "When is enough, enough?"

> Ecclesiastes 5:10 (NLT): *"Those who love money will never have enough."*

Second, it is sinful to hoard.

We talked about the parable of the rich fool with the overflowing barn in Luke 12 in the previous session.

These Scriptures teach that it is wise to save for unexpected hardship, but also that it is foolish to stockpile beyond our needs.

Saving versus Hoarding
Saving is putting money aside for APPROPRIATE goals.

So, what's the difference between saving and hoarding?

Saving is putting money aside for APPROPRIATE goals like retirement, education, etc.

Hoarding is continuing to put money aside after our goals are reached.

In other words, like the rich fool we think, "Our barns are full, so let's just make them bigger. Let's save more just for the sake of having more."

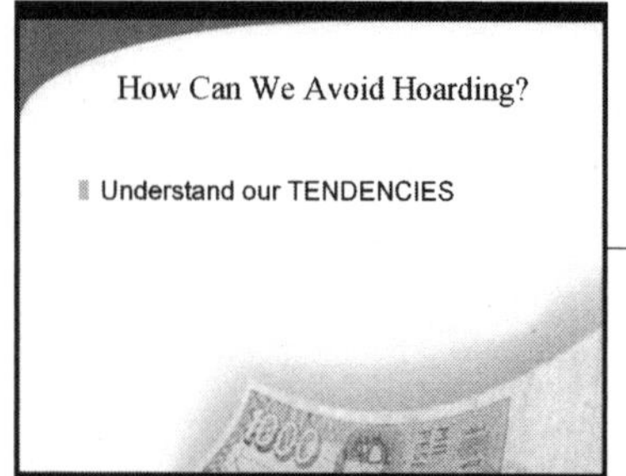
How Can We Avoid Hoarding?
Understand our TENDENCIES

How can we avoid hoarding?

First, we need to understand our TENDENCIES.

For example, some of us discovered on the Money Motivation Quiz in the pre-work that money represents security. If so, we may have the inclination to keep more of it than we reasonably need "just to be safe." On the other hand, some may be more relationally oriented and tend to spend their money on others rather than adequately preparing for the future. These people may need to be more disciplined in their saving habits.

Another way to avoid hoarding is to answer the difficult but absolutely critical question, "When is enough, enough?"

NOTES

The Wise Saver is:

One who builds, preserves, and invests with discernment.

The Mind and Heart of God on saving is:

- It is wise to save.

> Proverbs 21:20: *"In the house of the wise are stores of choice food and oil, but a foolish man devours all he has."*

- It is sinful to hoard. (Luke 12:16-21)

What's the difference between saving and hoarding?

- Saving is putting money aside for ________________ goals.
- Hoarding is continuing to put money aside after our goals are reached.

How can we avoid hoarding?

- Understand our ________________
- Answer the question, "When is enough, enough?"

> Ecclesiastes 5:10 (NLT): *"Those who love money will never have enough."*

That is a question that ultimately has to be answered between each one of us and God. But you can be certain that if we attempt to answer it by comparing what we have with what others have, the answer will always be, "Enough is *never* enough."

Ecclesiastes 5:10 says that "those who love money will never have enough" (NLT).

9 minutes

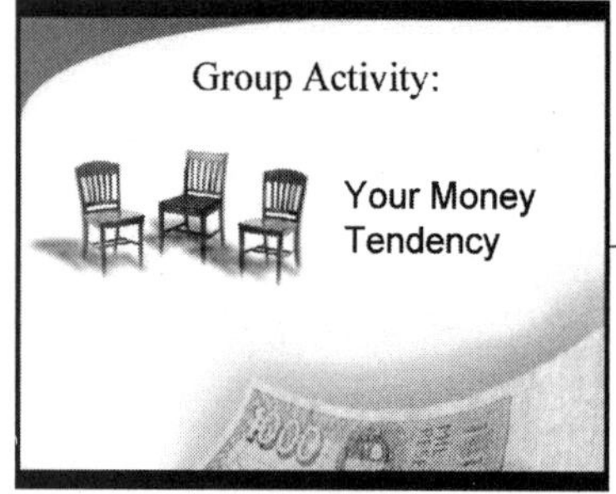
Group Activity:
Your Money Tendency

Let's take a closer look at our money tendency.

Group Activity: *Your Money Tendency*

Participant's Guide, page 41.

Objective
For participants to reflect on their money tendency and consider how they can move closer to God in this area.

Directions

1. Check the box below that applies to you. If you completed the Money Motivation Quiz in the pre-work, you can use those results instead.
2. Team up with two or three other people and answer the following questions:
   - What is one way your money tendency impacts you?
   - What is one step you can take to begin limiting that impact?

You will have 8 minutes to do this.

NOTES

Group Activity: *Your Money Tendency*

1. Check the box below that applies to you. If you completed the Money Motivation Quiz in the pre-work, you can use those results instead.

Money is important to me because it allows me:

- ❑ *Freedom—to do what I want to do. Independence is important to me. Money means having the freedom to do what I want.*
- ❑ *Security—to feel safe. Stability is important to me. Money means having protection from life's uncertainties.*
- ❑ *Power—to get ahead in life. Success is important to me. Money means having control over the things I value most.*
- ❑ *Love—to buy things for others. Relationships are important to me. Money means having the means to express my love to others and to build relationships.*

2. Team up with two or three other people and answer the following questions:

    - What is one way your money tendency impacts you?

    - What is one step you can take to begin limiting that impact?

Your Money Tendency

Money is important to me because it allows me:

- ❑ Freedom—to do what I want to do. Independence is important to me. Money means having the freedom to do what I want.
- ❑ Security—to feel safe. Stability is important to me. Money means having protection from life's uncertainties.
- ❑ Power—to get ahead in life. Success is important to me. Money means having control over the things I value most.
- ❑ Love—to buy things for others. Relationships are important to me. Money means having the means to express my love to others and to build relationships.

Call the group back together after 8 minutes.

Wrap-up (1 minute)

What were some of the ways your money tendency impacted you?

Solicit two or three comments from the group. Be sure to repeat their answers so everyone hears the response.

Possible responses:

- My money tendency is security. The way it affects me is that I worry a lot about not having enough even though God has been very good to us and we have everything we need. One step I could take is to memorize . . .
- Mine is love. I buy our children things thinking it will prove to them how much I love them.
- Mine is power. I tend to be control oriented. When I buy things for others I then feel like they owe me. I want to get more money for the power it gives me to control people and things.

NOTES

Group Activity: *Your Money Tendency*

1. Check the box below that applies to you. If you completed the Money Motivation Quiz in the pre-work, you can use those results instead.

Money is important to me because it allows me:

- ❑ *Freedom—to do what I want to do. Independence is important to me. Money means having the freedom to do what I want.*
- ❑ *Security—to feel safe. Stability is important to me. Money means having protection from life's uncertainties.*
- ❑ *Power—to get ahead in life. Success is important to me. Money means having control over the things I value most.*
- ❑ *Love—to buy things for others. Relationships are important to me. Money means having the means to express my love to others and to build relationships.*

2. Team up with two or three other people and answer the following questions:

- What is one way your money tendency impacts you?
- What is one step you can take to begin limiting that impact?

As we've discovered, money impacts us in a variety of ways, including our understanding of what it means to be a "wise saver." In the next session, we'll continue our discussion on saving.

SESSION SUMMARY

This concludes session two. We've covered the first two things you can do with money—earning and giving. And we've begun to talk about the third area, which is saving.

In the next session, we'll look at practical tips for saving and then explore the area of debt.

Break.

Session Three

SAVING AND DEBT

SESSION SNAPSHOT

OBJECTIVES

In this session, participants will:

1. Complete the savings category of the Spending Plan worksheet.
2. Reflect on who they are becoming as debtors.
3. Decide on an action step to take concerning their use of credit cards.
4. Complete the debt portion of the Spending Plan worksheet.

OUTLINE

I. Introduction

II. Discovery

A. Practical Tips on Saving
1. The Benefit of Saving
2. Three Kinds of Saving
3. Individual Activity: *Spending Plan Application*
4. Prioritizing the Four Uses of Money

B. Debt
1. Video: *The Debtor on the Street*
2. The Pull of the Culture vs. the Mind and Heart of God
3. Practical Tips on Debt
4. Individual Activity: *Credit Cards*
5. Credit Card Debt and Repayment
6. Individual Activity: *Spending Plan Application*

III. Session Summary

Video: *Out of Debt*

SAVING AND DEBT

TIME & MEDIA	CONTENTS

1 minute

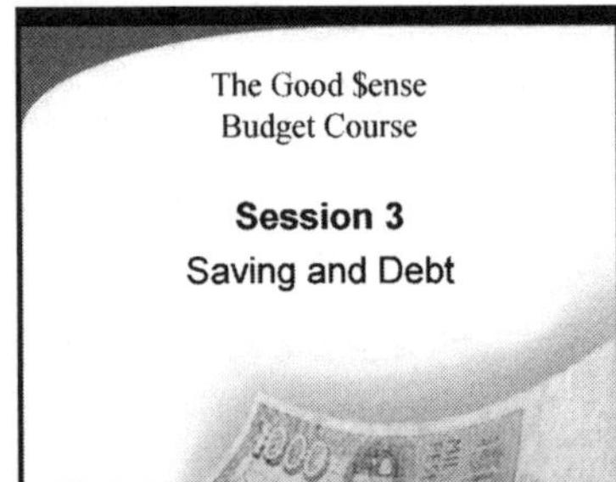

The Good $ense
Budget Course
Session 3
Saving and Debt

INTRODUCTION

Participant's Guide, page 43.

In the last session, we talked about who we are becoming as savers. In this session we'll complete the savings section, which includes filling out the savings category on the Spending Plan worksheet. We will then discuss debt and who we are becoming as debtors. We will take a look at how we use credit cards, and finally we'll complete the debt portion on our Spending Plans.

Turn to page 44.

DISCOVERY (45 minutes)

Practical Tips on Saving

Participant's Guide, page 44.

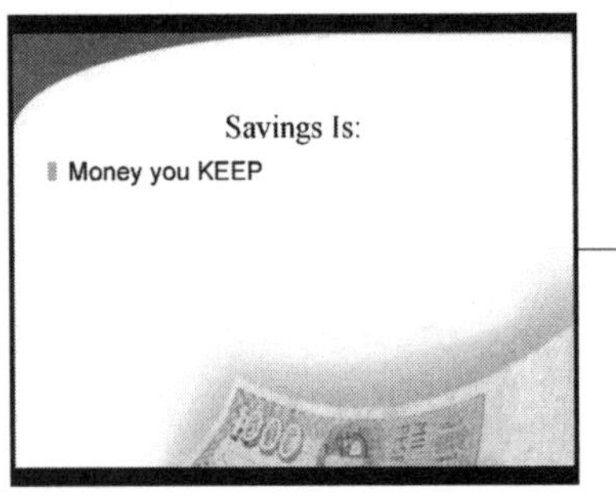

As we now move to discussing practical tips about saving, a good place to start is by defining the term.

→ Savings is money you KEEP!

NOTES

OBJECTIVES

In this session, you will:

1. Complete the savings category of the Spending Plan worksheet.
2. Reflect on who you are becoming as a debtor.
3. Decide on an action step to take concerning the use of credit cards.
4. Complete the debt portion of the Spending Plan worksheet.

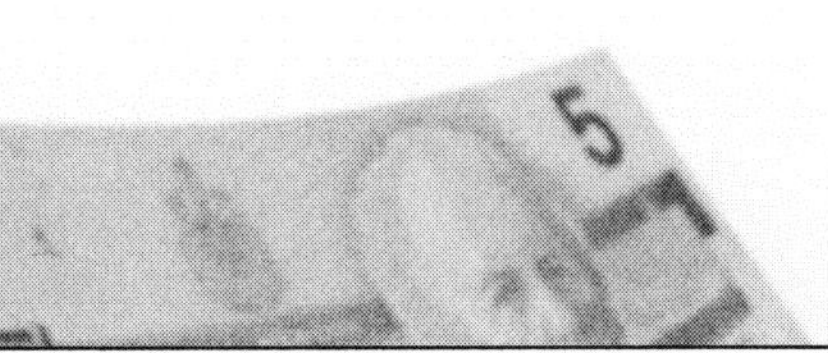

Practical Tips on Saving

Savings is:

- Money you ___________.
- Not money we have lost or given up.
- Future spending.

The Benefit of Saving

One huge benefit of saving is that it allows the very powerful force of compounding to work in our favor.

Compound interest is:

Interest earning interest, earning interest.

Compound interest example:

- $100 @ 10% = $10 interest
- $110 @ 10% = $11 interest
- The extra $1 is compound interest.

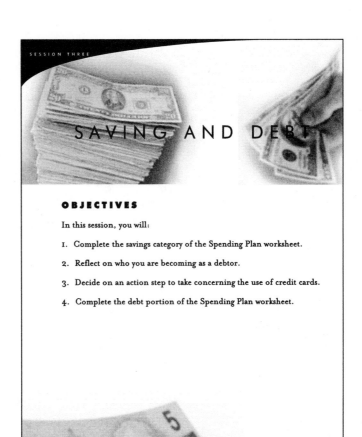

Note that when you buy a $65 sweater on sale for $40, you do not "save" $25—you *spend* $40. The next time you see a notice to, "Buy now and save 50 percent," you can respond by saying, "Thanks, but I'll *not* buy now and save 100 percent!"

Savings is not money we have somehow lost or given up. Saving is actually spending, but it's *future* spending.

4 minutes

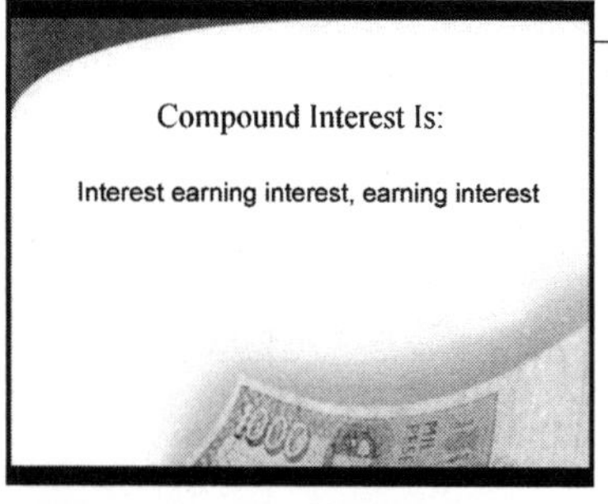

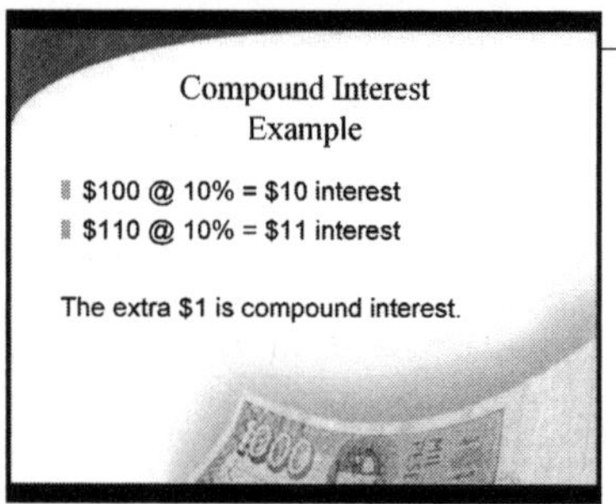

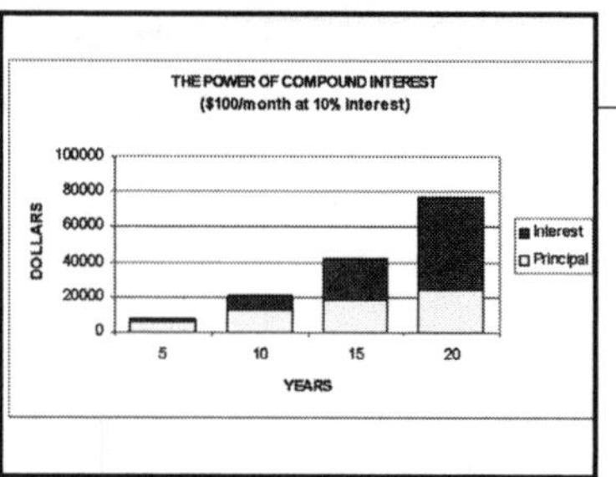

The Benefit of Saving

One huge benefit of saving is that it allows the very powerful force of compounding to work in our favor. Compound interest is defined as interest earning interest, earning interest.

For example if we invested $100 at 10 percent annual interest, we'd earn $10 in interest and have $110 at the end of one year. If we then left the entire $110 invested for a second year, we'd earn $11 in interest. The additional dollar earned the second year is compound interest—the interest earned by interest.

Participant's Guide, page 45.

It is an incredibly powerful concept. We can see the impact of compound interest in this graph.

The graph shows the growth that occurs by compound interest if we save $100 per month at 10 percent over a twenty-year period. Look at what happens by year twenty, the last bar on the right-hand side of the graph. The bottom portion of the bar represents the amount of money we put in—$1,200 per year for twenty years, which totals $24,000. The entire bar represents the total amount of money we now have: over $76,500. The difference between the two—represented by the top portion of the bar—is what we have gained through compound interest.

NOTES

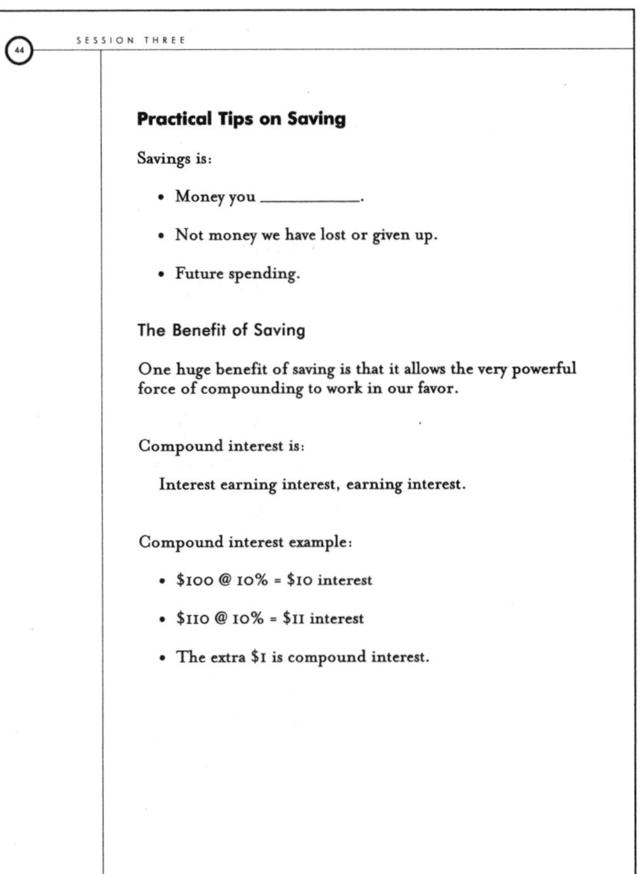

SESSION THREE 44

Practical Tips on Saving

Savings is:

- Money you ___________.
- Not money we have lost or given up.
- Future spending.

The Benefit of Saving

One huge benefit of saving is that it allows the very powerful force of compounding to work in our favor.

Compound interest is:

Interest earning interest, earning interest.

Compound interest example:

- $100 @ 10% = $10 interest
- $110 @ 10% = $11 interest
- The extra $1 is compound interest.

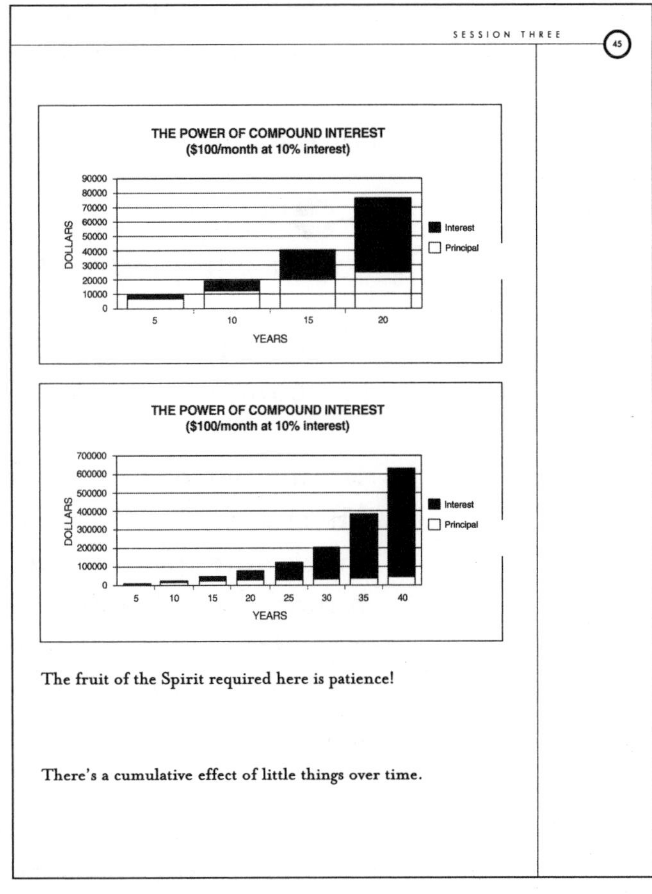

SESSION THREE 45

The fruit of the Spirit required here is patience!

There's a cumulative effect of little things over time.

Some of you may look at this and say, "I don't have twenty years until retirement." First of all, even if you had only ten years left, you would still have accumulated over $20,000 by saving $100 per month. Secondly, with an average life expectancy of eighty-seven years, beginning a saving plan in your middle and even later years still makes good sense.

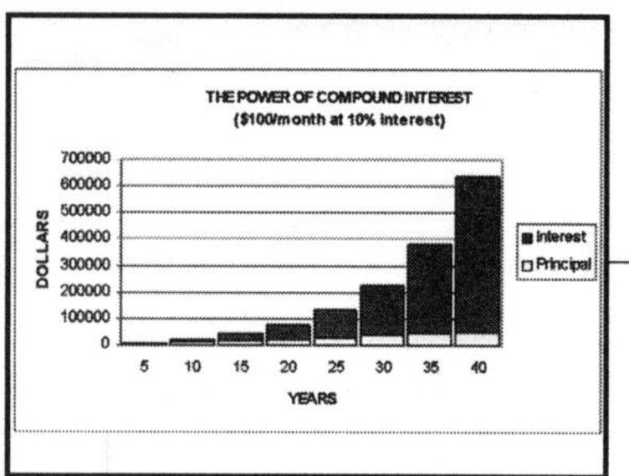

For those of you in your twenties and thirties, I want to encourage you even further by extending this graph out to forty years. You can see that by year forty, you would have almost $637,000.

One of the things to recognize about compounding is that it begins slowly but then grows very quickly.

→ The fruit of the Spirit required here is patience!

Time itself is your greatest ally in making compounding work for you. And there is no better time than right now to begin saving and having the impact of compound interest work for you—twenty-four hours a day, seven days a week, 365 days a year!

Here's one more thought.

→ Another way to look at this concept is that there's a cumulative effect of little things over time.

Just as a slow-dripping faucet can fill a bucket in one day, compound interest really adds up over time.

> If time permits, you can expand on how the cumulative effect applies to many areas of life. For example, writing a quick note to someone a few times a week adds up to over a hundred notes a year. A little bit of exercise each day has a significant impact on health and well-being. An in-depth explanation of this principle appears in the Appendix on page 109 of the Participant's Guide.

Now that you understand that compound interest can be a powerful ally, let's examine different kinds of savings.

NOTES

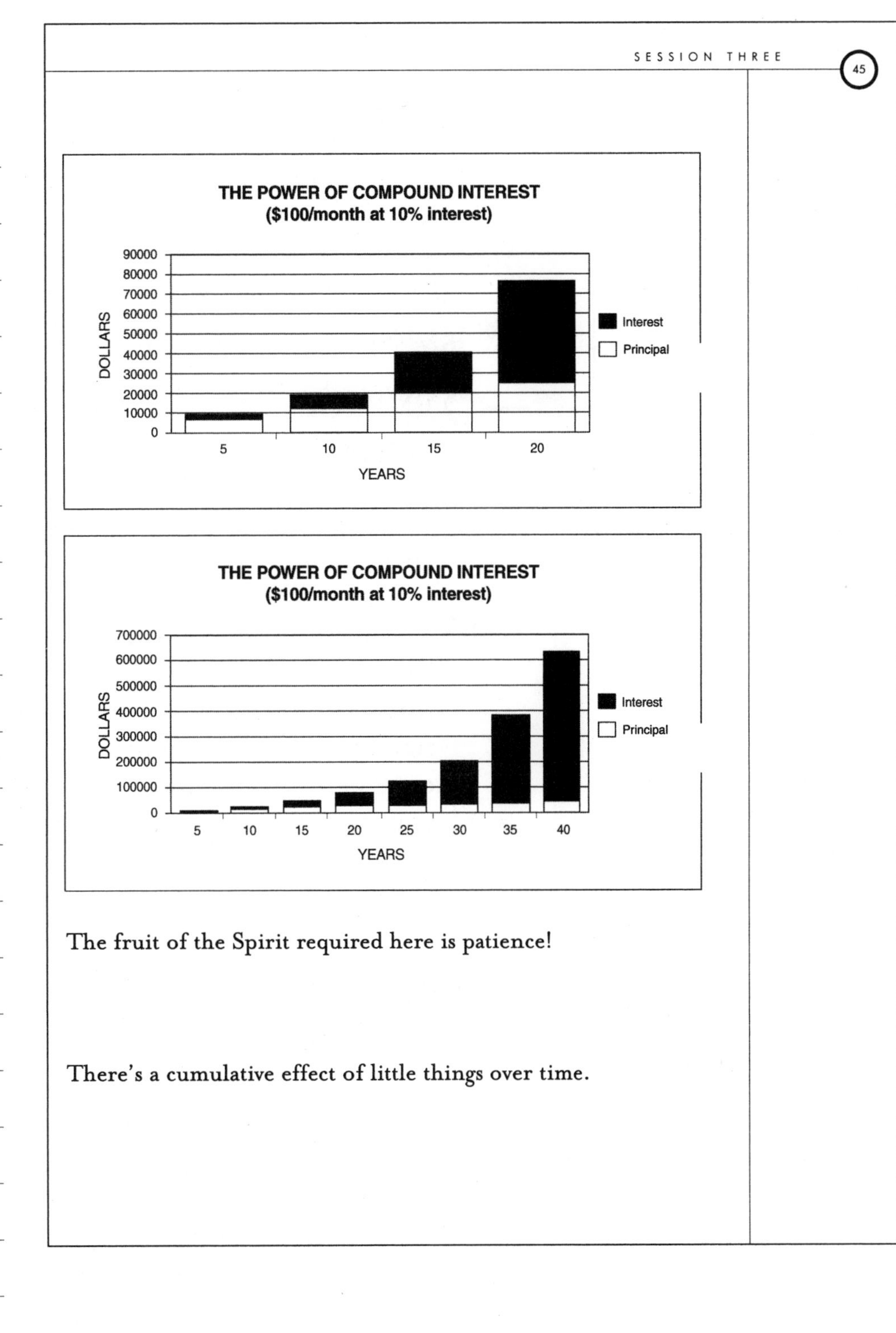

THE POWER OF COMPOUND INTEREST
($100/month at 10% interest)

THE POWER OF COMPOUND INTEREST
($100/month at 10% interest)

The fruit of the Spirit required here is patience!

There's a cumulative effect of little things over time.

Turn to page 46.

Three Kinds of Savings

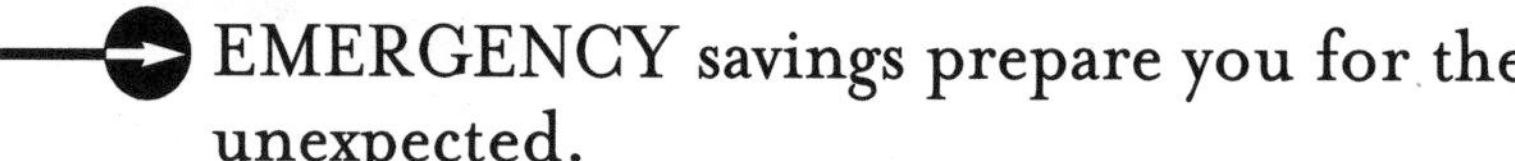
Participant's Guide, page 46.

Appropriate savings goals fall into three categories and should be addressed in the following order: emergency savings, replacement savings, and long-term savings.

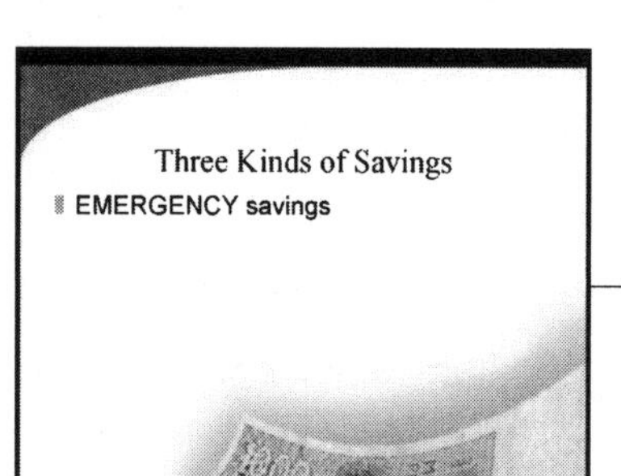

EMERGENCY savings prepare you for the unexpected.

This would include things like sudden unemployment or a serious illness.

A generally accepted goal for emergency savings is three months of basic living expenses, such as housing, food, and transportation costs. Since you need to be able to get these funds quickly when an emergency strikes, they should be kept in accounts you have easy access to, like a money market fund.

Replacement savings are for large expected purchases.

We know that things wear out and need to be replaced. This includes items such as major appliances, automobiles, and major home repairs such as replacing the roof, or carpeting.

Since these needs are more predictable, replacement savings could be invested in short-term certificates of deposit as well as money market funds.

In the early stage of building up savings, the emergency savings can double as emergency and replacement savings since replacing a needed item can become an emergency if the replacement funds aren't there! But once the emergency fund is in place, you can begin saving specifically for replacement needs.

NOTES

Three Kinds of Savings

________________ savings:

- Prepare you for the unexpected.
- Have three months of basic living expenses (such as housing, food, and transportation costs).
- Should be kept in accounts you have easy access to (like a money market fund).

Replacement savings:

- Are for large, expected purchases.
- Could be invested in short-term certificates of deposit as well as money market funds.

________________ savings:

- Are for planned circumstances that have long time frames.
- Take advantage of your employer's retirement plan if possible.

LONG-TERM savings are for planned circumstances that have long time frames, such as retirement or a young child's college education. A key tip for long-term savings is to take advantage of your employer's retirement plan if available.

How much you put into it will depend on other circumstances, but it is generally an excellent place for long-term savings. It provides tax-deferred growth and often offers employer matching funds.

7 minutes

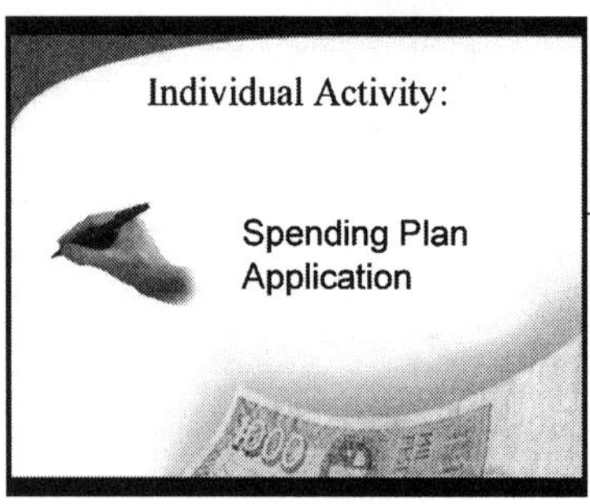
Individual Activity:
Spending Plan Application

Individual Activity: *Spending Plan Application*

Participant's Guide, page 47.

Objective
For participants to set short-term goals for savings.

Directions

1. Calculate an appropriate level of emergency savings. Consider three months of basic living expenses such as housing, food, and transportation.
2. Consider your current financial situation. Set a short-term goal for savings that will help you begin to build your emergency savings fund. If you already have an emergency savings fund, consider goals for replacement or long-term savings.
3. Fill in the savings category on your Spending Plan worksheet.

You have 7 minutes to do this.

Call the group back together after 7 minutes.

You now have a goal for savings. We'll show you ways to reach your goal in later sessions.

Now, turn to page 48.

NOTES

Three Kinds of Savings

__________________ savings:

- Prepare you for the unexpected.
- Have three months of basic living expenses (such as housing, food, and transportation costs).
- Should be kept in accounts you have easy access to (like a money market fund).

Replacement savings:

- Are for large, expected purchases.
- Could be invested in short-term certificates of deposit as well as money market funds.

__________________ savings:

- Are for planned circumstances that have long time frames.
- Take advantage of your employer's retirement plan if possible.

Individual Activity: *Spending Plan Application*

1. Calculate an appropriate level of emergency savings. Consider three months of basic living expenses such as housing, food, and transportation.
2. Consider your current financial situation. Set a short-term goal for savings that will help you begin to build your emergency savings fund. If you already have an emergency savings fund, consider goals for replacement or long-term savings.
3. Fill in the savings category on your Spending Plan worksheet.

4 minutes

Prioritizing the Four Uses of Money

Participant's Guide, page 48.

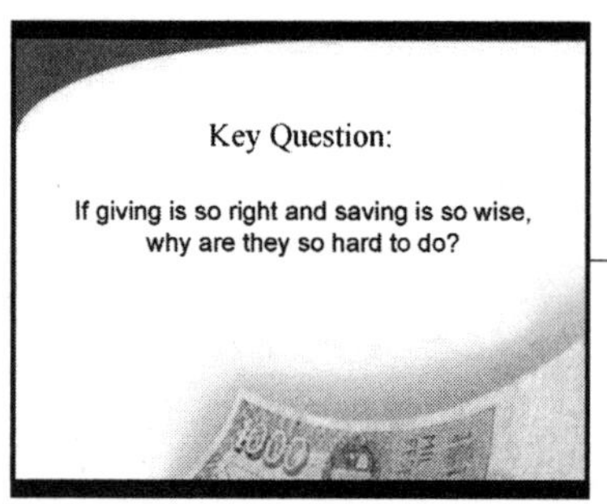

Having completed giving and saving, let's take a moment for reflection.

Here's a key question: If giving is so right and saving is so wise, why are they so hard to do?

Why do we so often feel like Paul in Romans 7:15 when he says, "I do not understand what I do. For what I want to do I do not do, but what I hate to do, I do." Part of the answer lies in the way we approach the four uses of money.

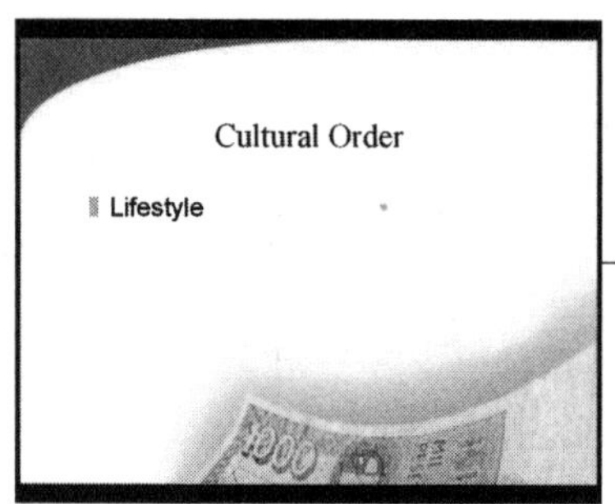

Cultural Order

The typical cultural order is to use money first on lifestyle.

We begin by thinking, "I've got this job, and this annual income. Where do I want to live? What sort of car do I want to drive? What type entertainment do I want to pursue? What kind of clothes do I want to wear?" Given our natural tendencies and the powerful Pull of the Culture, when we begin with lifestyle questions, we end up using all our income for these things.

If we use all our income for lifestyle, we will wind up in debt.

You may say, "But I've established a lifestyle that's just equal to what I'm making. I'm not spending a penny more than I'm making." But you also don't have any savings, so the first time the unexpected happens—like your car breaking down—the bill winds up on your credit card and you begin to spiral down into debt.

Saving comes next, but now we have debt payments, which make it hard to keep up with our lifestyle.

NOTES

Prioritizing the Four Uses of Money

Key Question: If giving is so right and saving is so wise, why are they so hard to do?

Cultural Order:

- Lifestyle
- Debt
- Saving
- Giving

God-honoring Order:

- Giving
- Saving
- Lifestyle

Transitional Order:

- Give . . . something
- Save . . . a little
- Debt . . . maximize repayment
- Lifestyle . . . spartan

Therefore, even though we know it's wise to save, we save very little or nothing at all.

Finally, there's giving.

Although we really would love to give, there's simply nothing left.

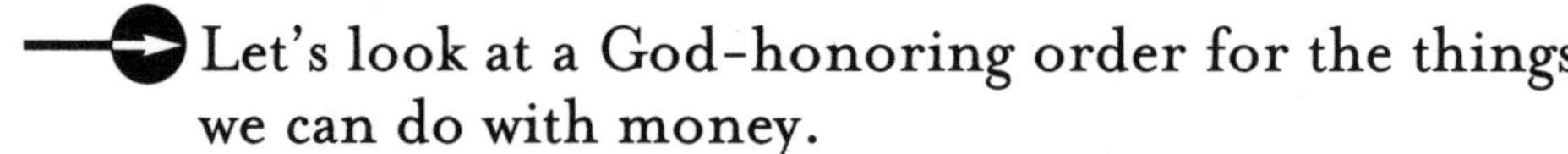

Let's look at a God-honoring order for the things we can do with money.

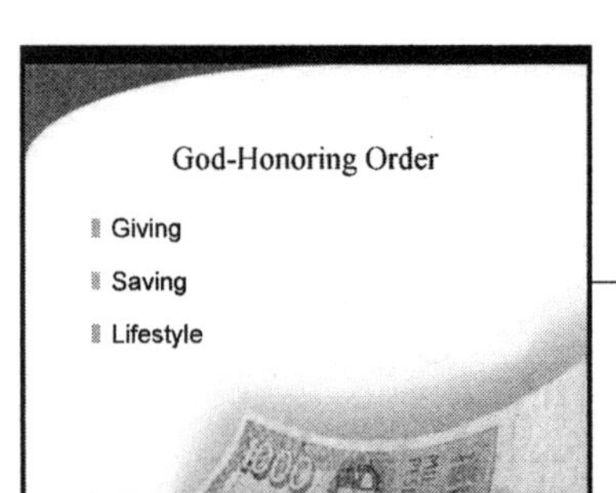

God-honoring Order

This order is giving, saving, lifestyle.

First, we decide how much to give. This will be the first check we write each pay period.

Secondly, we decide how much to save, and we save that amount right off the top as well.

The easiest way is through direct deposit from a paycheck right into a savings account.

Then, based on what is left, we establish our lifestyle.

Now we decide where we can afford to live, what kind of car we can afford to drive, how much we'll spend on clothes and entertainment, etc.

If we approach how we use our money in that order, there will be no fourth item on the list. We won't have debt because we will have emergency savings for when the unexpected occurs.

You may look at this order and think "But I *am* in debt. What do I do now? How do I get to the place of handling my money in the right order?" If that's your situation, there is a transitional order for you to follow.

NOTES

Prioritizing the Four Uses of Money

Key Question: If giving is so right and saving is so wise, why are they so hard to do?

Cultural Order:

- Lifestyle
- Debt
- Saving
- Giving

God-honoring Order:

- Giving
- Saving
- Lifestyle

Transitional Order:

- Give . . . something
- Save . . . a little
- Debt . . . maximize repayment
- Lifestyle . . . spartan

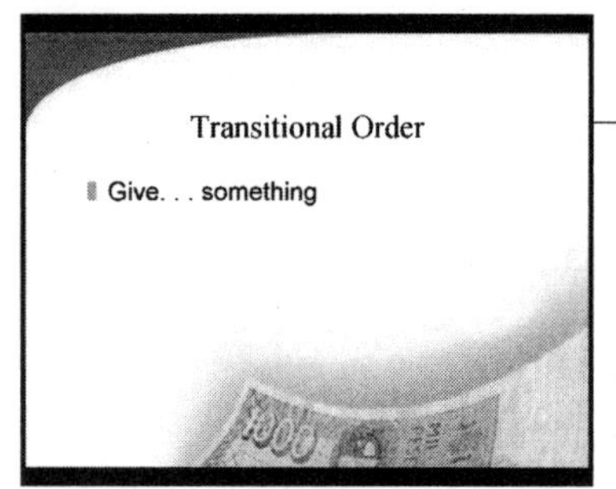

Transitional Order

First, put giving at the top. During the transition, the word to associate with giving is "something."

We've already said when we talked about giving that there's no excuse for not giving something. At this point, it may not be a whole lot, but it should be *something* . . . something based on gratitude for what we do have and not discontentment for what we do not have.

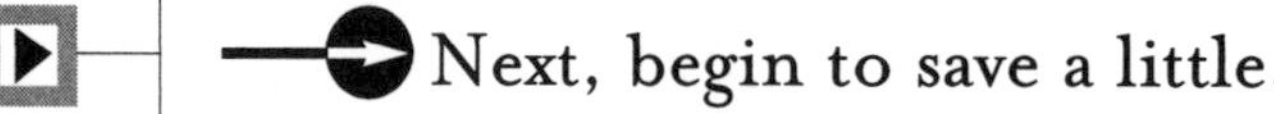

Next, begin to save a little.

As long as we have debt, it may not be much. Our key priority is to accelerate debt repayment but at the same time we want to begin to save a little. Begin the saving habit now! Your emergency savings will ultimately prevent future debt.

Third, pay debt. The phrase associated with debt is "maximize repayment."

We need to pay the maximum amount that we can in order to get out of debt as soon as possible. We will talk more about this shortly.

The final consideration is lifestyle. The word to associate with lifestyle in the transition period is "spartan."

By spartan we mean taking drastic short-term steps to reduce lifestyle expenses in order to maximize the amount of money to pay off debt. For example, rather than spending what we currently do on entertainment—going to the movies, eating out, etc.—we choose to rent a video for a few dollars, or perhaps even borrow one free from the library. Walks in the park and evenings spent playing board games with friends replace more expensive activities. We also reap the potential benefit of deepening relationships even as money to pay off debt increases.

NOTES

Prioritizing the Four Uses of Money

Key Question: If giving is so right and saving is so wise, why are they so hard to do?

Cultural Order:

- Lifestyle
- Debt
- Saving
- Giving

God-honoring Order:

- Giving
- Saving
- Lifestyle

Transitional Order:

- Give . . . something
- Save . . . a little
- Debt . . . maximize repayment
- Lifestyle . . . spartan

In a similar fashion, rather than spending hundreds of dollars on clothing for the latest seasonal change, we make a commitment to buy only the basic necessities and go back to the closet and dresser drawers for last year's clothing.

A spartan lifestyle involves looking at all the categories of the Spending Plan worksheet and identifying every possible area where short-term cutbacks can be made in order to take a big step toward debt repayment. Session four will help us find ways to do this.

The focus of the remainder of this session will be on the third point, maximizing debt repayment.

4 minutes

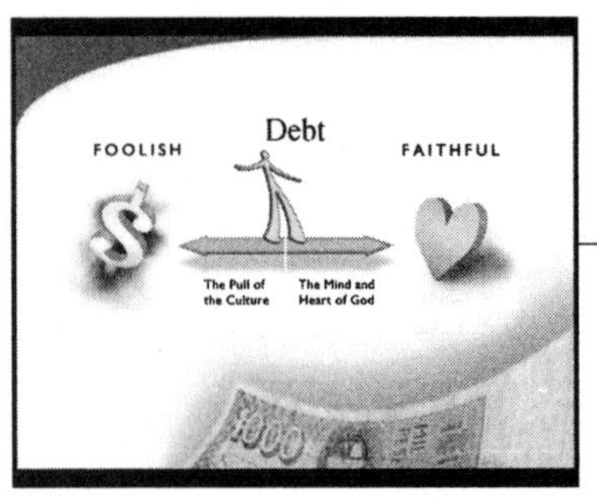

Debt

Participant's Guide, page 49.

Debt is the fourth area of our financial lives. Like the other areas, debt is about more than just finances—it's about who you *are* and who you are *becoming* as a debtor.

We're going to watch a short video to see what the typical person on the street has to say about debt.

Video: *The Debtor on the Street* (3 minutes)

View video: *The Debtor on the Street.*

Wrap-up (2 minutes)
What were some viewpoints you heard concerning debt?

NOTES

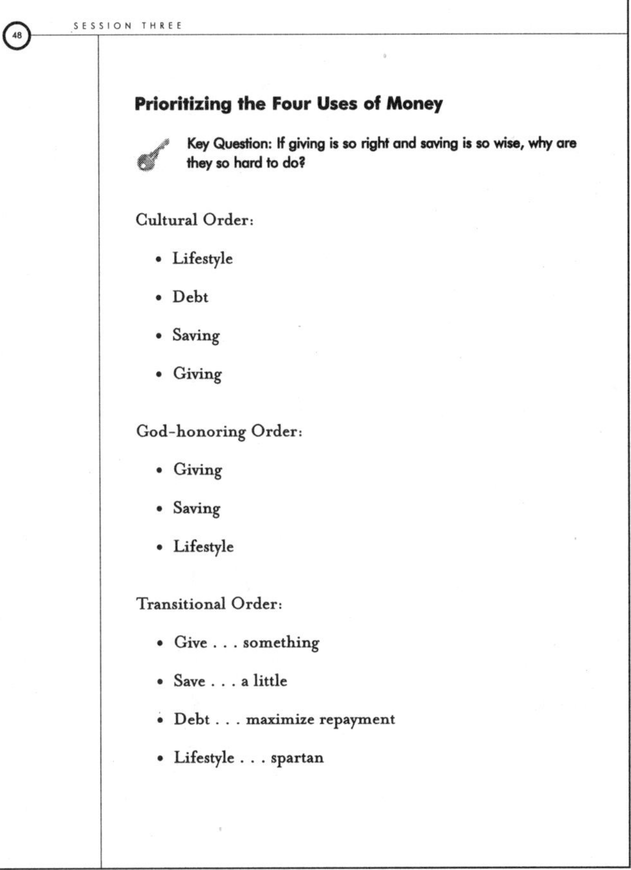

SESSION THREE 48

Prioritizing the Four Uses of Money

Key Question: If giving is so right and saving is so wise, why are they so hard to do?

Cultural Order:

- Lifestyle
- Debt
- Saving
- Giving

God-honoring Order:

- Giving
- Saving
- Lifestyle

Transitional Order:

- Give . . . something
- Save . . . a little
- Debt . . . maximize repayment
- Lifestyle . . . spartan

SESSION THREE 49

Debt

Video: *The Debtor on the Street*

Notes

The Pull of the Culture vs. the Mind and Heart of God

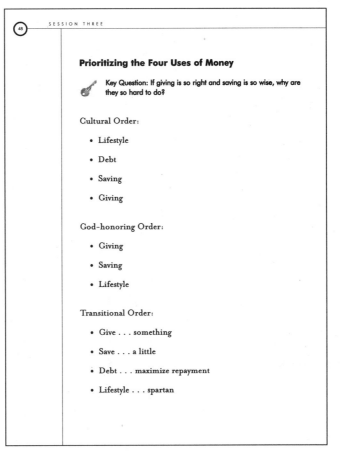

FOOLISH FAITHFUL

The Pull of the Culture

The Mind and Heart of God

Cultural Myth:

"Debt is expected and _______________________."

Solicit three or four comments from the group. Be sure to repeat their answers so everyone hears the response.

Possible responses:

- You can't avoid debt.
- I'm just going to ignore it.
- They get their interest, I get what I want. We're both happy.
- That's the way it is—everyone has debt.

Great responses and insights. Let's summarize our discussion of what we saw on the video by taking a look at the Pull of the Culture on the debtor.

5 minutes

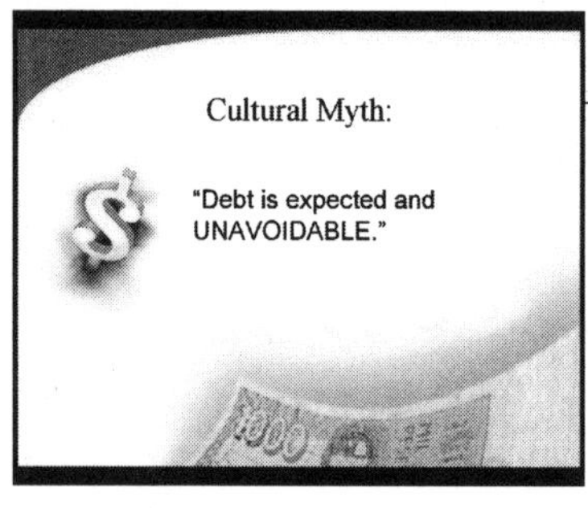
Cultural Myth:
"Debt is expected and UNAVOIDABLE."

The Pull of the Culture vs. the Mind and Heart of God

The dangerous and underlying cultural myth is, "Debt is expected and UNAVOIDABLE."

Many have bought into this assumption, and the consequences are staggering. According to a recent *Wall Street Journal* report, household borrowing in the United States increased 60 percent between 1995 and 2000. In 1999, almost $60 billion was paid in credit card *interest* alone!

While it's important to acknowledge that in some cases we incur debt for reasons beyond our control, in the majority of cases it is avoidable by living within our means and resisting the temptation of immediate gratification.

The myth that debt is expected and unavoidable is perpetuated by the fact that it is so encouraged and embraced by our culture. Historically, if you borrowed money it was assumed you had the means to repay it. Now, with over three billion credit card solicitations and 1.4 million bankruptcies per year in the U.S. alone, that obviously is no longer true.

NOTES

Debt

Video: *The Debtor on the Street*

Notes

The Pull of the Culture vs. the Mind and Heart of God

FOOLISH FAITHFUL

The Pull of the Culture | The Mind and Heart of God

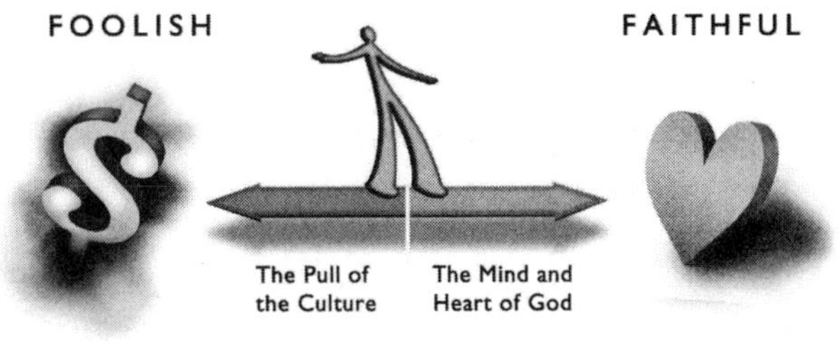

Cultural Myth:

"Debt is expected and ______________________."

Debt is now made to appear glamorous by dressing it up in a tuxedo and calling it "credit." Our culture promotes credit as painless and without negative consequences. Familiar phrases seductively ring in our ears:

- "Play now, pay later."
- "No money down. No payments until. . ."
- "You can afford it. Minimum payments are only. . ."
- "You deserve it."

Let's examine what God says about debt.

Turn to page 50.

The Cautious Debtor

Participant's Guide, page 50.

As we explore the Mind and Heart of God, we find that the Bible characterizes the God-honoring debtor as "cautious."

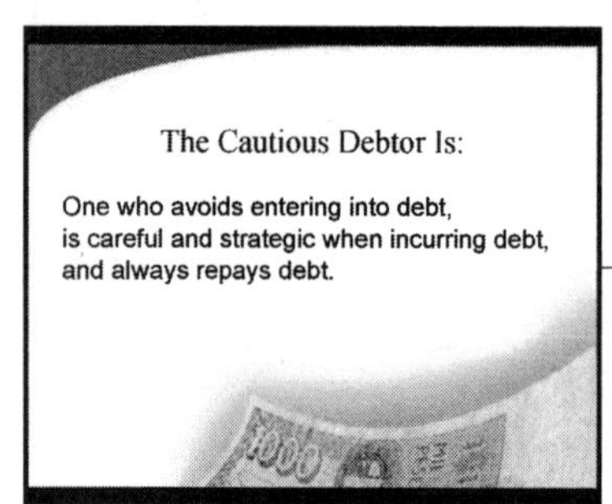
The Cautious Debtor Is:
One who avoids entering into debt,
is careful and strategic when incurring debt,
and always repays debt.

The cautious debtor is one who avoids entering into debt, is careful and strategic when incurring debt, and always repays debt.

There are both economic and spiritual dangers to debt.

The economic danger is that compound interest works against you.

If you were impressed by the graphs of compound interest at 10 percent that we discussed under saving, you should see the graph of how debt grows at credit card interest rates of 15 percent, 20 percent, and higher. At 18 percent, compounding will double the amount owed in four years.

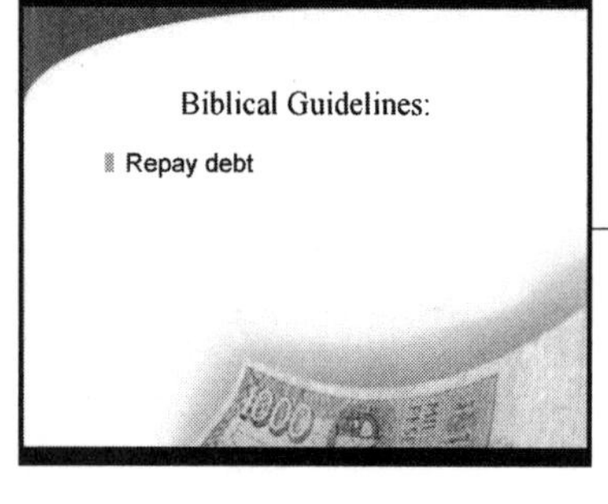
Biblical Guidelines:
Repay debt

Scripture has two guidelines for us about debt.

First, if we owe debt, we must repay it. Psalm 37:21 says, "The wicked borrow and do not repay..."

NOTES

Debt

Video: *The Debtor on the Street*

Notes

The Pull of the Culture vs. the Mind and Heart of God

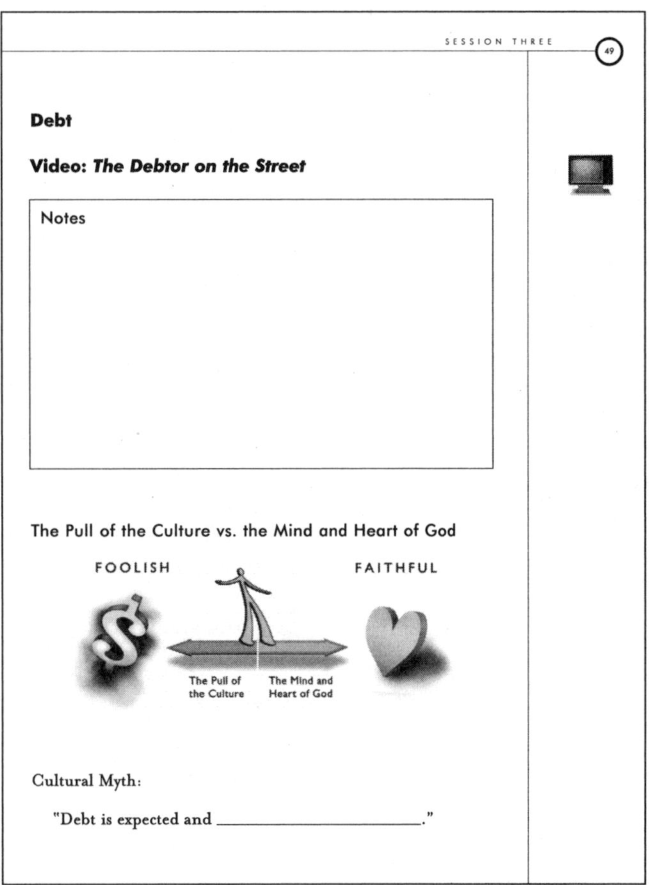

Cultural Myth:

"Debt is expected and ____________________."

The Cautious Debtor is:

One who avoids entering into debt, is careful and strategic when incurring debt, and always repays debt.

Economic danger of debt:

- Compound interest works against you.

Biblical guidelines:

- Repay debt.

Psalm 37:21: *"The wicked borrow and do not repay . . ."*

- __________ debt.

Proverbs 22:7: *"The borrower is servant to the lender."*

Second, and better yet, AVOID debt altogether because it produces bondage. When you owe someone money, they own a piece of you. Proverbs 22:7 says, "The borrower is servant to the lender."

Note: This section does not apply to collateralized debt such as a responsible first mortgage. It deals primarily with consumer debt on depreciating items.

Three Spiritual Dangers of Debt

Participant's Guide, page 51.

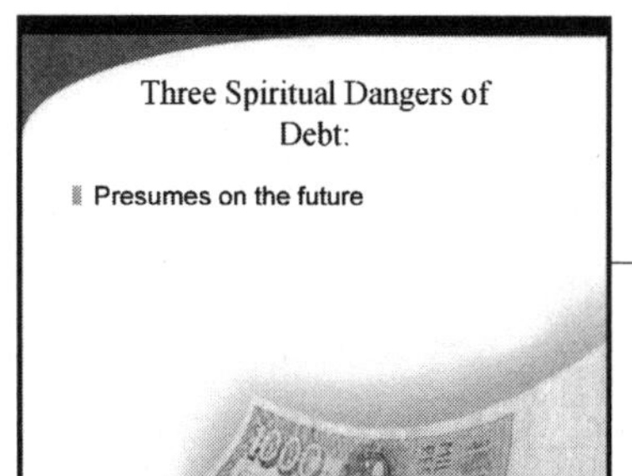

There are also three spiritual dangers of debt.

The first danger is that debt presumes on the future.

Every time we take on debt, we are presuming that we will be able to pay it back. The ad says, "You can afford a $120 monthly payment," and we believe it. While it may be true at the moment, we may not be able to pay it for the life of the loan.

James 4:14 says, "You do not even know what will happen tomorrow."

The second spiritual danger is that we deny God the opportunity to TEACH US.

He may wish to teach us about his love and provision, but we can deny him that opportunity. For example, I desire something I don't have the money for but I buy it anyway and put it on my credit card. I can just imagine God saying, "I'm so sorry you did that. I was going to have a friend give you that very thing. Not only have you denied me the opportunity to bless you and show you my love, but you've also placed yourself in bondage to debt."

NOTES

The Cautious Debtor is:

One who avoids entering into debt, is careful and strategic when incurring debt, and always repays debt.

Economic danger of debt:

- Compound interest works against you.

Biblical guidelines:

- Repay debt.

> Psalm 37:21: *"The wicked borrow and do not repay . . ."*

- __________ debt.

> Proverbs 22:7: *"The borrower is servant to the lender."*

Three Spiritual Dangers of Debt:

- Presumes on the future.

> James 4:14: *"You do not even know what will happen tomorrow."*

- Denies God the opportunity to __________________.

> Luke 12:30-31 (NLT): "Those things dominate the thoughts of most people, but your Father already knows your needs. He will give you all you need from day to day if you make the Kingdom of God your primary concern."

> Ecclesiastes 7:14: *"When times are good, be happy; when times are bad, consider: God has made the one as well as the other."*

- Fosters __________ and greed.

> Luke 12:15 (NLT): *"Beware! Don't be greedy for what you don't have. Real life is not measured by how much we own."*

In Luke 12:30-31 Jesus tells his disciples, "These things dominate the thoughts of most people, but your Father already knows your needs. He will give you all you need from day to day if you make the Kingdom of God your primary concern" (NLT).

There's another way God sometimes tries to teach us. It's through denial. For those of you who are parents, can you recall a time when your children wanted something that you didn't give them? Of course. Why do we sometimes deny our children? Because we know there are many things they want that are not in their best interests. That may be the way it is with God—he desires to teach us through denial, but we can circumvent his intentions by incurring debt to get what we want anyway.

Ecclesiastes 7:14 says, "When times are good, be happy; when times are bad, consider: God has made the one as well as the other."

The third spiritual danger is that debt often fosters ENVY and greed.

We all have a natural inclination to want more, and debt and credit can be used to satisfy that envious, greedy part of us.

Luke 12:15 says, "Beware! Don't be greedy for what you don't have. Real life is not measured by how much we own" (NLT).

We are back to the dilemma of choosing to follow the Pull of the Culture or seeking the Mind and Heart of God. We all want to move closer to the Mind and Heart of God as debtors, but how can we do it? Some of us are currently overwhelmed by the amount of debt we owe. Let's look at some practical tips on debt.

Turn to page 52.

NOTES

Three Spiritual Dangers of Debt:

- Presumes on the future.

James 4:14: *"You do not even know what will happen tomorrow."*

- Denies God the opportunity to ____________________.

Luke 12:30-31 (NLT): "Those things dominate the thoughts of most people, but your Father already knows your needs. He will give you all you need from day to day if you make the Kingdom of God your primary concern."

Ecclesiastes 7:14: *"When times are good, be happy; when times are bad, consider: God has made the one as well as the other."*

- Fosters ____________ and greed.

Luke 12:15 (NLT): *"Beware! Don't be greedy for what you don't have. Real life is not measured by how much we own."*

5 minutes

Practical Tips on Debt

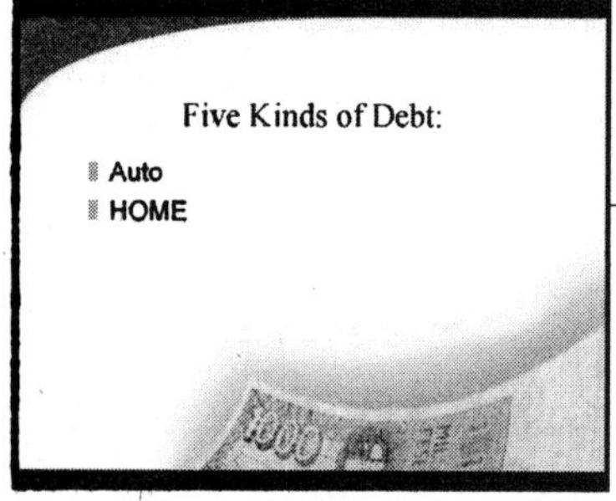

Participant's Guide, page 52.

It is helpful to understand that there are primarily five kinds of debt.

First, there are auto debt and home mortgage debt.

We're going to talk about these two kinds of debt in the next session.

Next are education debt and business debt.

In some cases, taking on these types of debt may be appropriate, but there are still real dangers to be aware of. We'll provide some cautions for educational loans in session four.

Finally, there is CREDIT CARD debt, which we often refer to as consumer debt.

We're going to focus on this type of debt right now, because it is the easiest debt to get into and the one that gets us into the most trouble.

How do you feel about this bold statement?

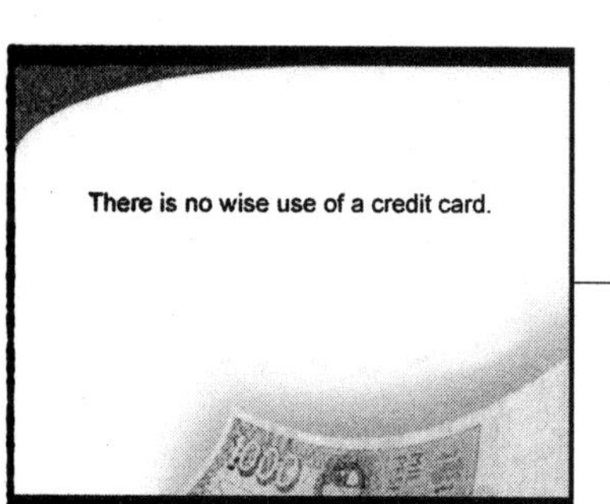

There is no wise use of a credit card.

"There's no wise use of a credit card."

Pause.

NOTES

Practical Tips on Debt

Five kinds of debt:

- Auto
- Home mortgage
- Education
- Business
- ____________________

"There's no wise use of a credit card."

Credit Card Studies:

- Family spending using a credit card versus cash:

  Amount spent (with a credit card) rose between 20 and 30 percent.

- Pocket camera purchase using cash versus credit card:

  Cash group paid an average of $29.58.

  Credit card group paid an average of $52.67.

Two Reasons Credit Card Users Spend More:

- Using a credit card is psychologically different than using cash.
- No ____________ of how much we've charged.

Solicit two or three comments from the group. Be sure to repeat their answers so everyone hears the response.

Possible responses:

- I travel, and I need a credit card to pay for hotels and rental cars.
- I carry one card with no annual fee. I pay it off each month and I even get frequent flyer miles.
- For safety reasons, I do not like to carry a lot of cash, so I use a credit card.

Most of us can't get by without a credit card. It's convenient, it's safe, it's often necessary for travel, and it's fast. We can pull into a gas station, get our gas, pay at the pump, and never have to enter the store. We can use the credit card on the phone and on the Internet.

You may have a no-fee card that you pay off every month, thereby paying no interest and, in addition, get frequent flyer miles.

If you use a credit card, that is the wisest way to use it. But studies have shown that even if we pay the balance every month, most of us who use credit cards spend significantly more than we would with cash or a check.

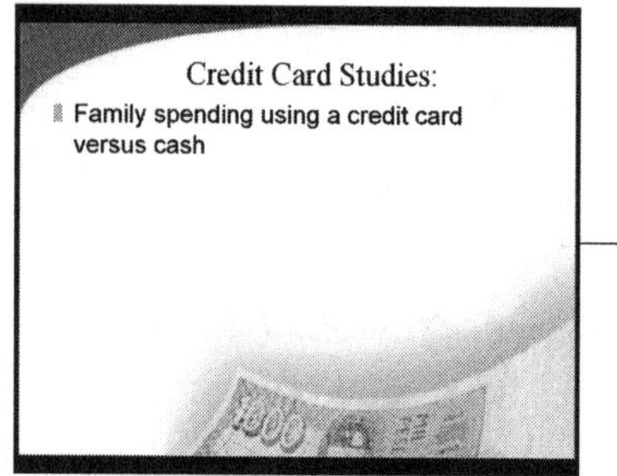
Credit Card Studies:
Family spending using a credit card versus cash

For example, in one study, researchers asked several hundred families to do all their buying with cash over a three-month period. At the end of three months, the same families were asked not to change their spending habits, but to use a credit card instead of cash to make their purchases.

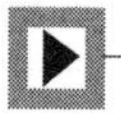

The amount spent rose between 20 and 30 percent.

In another study, Richard Feinberg, a consumer psychologist at Purdue University, instructed two groups of people to buy a pocket camera. He asked one group to pay cash for it and the other to buy it with a credit card.

NOTES

Practical Tips on Debt

Five kinds of debt:

- Auto
- Home mortgage
- Education
- Business
- ____________________

"There's no wise use of a credit card."

Credit Card Studies:

- Family spending using a credit card versus cash:

  Amount spent (with a credit card) rose between 20 and 30 percent.

- Pocket camera purchase using cash versus credit card:

  Cash group paid an average of $29.58.

  Credit card group paid an average of $52.67.

Two Reasons Credit Card Users Spend More:

- Using a credit card is psychologically different than using cash.
- No ____________ of how much we've charged.

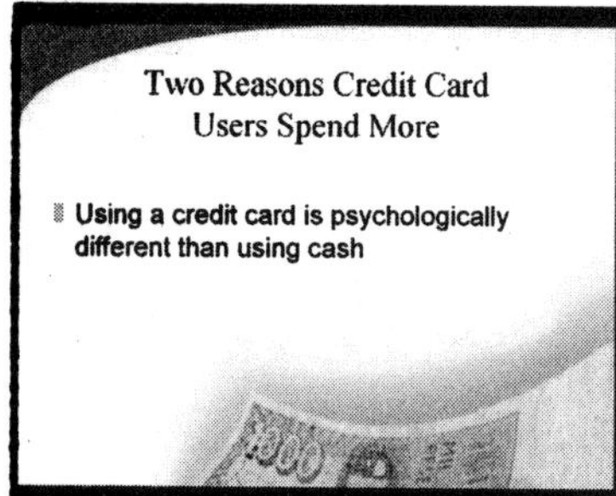

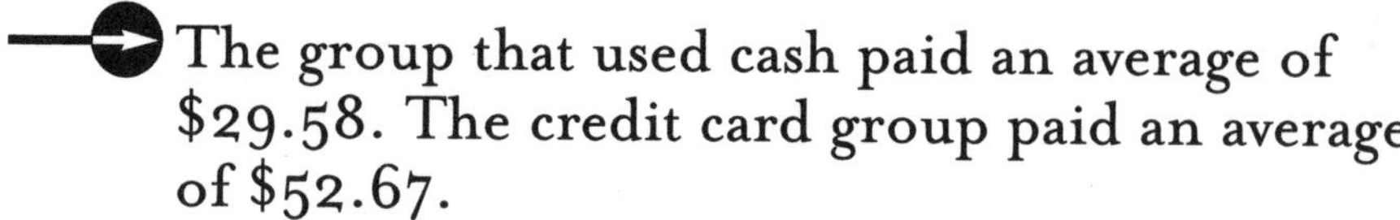

The group that used cash paid an average of $29.58. The credit card group paid an average of $52.67.

Let's consider for a moment two reasons why credit card users spend more.

First, using a credit card is psychologically different than using cash.

For example, let's say I make a purchase amounting to $37.88. The cashier takes my credit card and puts a receipt in front of me. I sign it and walk out the door. From a psychological standpoint, that transaction is very different than if I give the cashier a twenty, a ten, a five, and three singles, and I'm left with only twelve cents in my hand.

In the cash transaction, I receive very tangible evidence that the money is no longer available to me. I see those bills go to someone else and know that I have just twelve cents left. Even if I write a check, subtract the amount, and see my new balance, there will be some awareness that I now have less than before. There's no such feedback when all we do is sign a piece of paper.

The other reason we tend to spend more when we use a credit card is that we have no RECORD of total charges until the end of the month.

Have you ever opened your statement and been surprised at how high the balance was? You quickly scan through it looking for a billing error only to find that you really did make all those purchases.

Think for a minute. How much have you charged on your credit card during the last month? Almost none of us could answer that question accurately. If I really pressed you, your guess would almost always be less than what you actually spent.

NOTES

Practical Tips on Debt

Five kinds of debt:

- Auto
- Home mortgage
- Education
- Business
- ______________

"There's no wise use of a credit card."

Credit Card Studies:

- Family spending using a credit card versus cash:

  Amount spent (with a credit card) rose between 20 and 30 percent.

- Pocket camera purchase using cash versus credit card:

  Cash group paid an average of $29.58.

  Credit card group paid an average of $52.67.

Two Reasons Credit Card Users Spend More:

- Using a credit card is psychologically different than using cash.
- No __________ of how much we've charged.

Okay, now how many of you are persuaded to give up using a credit card? Seriously, I realize that most of you still feel a need for a credit card.

Participant's Guide, page 53.

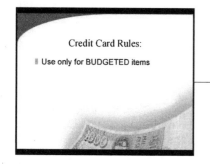

Credit Card Rules:
- Use only for BUDGETED items

Here are three credit card rules I'd like you to consider.

First, use credit cards only for BUDGETED items.

For some budgeted items a credit card is especially safe to use. For example, buying gas. You're not going to get carried away and overfill the tank and let it run all over the ground just because you're using your credit card! But, in many cases, you will need to ask the question, "Is this in the Spending Plan?"

The second rule is to pay the balance in full every month.

If you've used the card only for budgeted items, the money will be there to pay the balance due. Obviously, doing this will avoid all interest charges.

The third rule is that if you violate rule one or two, cut up your cards.

Do "plastic surgery!" You're in trouble. You're not in control. This decisive action will help you to stick to rules one and two.

In addition, there are three tips to keep in mind.

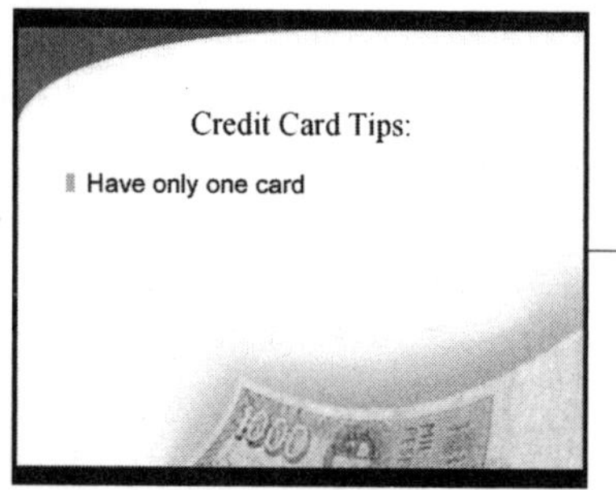
Credit Card Tips:
Have only one card

First, have only one card.

Doing so will reduce the temptation to overspend and will simplify bill paying. Select a card with no annual fee and start throwing all those offers for additional low-interest, no-fee cards in the trash. Don't even open them.

NOTES

Credit Card Rules:

- Use only for ______________________ items.
- Pay the balance in full every month.
- If you violate rule one or rule two, cut up your cards.

Credit Card Tips:

- Have only one card.
- Consider the use of a ___________ card.
- Consider deducting the amount from your checkbook balance.

Individual Activity: *Credit Cards*

In the space below, write down one action step you want to take with your credit card.

Action Step:

Second, consider the use of a DEBIT card.

A debit card can provide you many of the same advantages of credit cards, like convenience and safety, but it does not get you into credit problems. Note, however, that it still has some of the disadvantages we discussed previously, like a lack of psychological impact and having to wait until the end of the month to know how much we've actually spent.

Third, consider deducting the amount of your credit card purchase from your checkbook balance at the time of purchase.

This provides concrete evidence that you now have less money for other things and offsets the disadvantages discussed earlier.

Let's take a minute to think about what we've just talked about.

3 minutes

Individual Activity:
Credit Cards

Individual Activity: *Credit Cards*

Objective
For participants to decide on an action step to take with their credit cards.

Directions
In the space below, write down one action step you want to take with your credit card.

I'll give you a couple minutes to do this.

Call the group back together after 2 minutes.

Wrap-up (1 minute)
What are a couple of things you wrote down?

NOTES

SESSION THREE 53

Credit Card Rules:

- Use only for ______________ items.
- Pay the balance in full every month.
- If you violate rule one or rule two, cut up your cards.

Credit Card Tips:

- Have only one card.
- Consider the use of a __________ card.
- Consider deducting the amount from your checkbook balance.

Individual Activity: *Credit Cards*

In the space below, write down one action step you want to take with your credit card.

Action Step:

Solicit two or three comments from the group. Be sure to repeat their answers so everyone hears the response.

Possible responses:
- Use my credit card only for budgeted items.
- Begin to pay the balance in full each month.
- Eliminate many of the credit cards I currently carry.
- Replace my credit cards with a debit card.

4 minutes

Credit Card Debt and Repayment

Now we're going to take a closer look at the impact of credit card debt.

Turn to page 54.

Participant's Guide, page 54.

Here's an example that according to the Consumer Federation of America represents the average credit card debt owed per American family in 1998.

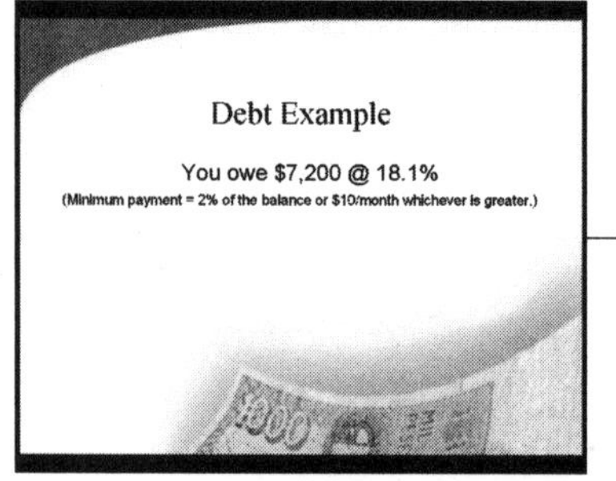

It was $7,200, with an average interest on that debt of 18.1 percent. This example assumes a fairly common minimum payment per month of 2 percent of the balance or $10, whichever is greater.

Let's assume you follow the credit card company's plan and pay only the minimum payment each month. The first month you pay 2 percent of $7,200 or $144. Over time, as you make some progress on reducing the $7,200, the minimum payment decreases to $140, then $135, etc. Following that plan, your repayment will take over thirty years and amount to over $23,000.

On the other hand, let's look at what happens if you pay $144 a month until the loan is completely repaid.

NOTES

Credit Card Rules:

- Use only for ____________________ items.
- Pay the balance in full every month.
- If you violate rule one or rule two, cut up your cards.

Credit Card Tips:

- Have only one card.
- Consider the use of a __________ card.
- Consider deducting the amount from your checkbook balance.

Individual Activity: *Credit Cards*

In the space below, write down one action step you want to take with your credit card.

Action Step:

Credit Card Debt and Repayment Example:

You owe $7,200 @ 18.1%		
Minimum Payment = 2% of the balance or $10—whichever is greater		
You Pay	Total Paid	Time (years)
$ Minimum/month	$23,049	30+
$144/month	$13,397	8
$144+100/month	$ 9,570	3

Key Question: Is God big enough and are you committed enough to find a little over three dollars a day somewhere in your expenditures that could go to debt repayment?

Principles for Accelerating Debt Repayment:

- Pay off your ________________ debt first.
- As a debt is repaid, roll the amount you were paying to the next largest debt.
- Incur no new debt!

You can do it!

That is, you don't decrease your payments when the credit card company says you can.

It might take some discipline, but your total repayment drops from over $23,000 to a little more than $13,000, and the debt gets paid off in ninety-four months or a little under eight years!

That's a huge step in the right direction, but let's consider an even better possibility.

If you were able to pay an extra $100 a month on top of the $144, the total repayment drops to $9,570 and is repaid in only forty months, a little over three years.

There are two important points in this illustration. First is the $9,500 repayment versus $23,000. The second and even more important point, however, is getting out of the bondage of debt in only three years versus more than thirty years!

I can guess what might be going through your mind. You're thinking, "Great in theory, but where am I going to get an extra $100 a month?"

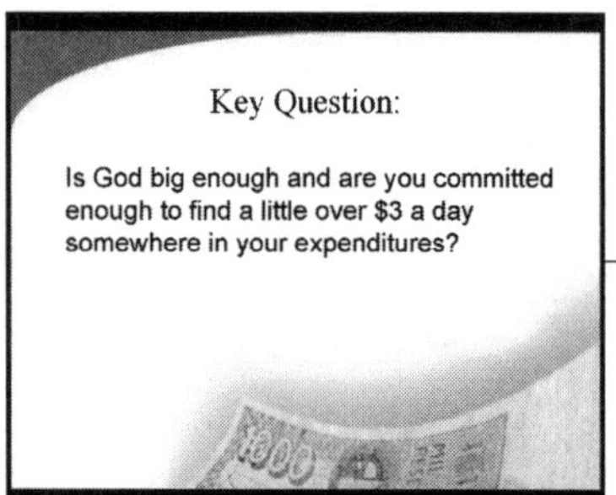
Key Question:
Is God big enough and are you committed enough to find a little over $3 a day somewhere in your expenditures?

To answer that question, I want you to first consider this question: Is God big enough and are you committed enough to find a little over three dollars a day somewhere in your expenditures that could go to debt repayment?

If so, in the next session, we will focus specifically on ways to reduce spending in order to free up that extra money.

Before we move to the Spending Plan Application, we're going to talk about two principles for accelerating debt repayment.

Principles for Accelerating Debt Repayment:
Pay off your SMALLEST debt first.

First, pay off your SMALLEST debt first.

NOTES

Credit Card Debt and Repayment Example:

You owe $7,200 @ 18.1%		
Minimum Payment = 2% of the balance or $10—whichever is greater		
You Pay	**Total Paid**	**Time (years)**
$ Minimum/month	$23,049	30+
$144/month	$13,397	8
$144+100/month	$ 9,570	3

Key Question: Is God big enough and are you committed enough to find a little over three dollars a day somewhere in your expenditures that could go to debt repayment?

Principles for Accelerating Debt Repayment:

- Pay off your ____________________ debt first.
- As a debt is repaid, roll the amount you were paying to the next largest debt.
- Incur no new debt!

You can do it!

The strategy is to take the smallest debt and, in addition to its minimum payment, pay whatever additional money you've been able to come up with toward that monthly payment.

You could argue that the greatest savings would occur by attacking the debt with the highest interest rate first. While this is true, the psychological benefit of getting one or more debts off the books very quickly far exceeds the few additional dollars it may cost.

Second, as a debt is repaid, roll the amount you were paying to the next largest debt, adding it to that debt's monthly payment.

Continue this strategy until all debts are paid. Do not decrease your debt repayment until all debts are paid off. Take advantage of the "snowball" effect of rolling over the payment for the last debt to the next one. This provides tremendous momentum to accelerate your debt repayment.

For more information on accelerating debt repayment, see pages 112-114 in the Appendix.

The final key point for getting out of debt is this:

Incur no new debt!

You must use discipline. Obviously, you will not make progress if you are continuing to incur new debt as the old is being paid.

If you do nothing more than stop going further into debt and take the first small step toward repayment, even if it is just reducing the balance a few dollars, you will have completely reversed the direction you were heading. This is a 180-degree turnaround! That's huge! I want to encourage you to take that step. Freeze your debt!

NOTES

Credit Card Debt and Repayment Example:

You owe $7,200 @ 18.1%		
Minimum Payment = 2% of the balance or $10—whichever is greater		
You Pay	**Total Paid**	**Time (years)**
$ Minimum/month	$23,049	30+
$144/month	$13,397	8
$144+100/month	$ 9,570	3

Key Question: Is God big enough and are you committed enough to find a little over three dollars a day somewhere in your expenditures that could go to debt repayment?

Principles for Accelerating Debt Repayment:

- Pay off your ____________________ debt first.
- As a debt is repaid, roll the amount you were paying to the next largest debt.
- Incur no new debt!

You can do it!

Now, let's look at the debt payment category on our Spending Plan worksheets.

7 minutes

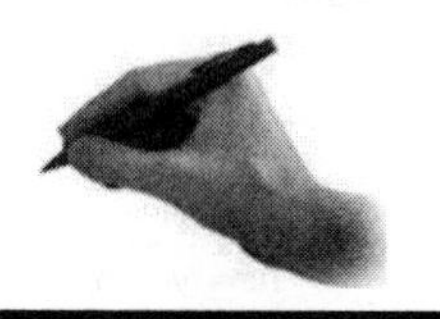

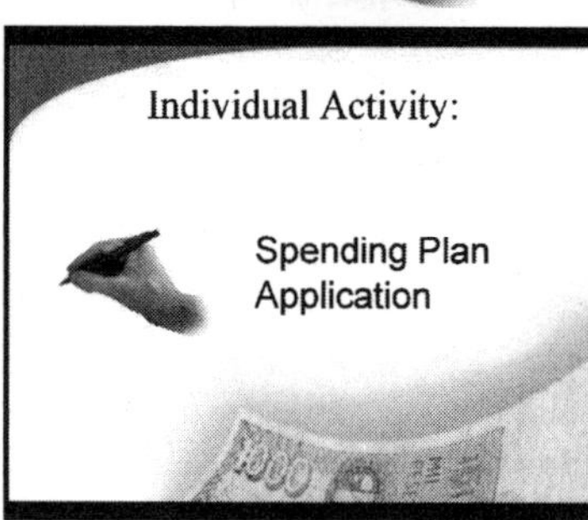
Individual Activity:
Spending Plan Application

Individual Activity: *Spending Plan Application*

Participant's Guide, page 55.

Objective
To have participants document debt reduction payments on the Spending Plan worksheet.

Directions

1. Using your pre-work information from the "What I Own and What I Owe" sheet, list each of your debts and fill in the monthly minimum payments on your Spending Plan worksheet. If you did not complete the pre-work, estimate your monthly minimum payment for each debt.
2. Set a tentative goal for how much additional payment you plan to make each month.
3. Apply this additional payment to your smallest debt.

You have 5 minutes to do this.

Call the group back together after 5 minutes.

Wrap-up
Now that you've put down an amount for your debt payments, let me offer an additional bit of motivation for you to make it a top priority.

Turn to page 56.

Participant's Guide, page 56.

NOTES

SESSION THREE
55

Individual Activity: *Spending Plan Application*

1. Using your pre-work information from the "What I Own and What I Owe" sheet, list each of your debts and fill in the monthly minimum payments on your Spending Plan worksheet.

   If you did not complete the pre-work, estimate your monthly minimum payment for each debt.

2. Set a tentative goal for how much additional payment you plan to make each month.

3. Apply this additional payment to your smallest debt.

Debt repayment is a great investment! Many people are looking for some advice on investing. Before looking for stocks or mutual funds to invest in, ask yourself the question, "Do I have any consumer debt?" If so, you have a wonderful investment opportunity.

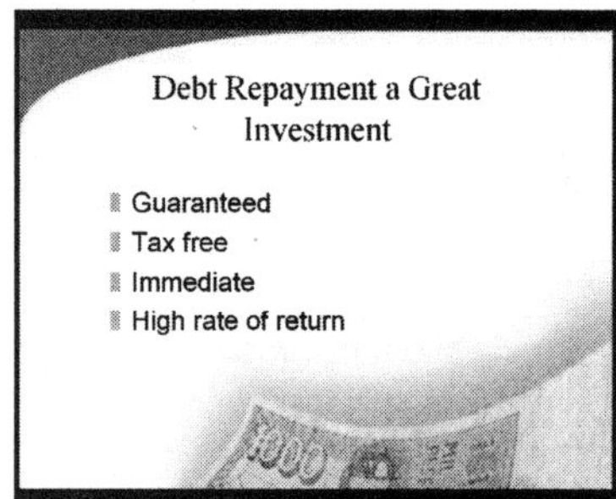
Debt Repayment a Great Investment
Guaranteed
Tax free
Immediate
High rate of return

It's guaranteed, tax free, immediate, and offers a high rate of return on your investment.

Pay off your credit cards!

At this point it's important to acknowledge that some of us are in debt for reasons totally beyond our control: an accident, an illness, an unavoidable job loss, etc. I want to be very sensitive to these situations. But others of us are in debt because we didn't have a plan, we didn't discipline ourselves, and we let the culture pull us out of control. In these cases, debt is not the problem; debt is a symptom. It could be a symptom of lifelong overspending patterns you grew up with in your family of origin. Or perhaps it is connected to feelings of insecurity or a lack of self-esteem.

If debt is a symptom of a deeper issue for you, take whatever steps are necessary to discover and eliminate the root issue. Divest yourself of behaviors that feed the problem. Throw away catalogs that come in the mail, don't take mall walks or go window-shopping, etc.

If part of the problem is trying to keep up with your neighbors, go outside tonight and yell out at the top of your lungs, "You win! You win the newest car, biggest boat, best landscaping, and most beautiful interior decorating contests! I'm out of this insane competition!" Resolve today to seek assistance and accountability for the problem you have that is creating debt.

NOTES

Debt repayment is a great investment!

- Guaranteed
- Tax free
- Immediate
- High rate of return

Pay off your credit cards!

Video: ***Out of Debt***

Notes

6 minutes

SESSION SUMMARY

To wrap up our discussion on debt, we're going to watch a video that tells stories of those who have successfully overcome it.

Video: *Out of Debt* (5 minutes)

View video: *Out of Debt.*

This video demonstrates the struggle and sacrifice required to overcome debt, but it also serves as an inspiration that it can be done—and that *you* can do it. I'm now going to give you a minute to talk with God about what is on your heart. If you're here with someone, you may want to pray together.

Pause a minute to allow participants to pray.

Let's wrap up this time with prayer.

Father, the Pull of the Culture is so very strong in this area. Lift up each person here today. Guide and encourage them to take the right steps and make the difficult choices necessary to lead them out of consumer debt and into financial freedom and faithfulness, amen.

Break.

Session Four

SPENDING

SESSION SNAPSHOT

OBJECTIVES

In this session, participants will:

1. Reflect on "driving their stake" lifestyle-wise.
2. Set short-term goals for the housing, auto/transportation, insurance, household/personal and entertainment spending categories on their Spending Plan worksheets.
3. Identify action steps to reduce expenses in these categories.

OUTLINE

I. Introduction

II. Discovery

A. Spending
1. The Pull of the Culture versus the Mind and Heart of God
2. Driving Your Stake
3. Individual Activity: *Driving Your Stake Lifestyle-wise*

B. Spending Categories
1. Housing
2. Individual Activity: *Spending Plan Application*
3. Auto/Transportation
4. Insurance
5. Individual Activity: *Spending Plan Application*
6. Household/Personal
7. Individual Activity: *Household/Personal and Entertainment Ideas and Spending Plan Application*

III. Session Summary

SPENDING

TIME & MEDIA	CONTENTS

1 minute

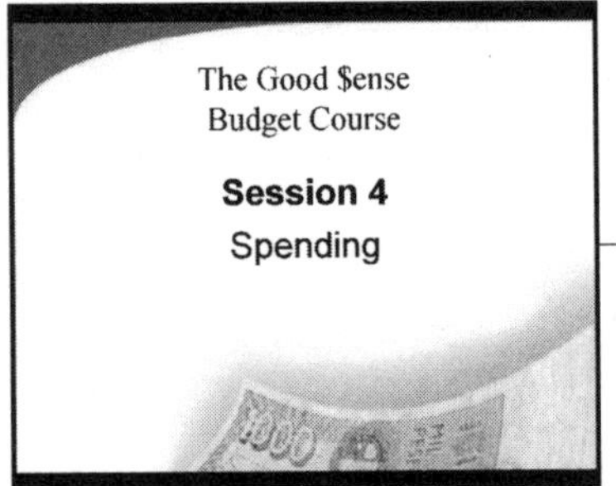

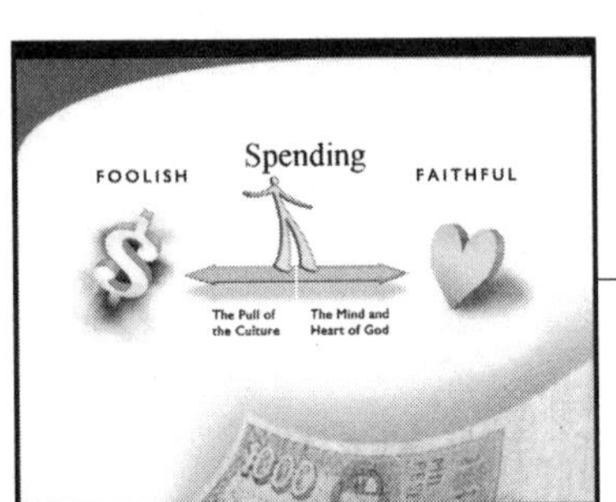

INTRODUCTION

Participant's Guide, page 57.

The fifth and final area of our financial lives is spending. It is within this area that we can find the money to help in our debt reduction efforts and to increase giving and saving.

Up to this point, we have focused on the concept of *more*—how we can give more, save more, and pay off more debt. The mindset for this session is *less*. We will look at how we can spend less while still meeting our needs and the needs of those dependent on us. As we discussed in previous sessions, this is another area that is about more than just finances. It's about who you *are* and who you are *becoming* as a consumer.

In this session you'll have the opportunity to reflect on what "driving your stake" lifestyle-wise would mean to you. You'll also be able to set short-term goals for the spending categories and finally, identify some action steps to reduce expenses.

DISCOVERY (49 minutes)

Spending

Let's start by taking a look at the Pull of the Culture on the consumer.

NOTES

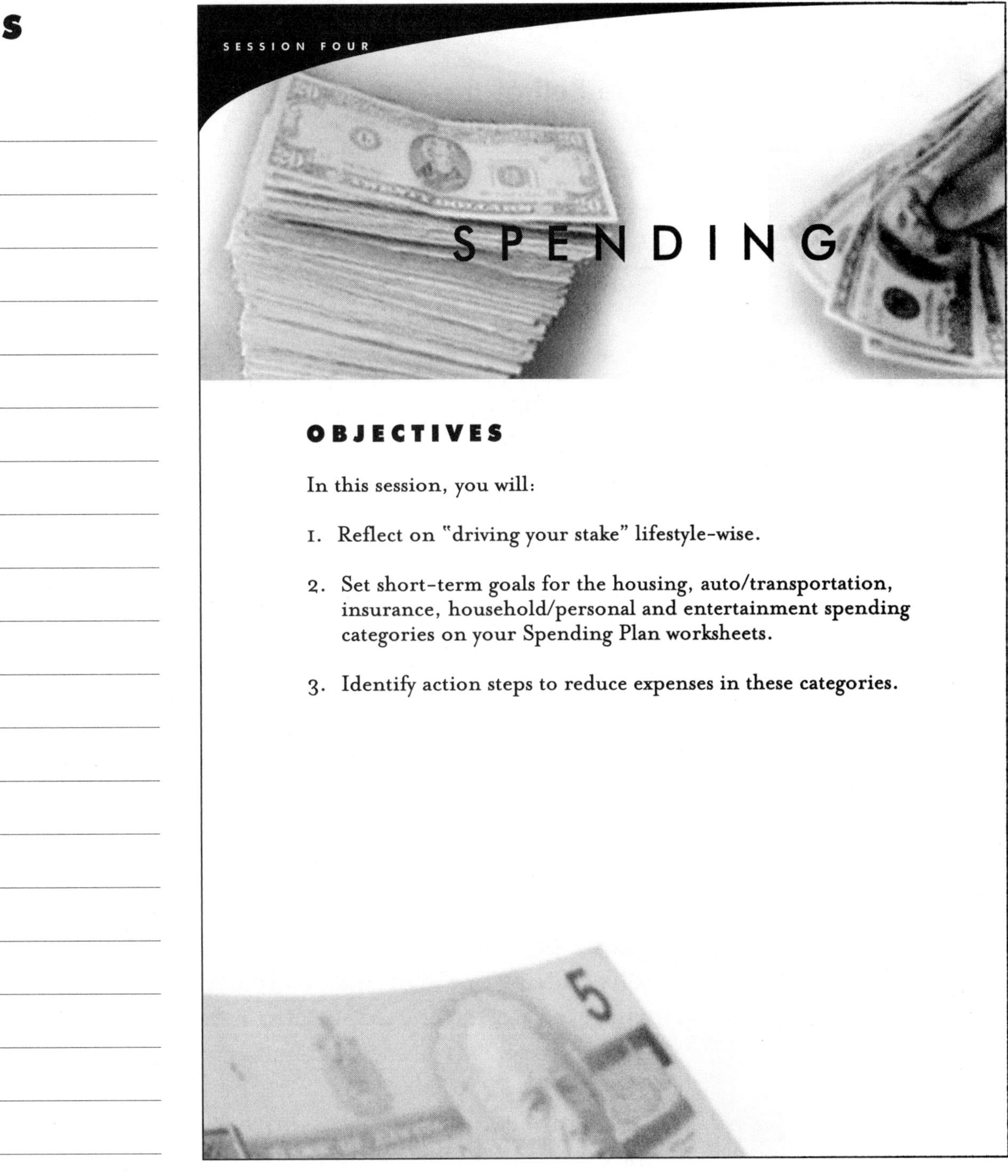

OBJECTIVES

In this session, you will:

1. Reflect on "driving your stake" lifestyle-wise.
2. Set short-term goals for the housing, auto/transportation, insurance, household/personal and entertainment spending categories on your Spending Plan worksheets.
3. Identify action steps to reduce expenses in these categories.

Turn to page 58.

3 minutes

The Pull of the Culture vs. the Mind and Heart of God

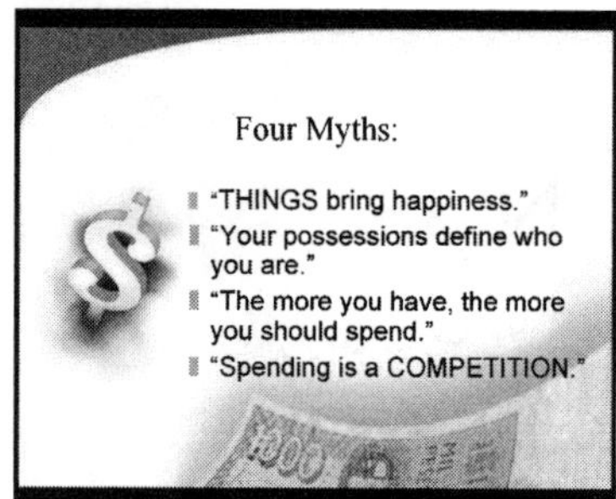

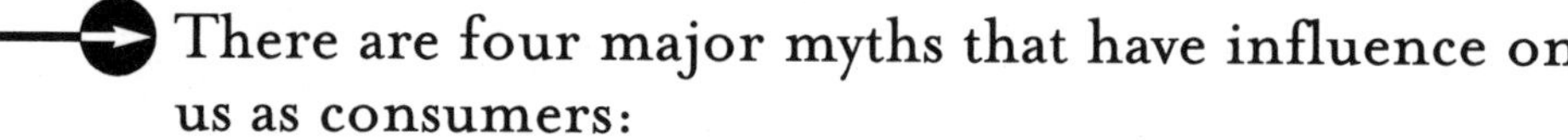
Participant's Guide, page 58.

There are four major myths that have influence on us as consumers:

- "THINGS bring happiness."
- "Your possessions define who you are."
- "The more you have, the more you should spend."
- "Spending is a COMPETITION."

These statements are not entirely new to us since they flow out of cultural myths we've discussed throughout the course. Let's look at each one.

"Things bring happiness." The aim of advertising is to make us discontent with what we have and to convince us that happiness lies in possessing one more thing. "Wear me, drink me, drive me, buy me at the 'Stuff-mart,' and you'll be successful, healthy, wealthy, and wise!"

"Your possessions define who you are." Our culture also tells us that our worth as individuals is somehow tied into whatever we have, and we compare ourselves to others on that basis.

"The more you have, the more you should spend." We have bought into the belief that as our incomes go up, we should purchase bigger houses, sportier cars, and trendier clothes to keep up with it.

"Spending is a competition." The Joneses are the opposing team. And sadly, the research shows that many of us are no longer just trying to keep up with our neighbors, but through the influence of the media, we're trying to keep up with those several income levels above us.

NOTES

Spending

The Pull of the Culture vs. the Mind and Heart of God

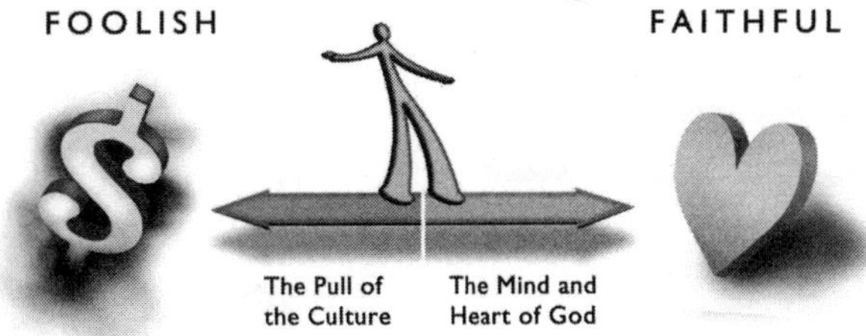

Four Myths:

- "__________ bring happiness."
- "Your possessions define who you are."
- "The more you have, the more you should spend."
- "Spending is a ______________________."

The Prudent Consumer is:

One who enjoys the fruits of their labor yet guards against materialism.

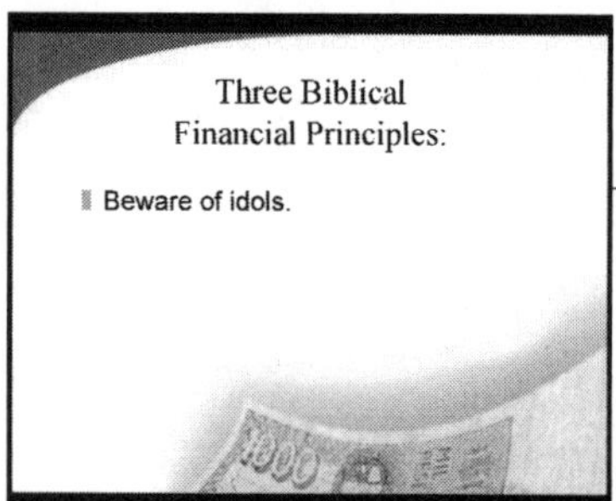

The Prudent Consumer

Now, let's look at the Mind and Heart of God on spending. The Bible characterizes the God-honoring consumer as "prudent."

The prudent consumer: one who enjoys the fruits of their labor yet guards against materialism.

Participant's Guide, page 59.

Let's examine three Biblical Financial Principles about our behavior as consumers.

First, beware of idols.

In Deuteronomy 5:7-8, God declares himself to be a jealous God and commands that we have no other gods before him. Yet, since the beginning of time, we have wrestled with the temptation to replace God with things. Today we call it materialism, which we need to recognize as a competing theology.

In Romans 1:25 the Apostle Paul described the wicked as those who "worshiped and served created things rather than the Creator."

In contrast, God desires us to seek first the kingdom, and have faith that all these things will be given to us as well.

Second, guard against GREED.

In Luke 12:15, Jesus says, "Beware! Don't be greedy for what you don't have. Real life is not measured by how much we own."

In contrast to greed, the Bible calls us to seek moderation. Proverbs 30:8 says, "Give me neither poverty nor riches. Give me just enough to satisfy my needs" (NLT).

NOTES

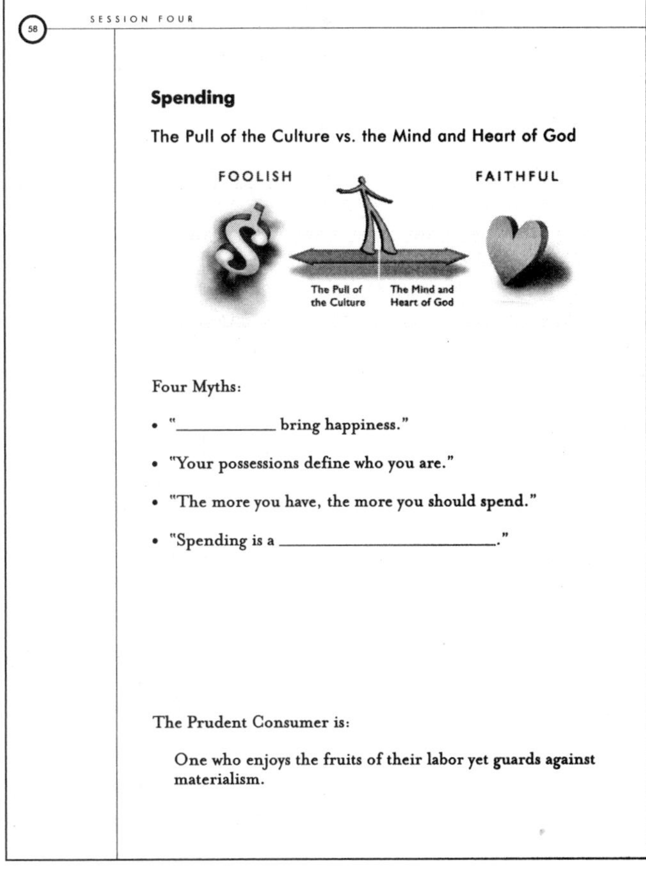

Four Myths:

- "__________ bring happiness."
- "Your possessions define who you are."
- "The more you have, the more you should spend."
- "Spending is a ____________________."

The Prudent Consumer is:

One who enjoys the fruits of their labor yet guards against materialism.

Three Biblical Financial Principles:

- Beware of idols.

> Romans 1:25: *They "worshiped and served created things rather than the Creator."*

- Guard against __________.

> Luke 12:15 (NLT): *"Beware! Don't be greedy for what you don't have. Real life is not measured by how much we own."*

- Be __________.

> Philippians 4:12: *"I know what it is to be in need, and I know what it is to have plenty. I have learned the secret of being content in any and every situation, whether well fed or hungry, whether living in plenty or in want."*

Contentment with and gratitude for what we have is the antidote to greed and envy.

God wants us to recognize our immeasurable value as his beloved children and to not associate our value with the possession of material things.

When we practice __________________ and learn contentment, we become free to be a blessing to others.

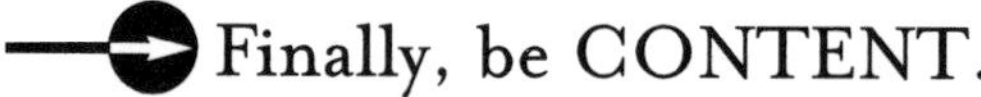

Finally, be CONTENT.

In Philippians 4:12 Paul explains that he has learned to be content in all circumstances. He writes, "I know what it is to be in need, and I know what it is to have plenty. I have learned the secret of being content in any and every situation, whether well fed or hungry, whether living in plenty or in want."

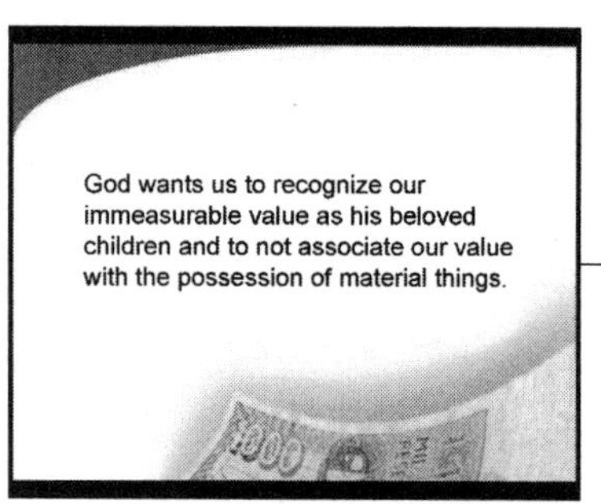
God wants us to recognize our immeasurable value as his beloved children and to not associate our value with the possession of material things.

Contentment with and gratitude for what we have is the antidote to greed and envy.

Once again, remember that God wants us to recognize our immeasurable value as his beloved children and to not associate our value with the possession of material things.

As we seek to become prudent consumers, God reminds us in 1 Timothy 6 that he "richly supplies us with everything for our enjoyment," yet instructs us to put our hope in him and not in the uncertainty of wealth. He further instructs us to "do good, to be rich in good deeds, and to be generous and willing to share."

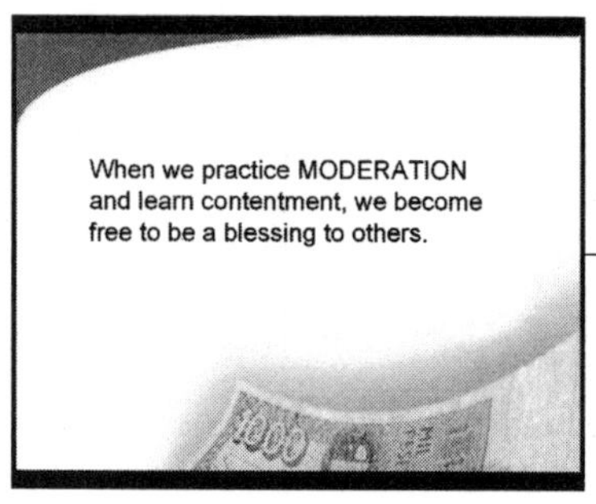
When we practice MODERATION and learn contentment, we become free to be a blessing to others.

In the context of spending, when we practice MODERATION and learn contentment, we become free to be a blessing to others.

Turn to page 60.

1 minute

Driving Your Stake

Participant's Guide, page 60.

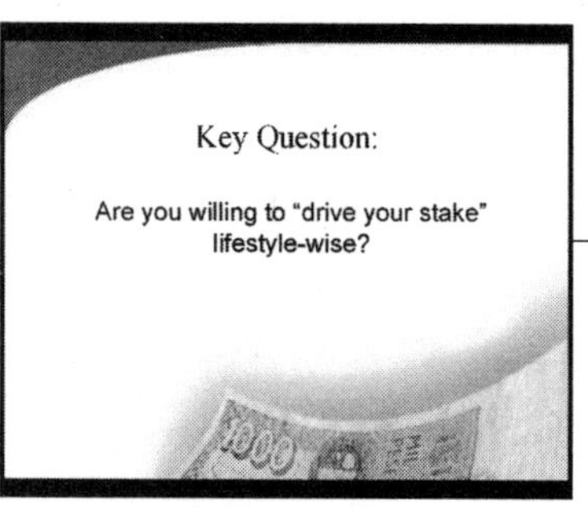
Key Question:
Are you willing to "drive your stake" lifestyle-wise?

Understanding this challenge of being content and seeking moderation raises a key question: Are you willing to "drive your stake" lifestyle-wise?

What does this mean?

NOTES

Three Biblical Financial Principles:

- Beware of idols.

> Romans 1:25: *They "worshiped and served created things rather than the Creator."*

- Guard against ____________.

> Luke 12:15 (NLT): *"Beware! Don't be greedy for what you don't have. Real life is not measured by how much we own."*

- Be ____________.

> Philippians 4:12: *"I know what it is to be in need, and I know what it is to have plenty. I have learned the secret of being content in any and every situation, whether well fed or hungry, whether living in plenty or in want."*

Contentment with and gratitude for what we have is the antidote to greed and envy.

God wants us to recognize our immeasurable value as his beloved children and to not associate our value with the possession of material things.

When we practice ____________________ and learn contentment, we become free to be a blessing to others.

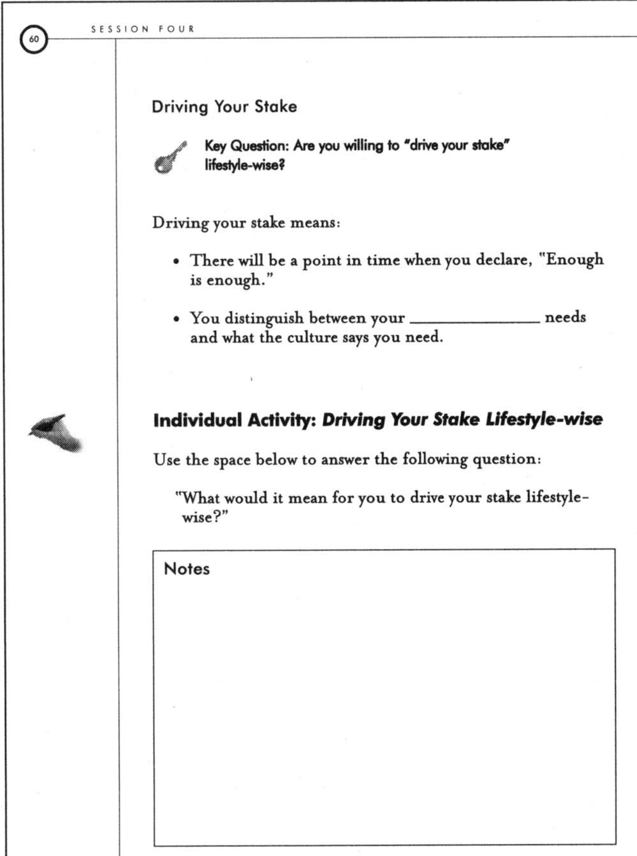

Driving Your Stake

Key Question: Are you willing to "drive your stake" lifestyle-wise?

Driving your stake means:

- There will be a point in time when you declare, "Enough is enough."
- You distinguish between your ________________ needs and what the culture says you need.

Individual Activity: *Driving Your Stake Lifestyle-wise*

Use the space below to answer the following question:

"What would it mean for you to drive your stake lifestyle-wise?"

Notes

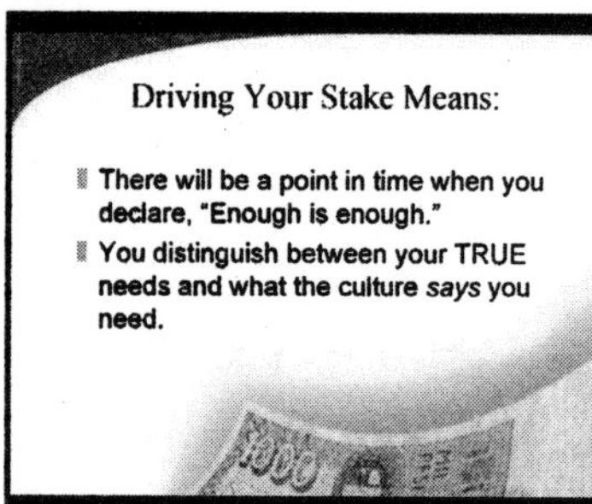
Driving Your Stake Means:
There will be a point in time when you declare, "Enough is enough."
You distinguish between your TRUE needs and what the culture *says* you need.

It basically means that there will be a point in time when you declare, "Enough is enough." You distinguish between your needs and your wants, between your TRUE needs and what the culture *says* you need.

For example, will there be a point in time where you would say, "You know, this house is big enough. It keeps me warm in the winter. It keeps me dry in the summer. Even if I made $10,000 a year, $50,000 a year, or $100,000 a year more and could afford a bigger house in a 'nicer' neighborhood, I'm not going to buy it. I'm driving my stake lifestyle-wise."

Similarly, you could also say, "The kind of car I drive now gets me reliably from point A to point B. Even if I could afford a much more expensive car, I'm not going to buy it. I'm driving my stake lifestyle-wise."

I don't know where you are in this regard, but I would challenge you to drive that stake somewhere. For some, maybe your stake is still out there a ways. For example, your family is growing and you're living in a very small house. It's okay to wait on driving your stake regarding housing.

For others, maybe you could drive your stake right where you are now and declare that enough is enough or maybe you are at a place where God is nudging you to downsize and drive your stake back from where it is now.

The key question we need to ask ourselves as prudent consumers is, When is enough enough? As we've already said, if our treasure is in earthly things, enough will never be enough. Enough has much more to do with an attitude we adopt than with a numerical goal.

Because this is such a key question, and because we're not often challenged to consider it, let's take a moment to think about this now.

NOTES

Driving Your Stake

Key Question: Are you willing to "drive your stake" lifestyle-wise?

Driving your stake means:

- There will be a point in time when you declare, "Enough is enough."
- You distinguish between your ________________ needs and what the culture says you need.

Individual Activity: *Driving Your Stake Lifestyle-wise*

Use the space below to answer the following question:

"What would it mean for you to drive your stake lifestyle-wise?"

Notes

3 minutes

Individual Activity:
Driving Your Stake Lifestyle-wise

Individual Activity: *Driving Your Stake Lifestyle-wise*

Objective
For participants to reflect on what it would mean to them to "drive their stake" lifestyle-wise.

Directions
Use the space below to answer the following question: What would it mean for you to drive your stake lifestyle-wise?

Call the group back together after 2 minutes.

Wrap-up (1 minute)
What types of responses did you come up with?

Solicit two or three comments from the group. Be sure to repeat their answers so everyone hears the response.

Possible responses:
- "I'm going to stop trying to keep up with the Jones's."
- "We can downsize our house when our children no longer live with us."
- I'll reconsider the car I'm going to buy."

Again, we face the dilemma between choosing to follow the Pull of the Culture or seeking the Mind and Heart of God. And the question is, What are you becoming as a consumer? Are you becoming more financially faithful, or are you foolishly allowing the culture to pull you away from God?

Spending Categories

Keeping this in mind, let's take a look at the remaining spending categories on the Spending Plan worksheet.

NOTES

Driving Your Stake

Key Question: Are you willing to "drive your stake" lifestyle-wise?

Driving your stake means:

- There will be a point in time when you declare, "Enough is enough."
- You distinguish between your ______________ needs and what the culture says you need.

Individual Activity: *Driving Your Stake Lifestyle-wise*

Use the space below to answer the following question:

"What would it mean for you to drive your stake lifestyle-wise?"

Notes

4 minutes

Housing

Participant's Guide, page 61.

The first category is housing. For most of us, whether we own or rent, housing is the biggest expenditure we'll have in our lifetime.

Mortgage / Taxes / Rent
Notice that the first category on your Spending Plan worksheet under housing is mortgage and taxes or rent.

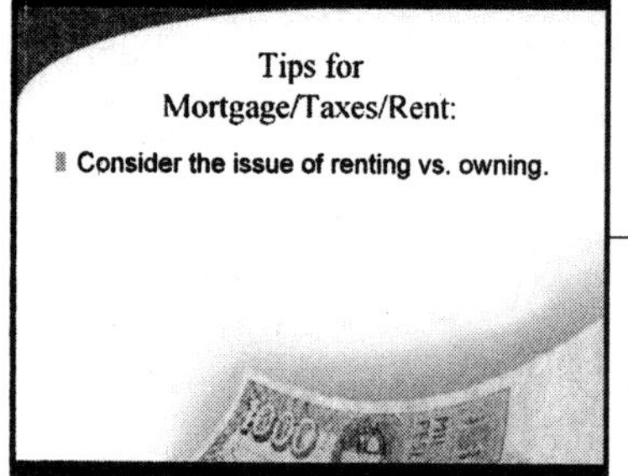

There are several tips for this category.

First, let's consider the issue of renting versus owning.

There's a commonly held belief that it's always best to own—that those who rent are just throwing money away. While there are many emotional advantages to ownership and often financial advantages, home ownership can also have financial disadvantages.

For example, a home can depreciate as well as appreciate in value. And your personal circumstances may not be optimal for homeownership. For example, buying a home when there is a good chance you may move in a year or two may not make good financial sense. Considering all the expense of purchasing, moving, and reselling, it may be wiser to rent. Perhaps you lack the cash to make a reasonable down payment. Rather than taking on private mortgage insurance and a debt that will make you "house poor," it may be wiser to rent inexpensively until you have saved enough for a larger down payment.

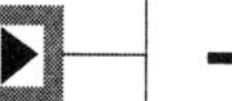

Second, if and when you do decide to purchase a home and have a mortgage, think PREPAYMENT.

NOTES

Housing

Tips for Mortgage/Taxes/Rent:

- Consider the issue of renting versus owning.
- Think ______________ of mortgage.
- Beware of basing a mortgage on ______________.
- Exercise caution with regard to equity loans.
- Consider an extended household.

Maintenance and Repairs:

- Become a Mr. or a Ms. "Fix-it."

Utilities:

- Control the thermostat.
- Use phones wisely.
- Evaluate options for Internet and cable services.

You can reduce the term of your mortgage by a significant number of years and also reduce interest costs substantially by making one extra payment per year. For example, a thirty-year, 7.5 percent mortgage would be paid off seven years sooner; a 10 percent mortgage would be paid off nine years sooner. Making one additional payment each year may not be possible at first, but think about budgeting for it in the future or using any unexpected income for this purpose. Prepayment can make a tremendous difference in the term of the mortgage and obviously in the amount of interest you'll pay.

Third, beware of basing a mortgage on TWO INCOMES.

The mortgage companies may tell you differently, but think back to our discussion earlier about how to handle two incomes. It is wise to cover all your basic living costs, including housing, with one income. Rather than mortgaging your future flexibility and being forever dependent on two incomes, delay purchasing a home until you can cover the payments with one income. Wait a couple years, make some sacrifices, save a significant portion of that second income, and then make a down payment, that enables you to pay the mortgage out of one salary.

Fourth, exercise extreme caution with regard to equity loans.

Home equity loans are rapidly becoming the ultimate credit card. Some companies now allow borrowers to make automatic transfers of credit card balances into a home loan. There's no telling where this will all end, but to use a home equity loan to allow continued spending beyond your means is a trap that places your home in danger. Don't fall into it. Don't allow a home equity loan to be a means to fund short-term spending with long-term debt.

NOTES

Housing

Tips for Mortgage/Taxes/Rent:

- Consider the issue of renting versus owning.
- Think ____________________ of mortgage.
- Beware of basing a mortgage on ____________________.
- Exercise caution with regard to equity loans.
- Consider an extended household.

Maintenance and Repairs:

- Become a Mr. or a Ms. "Fix-it."

Utilities:

- Control the thermostat.
- Use phones wisely.
- Evaluate options for Internet and cable services.

A final issue to consider in this category is whether an extended household is an option.

My guess is that there are empty bedrooms in some of your homes and apartments. There are a lot of people within the body of Christ who would benefit from occupying those rooms. Could you allow someone to share your home at a very reasonable "rent," thereby reducing expenses for both of you while simultaneously allowing them to experience living in a Christian home? It can be a "win-win" situation with lots of blessing on both sides as we actually live out being the family of God.

Now, let's move to the second housing expense on your Spending Plan worksheet, maintenance and repairs.

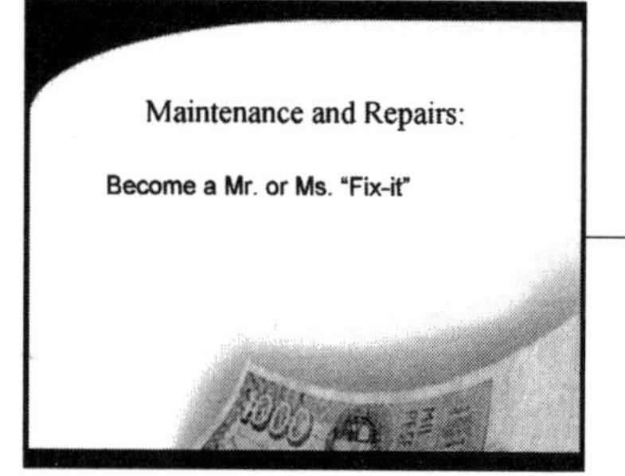

Maintenance and Repairs

The advice here is to become a Mr. or a Ms. "Fix-it."

If you're going to own a home, learn basic repairs like changing a washer in the faucet, and the importance of preventative maintenance tasks such as changing furnace and air conditioning filters and cleaning leaves out of your gutters. Doing these things yourself greatly reduces expenses and prevents costly repairs later. Check the library for books on this subject.

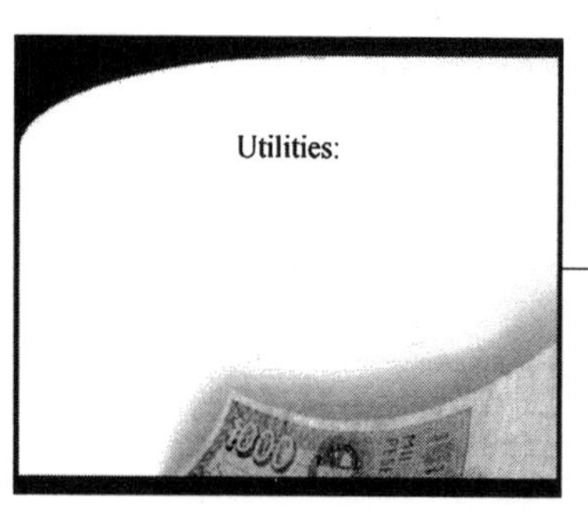

Utilities

The other expense on your worksheet under housing is utilities.

Here are three guidelines for reducing utilities costs.

First, control the thermostat.

NOTES

Housing

Tips for Mortgage/Taxes/Rent:

- Consider the issue of renting versus owning.
- Think ______________ of mortgage.
- Beware of basing a mortgage on ______________.
- Exercise caution with regard to equity loans.
- Consider an extended household.

Maintenance and Repairs:

- Become a Mr. or a Ms. "Fix-it."

Utilities:

- Control the thermostat.
- Use phones wisely.
- Evaluate options for Internet and cable services.

A couple degrees on the thermostat can make a significant difference in your heating and air-conditioning bills. In addition, make sure weather stripping and caulking are in good repair. Often your utility company provides free information on how to reduce costs. The month-after-month savings in utility costs is a great example of the cumulative-effect principle we discussed previously.

→ Second, use phones wisely.

Make sure you have the best long-distance plan for your needs. Then ask yourself which phone extras like call waiting, caller I.D., voicemail, etc., you really need. Also, limit cell phone use. This is a high-expense item that can become addictive. Use it for emergency purposes and not just convenience. Notice that most companies offer the first month free. Why? So, by the time regular monthly charges kick in, you've already established the habit of using the phone on a frequent basis.

If appropriate for your audience, point out that many families now have multiple cell phones, which can be a significant monthly expense.

→ Finally, evaluate options for Internet and cable services.

Explore some of the free services available, and check out the various packages provided by Internet companies. With cable, be aware that some lower cost versus premium plans aren't readily available unless you pursue them aggressively.

Turn to page 62.

NOTES

Housing

Tips for Mortgage/Taxes/Rent:

- Consider the issue of renting versus owning.
- Think ______________________ of mortgage.
- Beware of basing a mortgage on ___________________.
- Exercise caution with regard to equity loans.
- Consider an extended household.

Maintenance and Repairs:

- Become a Mr. or a Ms. "Fix-it."

Utilities:

- Control the thermostat.
- Use phones wisely.
- Evaluate options for Internet and cable services.

8 minutes

Individual Activity:

Spending Plan Application

Individual Activity: *Spending Plan Application*

Participant's Guide, page 62.

Objective
For participants to set short-term goals for the housing category on their Spending Plan worksheets.

Directions

1. Look at your pre-work sheet for what you currently spend for housing.

   If you didn't complete the pre-work, use your best estimate of housing expenses. The percent guidelines on the Spending Plan worksheet can help you.

2. Consider some of the issues discussed regarding housing. Write down at least one action step that you plan to take under this category.

3. Set short-term goals for housing expenses, and fill in this category of your Spending Plan worksheet.

You have 8 minutes to do this.

Call the group back together after 8 minutes.

If time allows, you may want to give participants more time to work.

3 minutes

Auto/Transportation

Participant's Guide, page 63.

What's the next biggest category after housing?

Pause briefly for participants' responses.

Yes, auto or transportation. Car expenses can eat you alive financially.

NOTES

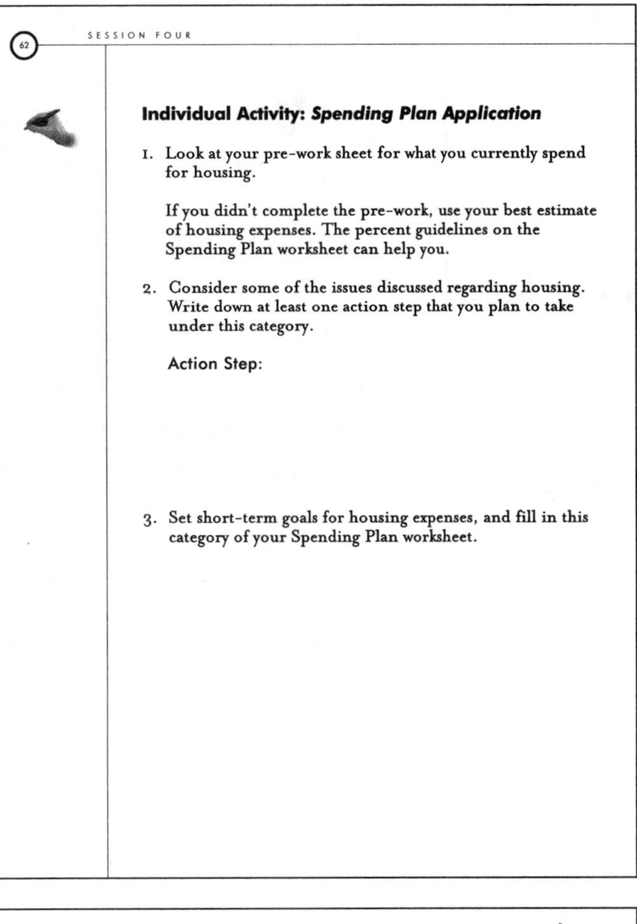

Individual Activity: *Spending Plan Application*

1. Look at your pre-work sheet for what you currently spend for housing.

   If you didn't complete the pre-work, use your best estimate of housing expenses. The percent guidelines on the Spending Plan worksheet can help you.

2. Consider some of the issues discussed regarding housing. Write down at least one action step that you plan to take under this category.

   Action Step:

3. Set short-term goals for housing expenses, and fill in this category of your Spending Plan worksheet.

Auto/Transportation

Transportation Quiz:

- What is the least expensive car you can own?

  ____

- When is it economically wise to buy a new (never-owned) car?

  ____

- What are the economic advantages to leasing?

  ____

- What is the proper mileage at which it is best to unload the old car?

  ____

Statistics:

Average reliability	*Average trade-in*
Life = 10.2 years	*Time = 4 years*
Mileage = 120,000	*Mileage = 50,000*

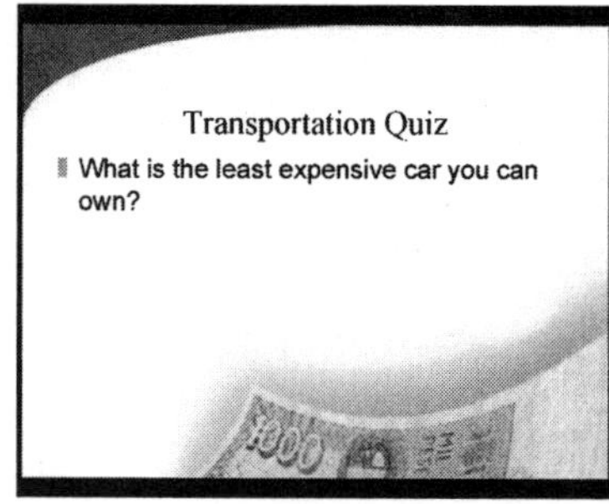

Let's take a quick quiz to test your knowledge of this area.

First question, What is the least expensive car you can own?

Pause briefly for participants' responses.

The answer is, the car you already own. The only time this might not be the case is if you are driving a very expensive car you really can't afford. Otherwise, the car you have is the car to drive. Keep good, clean, fresh oil in it. Drive it sensibly. Make it last. We'll talk about this more in a moment.

When is it economically wise to buy a new, never-owned car?

Pause briefly for participants' responses.

The answer is, *never.* It is not sinful to buy a brand-new, never-owned car. But from a purely financial standpoint, it's not the wisest thing to do. Why? Because of the huge depreciation during the first and second years, which may be thirty to forty percent of the original cost. If you buy a one- or two-year-old car, you pay much less for it than a new car, and you've got a car that's still reliable for years and years to come.

What are the economic advantages to leasing?

Pause briefly for participants' responses.

There aren't any—unless you're a car dealer. Although you do pay less each month, you don't own anything at the end of the lease. And there can be significant additional charges if you go over the mileage allocation or if wear and tear exceeds what the dealer considers normal. Leases are also difficult for the average person to understand, so comparing costs is very difficult.

NOTES

Auto/Transportation

Transportation Quiz:

- What is the least expensive car you can own?

  ____

- When is it economically wise to buy a new (never-owned) car?

  ____

- What are the economic advantages to leasing?

  ____

- What is the proper mileage at which it is best to unload the old car?

  ____

Statistics:

Average reliability	*Average trade-in*
Life = 10.2 years	*Time = 4 years*
Mileage = 120,000	*Mileage = 50,000*

It can be argued that if you want a new car every several years and you don't put many miles on it and you take good care of it, leasing can be a viable option to buying. However, this is based on getting a new car every several years, which we've already clarified as unwise financially.

What's the proper mileage at which it's best to unload the old car?

Pause briefly for participants' responses.

Actually there's no specific answer to this question. The answer is, when it approaches the point that maintenance expenses exceed the value of the car. Generally, this happens at a much higher mileage level than most people expect.

Let's look closely at some statistics that reveal the truth about new cars.

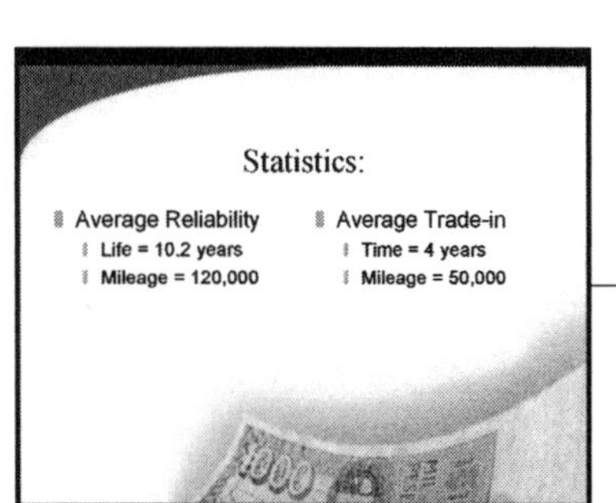

According to recent research:

The average reliable life of a new car is 10.2 years and 120,000-plus miles.

The average time at which a new car is traded in is less than four years and under 50,000 miles.

Obviously, lots of folks are getting rid of their cars well before reliability becomes an issue.

Again, hold onto your car, treat it well, keep the fluids changed, and drive it for an extended period of time. If you do, you can pay cash for your next car! Let me show you how.

NOTES

Auto/Transportation

Transportation Quiz:

- What is the least expensive car you can own?

  ____

- When is it economically wise to buy a new (never-owned) car?

  ____

- What are the economic advantages to leasing?

  ____

- What is the proper mileage at which it is best to unload the old car?

  ____

Statistics:

Average reliability

Life = 10.2 years

Mileage = 120,000

Average trade-in

Time = 4 years

Mileage = 50,000

Turn to page 64.

Participant's Guide, page 64.

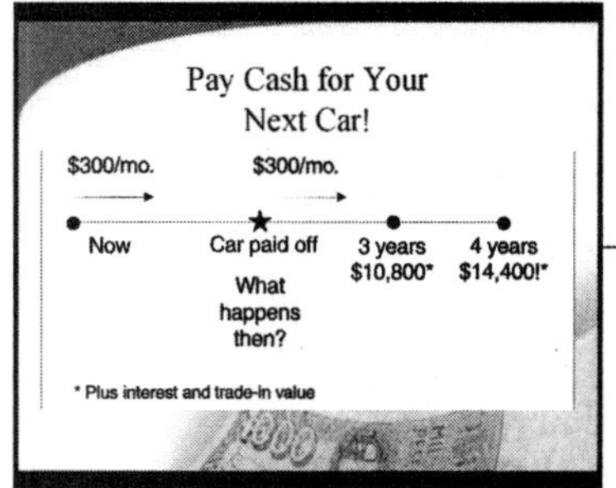

Let's assume you currently have a monthly car payment of $300. At some point, you'll pay the car off. What happens then? One of two things normally occurs. In many cases we think, "The car is paid off, so it's time to get a new car." I hope we've already shown that that's not necessarily true. Remember that a car can provide reliable service for at least ten years.

The other thing that often happens is we say, "Great! The car is paid off. I now have $300 a month to spend on something else." We make no provision for when we will need to buy the next car.

When you get to the point of paying off your car, commit to keeping your car for another three or four years and continue the $300 per month payments. Who do you pay them to? Yourself! You've been making the payments. They're in your Spending Plan. Continue to put that amount into an interest-bearing account. Use direct deposit if possible. Let's look at what happens if you pay yourself for the next three or four years.

→ By saving $300 a month, $3,600 a year, you'd have $10,800 at the end of three years, or $14,400 after four years. Plus you'd have interest and the trade-in value of your current car so that *you can pay cash for your next car!*

And, if you keep that car for six to eight years, your payment to yourself could be much lower than your existing car payment.

I want to encourage you to seriously consider this option. It will take some discipline, but it's worth it.

NOTES

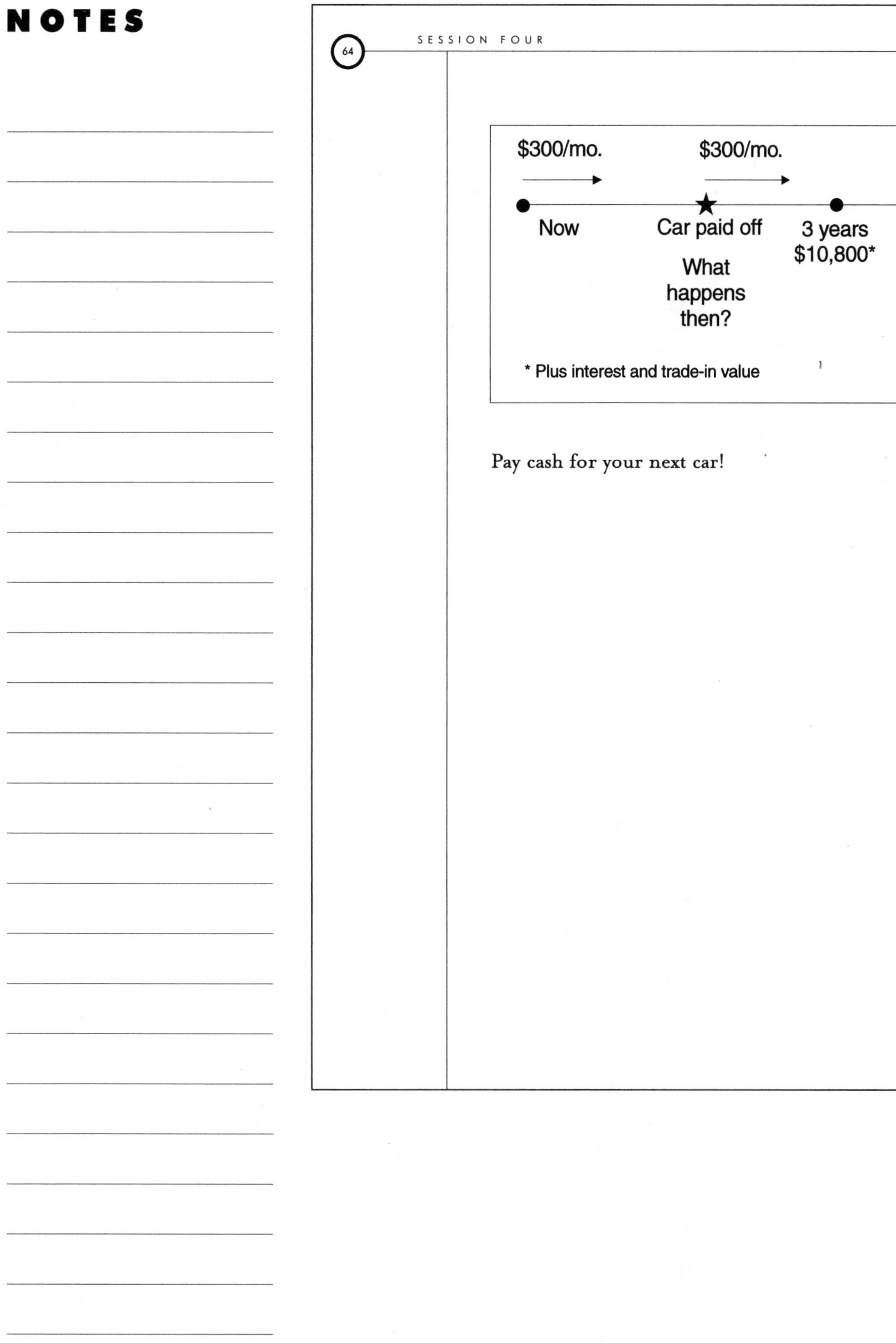
64
SESSION FOUR
$300/mo.
$300/mo.
Now
Car paid off
What happens then?
3 years $10,800*
4 years $14,400!*
* Plus interest and trade-in value
Pay cash for your next car!

2 minutes

Insurance

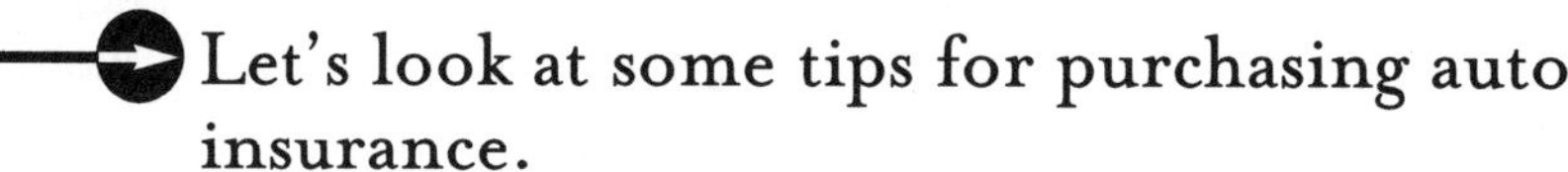
Participant's Guide, page 65.

The next category on your Spending Plan worksheet is insurance. It is one of the least understood and least monitored areas of personal finances.

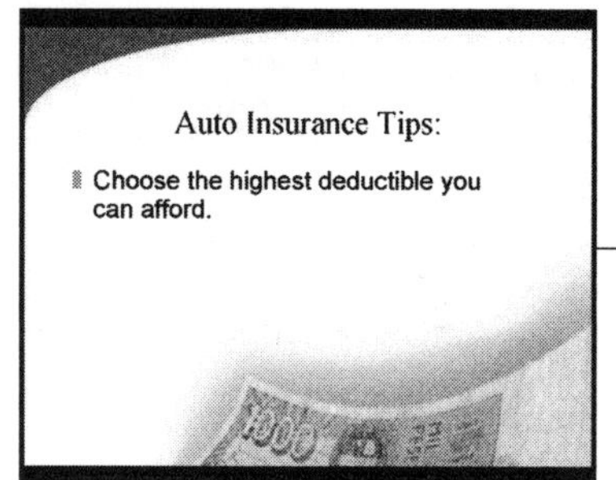

Auto Insurance

Let's look at some tips for purchasing auto insurance.

First of all, choose the highest deductible you can afford.

"Catastrophic" is the key word for insurance.

It's to protect you from major loss. For example, a $100 deductible is much more costly than a $250 or $500 deductible. Is a $250 loss on a car a catastrophic loss? It isn't for most of us. Although I'd hate to pay $250 rather than $100 if I were in an accident, it is worth it if I've saved premium costs over a few years.

Shop for it.

Often there are significant differences between companies in terms of rates, coverage, and service. Various websites provide comparative rate information. Check with a rating service like A.M. Best Company—ambest.com—to be sure the company is sound.

COMBINE policies.

For example, combining auto and homeowners insurance and having all cars on one policy usually results in significant discounts.

Look for other discounts.

Most companies offer good student, good driver, and low mileage discounts.

NOTES

Insurance

Auto Insurance Tips:

- Choose the highest deductible you can afford.

  "Catastrophic" is the key word for insurance.

- Shop for it.
- ________________ policies.
- Look for other discounts.
- Consider eliminating ________________ coverage on an older car.

Life Insurance:

- Consider a renewable term policy.
- Consider whether life insurance is necessary.

Other:

- Consider disability insurance.
- Consider long-term healthcare insurance.

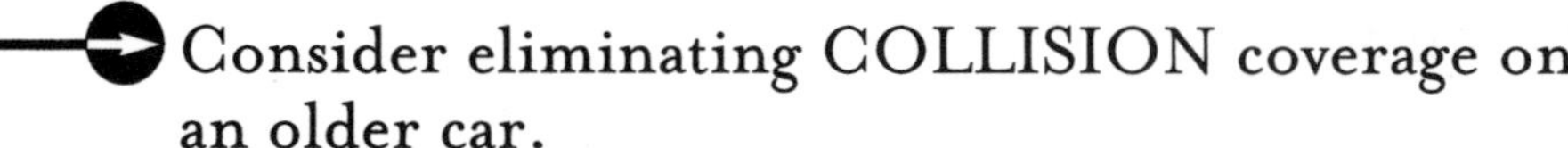

Consider eliminating COLLISION coverage on an older car.

Remember that the purpose of insurance is to cover catastrophic loss. If the car's value has decreased to the point where you could afford to replace it, it does not fall into the catastrophic loss category. Dropping collision coverage would then save the largest part of your premium.

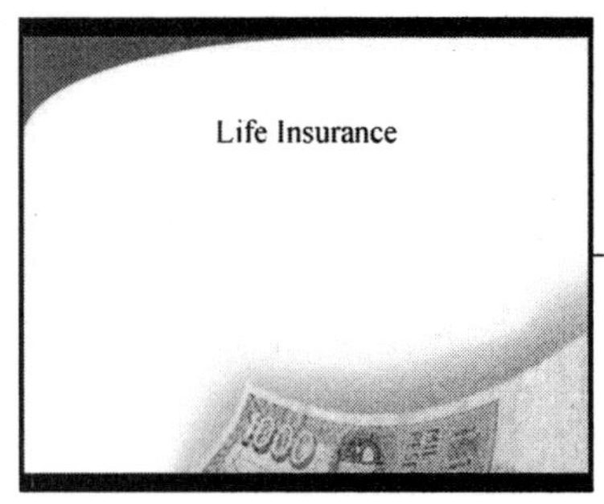

Life Insurance

Now, let's look at life insurance. It has a biblical foundation. As we discussed earlier, we are called as Christians to provide for those who are dependent on us. If you're the head of a household with children, part of the way to provide for them is to have insurance in the event that something happens to you.

A problem with life insurance is that when we need it the most, we can afford it the least. We need it most when our families are young and, generally speaking, our income is the lowest and our expenses the highest.

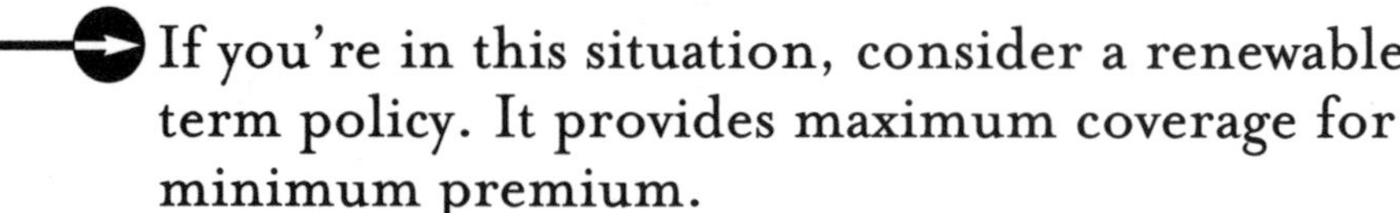

If you're in this situation, consider a renewable term policy. It provides maximum coverage for minimum premium.

Also consider whether life insurance is necessary.

It may not be if you are single with no dependents or if your children are grown and on their own, assets have accumulated, and both spouses have the ability to earn money. In those cases, you may not need life insurance except perhaps as part of an overall estate plan. Given the variety of insurance products available, it's a good idea to consult with one or two trusted professionals prior to making this kind of decision.

There are two more points under insurance.

NOTES

Insurance

Auto Insurance Tips:

- Choose the highest deductible you can afford.

  "Catastrophic" is the key word for insurance.

- Shop for it.
- ________________ policies.
- Look for other discounts.
- Consider eliminating ________________ coverage on an older car.

Life Insurance:

- Consider a renewable term policy.
- Consider whether life insurance is necessary.

Other:

- Consider disability insurance.
- Consider long-term healthcare insurance.

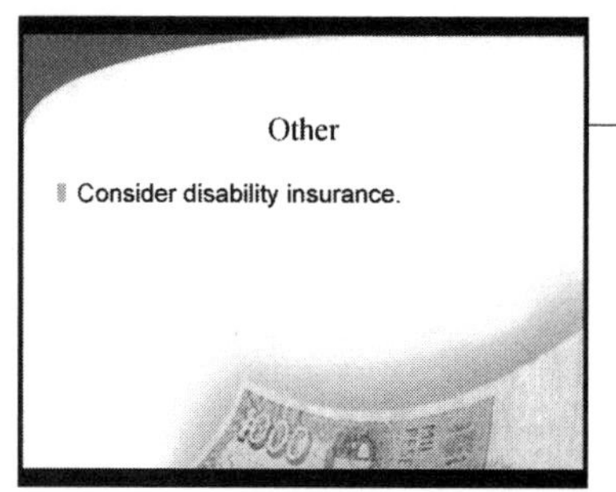
Other
Consider disability insurance.

Disability Insurance

First, consider disability insurance.

If you are not covered through an employer, you need to have disability as part of your insurance plan. Until later in life, there is a greater chance of being disabled than there is of dying.

The second point is, consider long-term healthcare insurance.

As we grow older, health problems requiring a nursing home or in-home care can create major financial problems. As you enter your sixties, it may be wise to investigate long-term healthcare insurance.

Let's take some time now to work on our Spending Plan worksheets.

Turn to page 66.

8 minutes

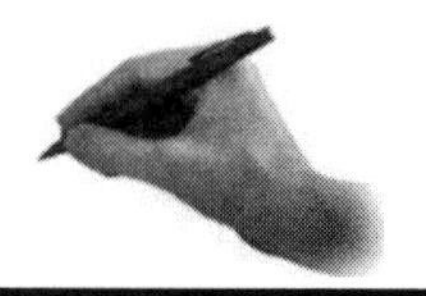

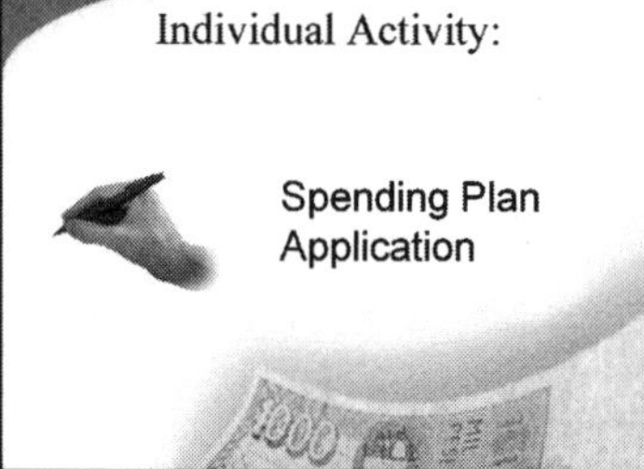
Individual Activity:
Spending Plan
Application

Individual Activity: *Spending Plan Application*

Participant's Guide, page 66.

Objective
To allow participants to set short-term goals for the auto/transportation and insurance categories on their Spending Plan worksheets.

Directions

1. Look at your pre-work sheet for what you currently spend on the auto/transportation and insurance categories.

   If you didn't complete the pre-work, use your best estimate of expenses. The percent guidelines on the Spending Plan worksheet can help you.

2. Consider any ways you can reduce these expenses. Write down at least one action step you plan to take.

NOTES

SESSION FOUR 65

Insurance

Auto Insurance Tips:

- Choose the highest deductible you can afford.

  "Catastrophic" is the key word for insurance.
- Shop for it.
- ________________ policies.
- Look for other discounts.
- Consider eliminating ________________ coverage on an older car.

Life Insurance:

- Consider a renewable term policy.
- Consider whether life insurance is necessary.

Other:

- Consider disability insurance.
- Consider long-term healthcare insurance.

SESSION FOUR

Individual Activity: *Spending Plan Application*

1. Look at your pre-work sheet for what you currently spend on the auto/transportation and insurance categories.

   If you didn't complete the pre-work, use your best estimate of expenses. The percent guidelines on the Spending Plan worksheet can help you.
2. Consider any ways you can to reduce these expenses. Write down at least one action step you plan to take.

   Action Step:
3. Set short-term goals for these categories, and fill in your Spending Plan worksheet.

3. Set short-term goals for these categories and fill in your Spending Plan worksheet.

You'll have 8 minutes to do this.

Call the group back together after 8 minutes.

2 minutes

If time allows, you may want to give participants more time to work.

Household/Personal

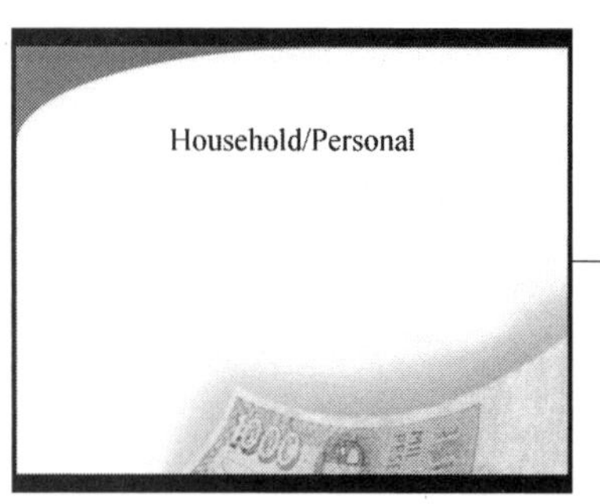

Participant's Guide, page 67.

The next category on the Spending Plan worksheet is household/personal.

We are going to look closely at the expenses in this category through an individual activity, but first, I'd like to comment on three things: clothing, books and magazines, and gambling.

Clothing

Let's start with clothing.

If you buy clothes to feel better about yourself when you don't really need those clothes, let me encourage you to seek help in getting to the bottom of this issue. God doesn't want you pegging your worth on what you're wearing.

If you're raising kids, talk with them about the peer pressure they may feel to have designer clothes. Point out that their value as a friend is not a reflection of what they wear but that their value comes from being a beloved child of their heavenly Father. That is the truth we want to build into our children rather than reinforcing the message of a culture that says their value is based on what designer label is on their clothing. Your children may not immediately embrace this truth, but be consistent in using teachable moments to reinforce it.

NOTES

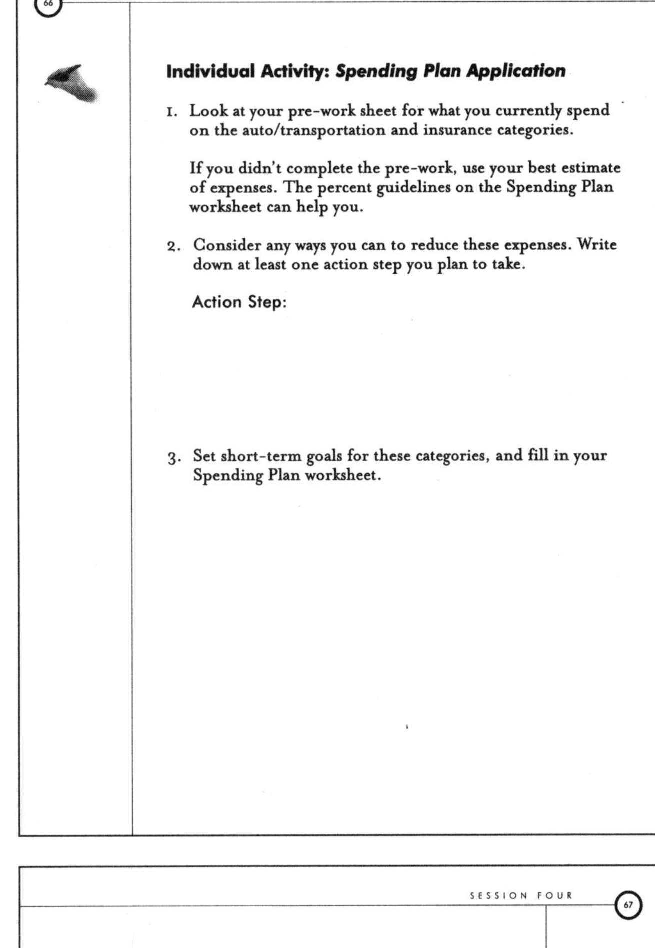

Individual Activity: *Spending Plan Application*

1. Look at your pre-work sheet for what you currently spend on the auto/transportation and insurance categories.

   If you didn't complete the pre-work, use your best estimate of expenses. The percent guidelines on the Spending Plan worksheet can help you.

2. Consider any ways you can to reduce these expenses. Write down at least one action step you plan to take.

   Action Step:

3. Set short-term goals for these categories, and fill in your Spending Plan worksheet.

Household/Personal

Clothing

Books and Magazines

> Philippians 4:8 (NLT): *"Fix your thoughts on what is true and honorable and right. Think about things that are pure and lovely and admirable. Think about things that are excellent and worthy of praise."*

Gambling

Think about what lies behind your gambling, and reflect on what God says in:

- Luke 12:15
- Proverbs 28:19-20

Books and Magazines

Let's move on to books and magazines.

The first question is, *Do* you read what you subscribe to? The second question is, *Should* you read it? You've heard the saying, "Garbage in, garbage out." It applies to computers, and it applies to the human mind.

I'm going to digress just a second from purely financial matters and put in a word about an issue that's often hard to talk about—pornography. Pornography is an aggressive cancer in our society. It is addictive, it impacts behavior, and it will shatter any intimate relationship you have. If you are into pornography, get help and get out of it.

Philippians 4:8 says, "Fix your thoughts on what is true and honorable and right. Think about things that are pure and lovely and admirable. Think about things that are excellent and worthy of praise" (NLT).

Gambling

Now, a word about gambling.

Although gambling is not listed specifically on your Spending Plan worksheet, it is worth mentioning since it has become a major issue within our society. In 1991, gambling was legal in only three U.S. states. Now it's legal in forty-seven out of fifty states. According to a recent news report, in 1974, $17 million was wagered in legal gambling in the United States. In 1998, that figure was $600 billion. An estimated 4.2 million Americans are addicted to gambling.

If this is an area of expense for you, be honest and include it as a part of your Spending Plan worksheet, perhaps under entertainment.

NOTES

Household/Personal

Clothing

Books and Magazines

Philippians 4:8 (NLT): *"Fix your thoughts on what is true and honorable and right. Think about things that are pure and lovely and admirable. Think about things that are excellent and worthy of praise."*

Gambling

Think about what lies behind your gambling, and reflect on what God says in:

- Luke 12:15
- Proverbs 28:19-20

I also want to encourage you to think about what lies behind your gambling and reflect on what God says about greed in Luke 12:15, and about avoiding get-rich-quick schemes in Proverbs 28:19-20.

Now, let's move to the activity for this category.

Turn to page 68.

15 minutes

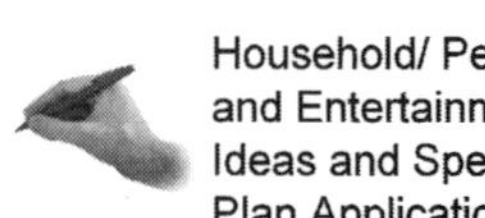

Individual Activity:

Household/ Personal and Entertainment Ideas and Spending Plan Application

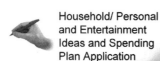

Individual Activity: *Household/Personal and Entertainment Ideas and Spending Plan Application*

Participant's Guide, page 68. Note that pages 69–80 of the Participant's Guide are not shown in this book.

Objective
For participants to generate ideas and set short-term goals for the household/personal and entertainment categories on their Spending Plan worksheet.

Directions

1. Look at your pre-work for what you currently spend on the following household/personal expenses: food, clothes/dry cleaning, gifts, books/magazines, allowances, personal technology, education, and the following entertainment expenses: going out, travel, and other.

   If you didn't complete the pre-work, use your best estimates of expenses. The percent guidelines on the Spending Plan worksheet can help you.

2. Select three categories you think have the most potential to be reduced, and read the information on pages 69–80 pertaining to these expenses. Write down at least one idea that can help you reduce each expense, and set a short-term goal on your Spending Plan worksheet.

3. Set goals for all remaining household/personal and entertainment expenses.

NOTES

Household/Personal

Clothing

Books and Magazines

> Philippians 4:8 (NLT): *"Fix your thoughts on what is true and honorable and right. Think about things that are pure and lovely and admirable. Think about things that are excellent and worthy of praise."*

Gambling

Think about what lies behind your gambling, and reflect on what God says in:

- Luke 12:15
- Proverbs 28:19–20

Individual Activity: *Household/Personal and Entertainment Ideas and Spending Plan Application*

1. Look at your pre-work for what you currently spend on the following household/personal expenses: food, clothes/dry cleaning, gifts, books/magazines, allowances, personal technology, and education and the following entertainment expenses: going out, travel, and other.

   If you didn't complete the pre-work, use your best estimates of expenses. The percent guidelines on the Spending Plan worksheet can help you.

2. Select three categories you think have the most potential to be reduced, and read the information on pages 69–80 pertaining to these expenses. Write down at least one idea that can help you reduce each expense, and set a short-term goal on your Spending Plan worksheet.

   Ideas:

3. Set goals for all remaining household/personal and entertainment expenses.

Note: If you have children, the section on allowances contains some excellent tips for teaching your children about money.

I'll give you 14 minutes to work on this.

Call the group back together after 14 minutes.

Wrap-up (1 minute)

What ideas did you come up with?

Solicit four or five comments from the group. Be sure to repeat their answers so everyone hears the response.

Possible responses:

- I'm going to plan menus ahead of time and always take a list with me when I go grocery shopping.
- We're going to limit how much we spend on family gifts.
- We're going to re-think our plans for how to finance our childrens' college education.

SESSION SUMMARY

We have now completed the spending categories of housing, transportation/auto, insurance, and household/personal. In the next session, we will complete the Spending Plan worksheet.

Break.

Session Five

BALANCING THE SPENDING PLAN

SESSION SNAPSHOT

OBJECTIVES

In this session, participants will:

1. Complete the professional services and miscellaneous small cash expenditures categories on their Spending Plan worksheets.
2. Balance their Spending Plan worksheets.

OUTLINE

I. Introduction

II. Discovery

A. Spending Categories
1. Professional Services
2. Miscellaneous Small Cash Expenditures
3. Individual Activity: *Spending Plan Application*
4. Adjusting the Spending Plan
5. Individual Activity: *Adjusting the Spending Plan*

III. Session Summary

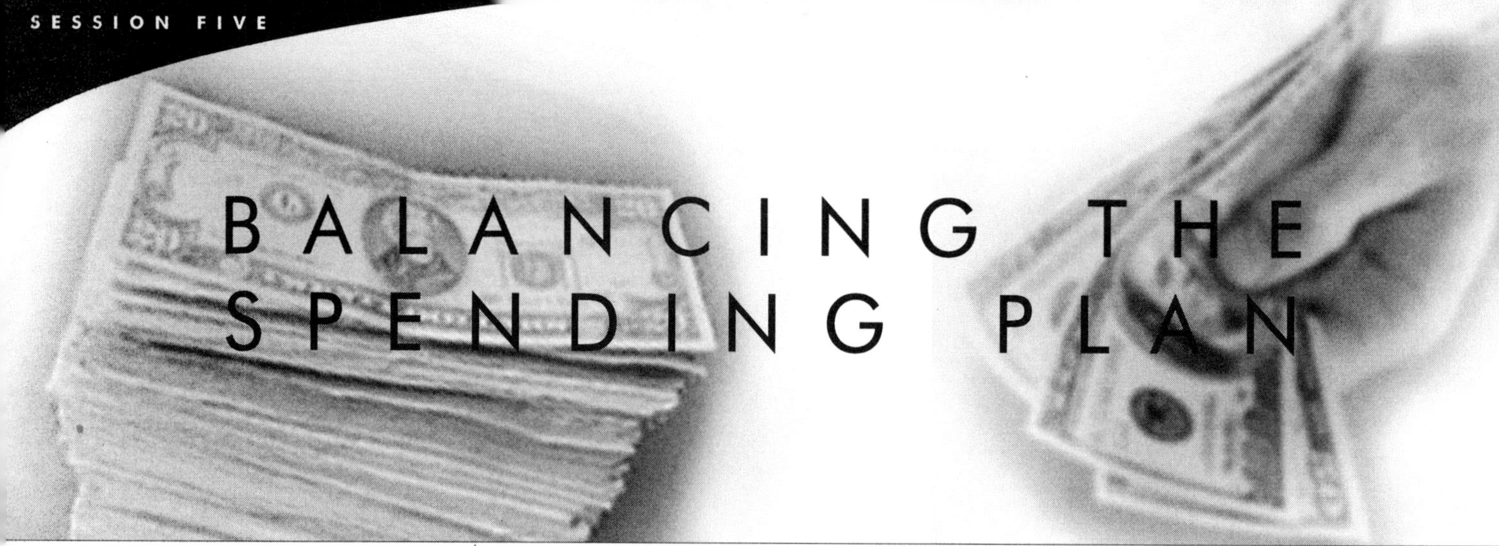

BALANCING THE SPENDING PLAN

TIME & MEDIA	CONTENTS

INTRODUCTION

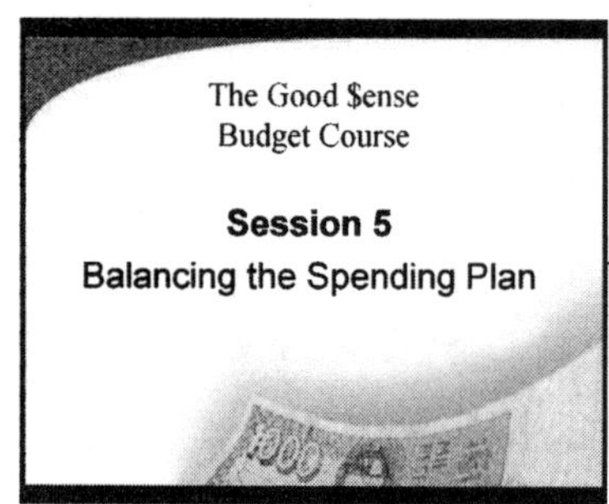

The Good $ense
Budget Course
Session 5
Balancing the Spending Plan

Participant's Guide, page 81.

In this session, we will complete the remaining categories of our Spending Plan worksheet and then bring our plans into balance.

Turn to page 82.

DISCOVERY (50 minutes)

2 minutes

Spending Categories

Professional Services

Participant's Guide, page 82.

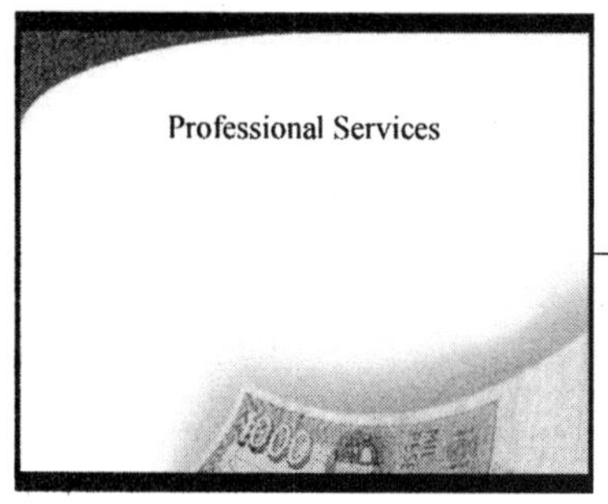

→ Let's look at the professional services category on your Spending Plan worksheet.

You can see that this category includes the expenses for child care, medical, dental, and prescriptions, as well as service professionals such as lawyers or counselors.

I'd like to offer guidelines in two of these areas: child care and other service professionals.

→ First, let's talk about child care.

NOTES

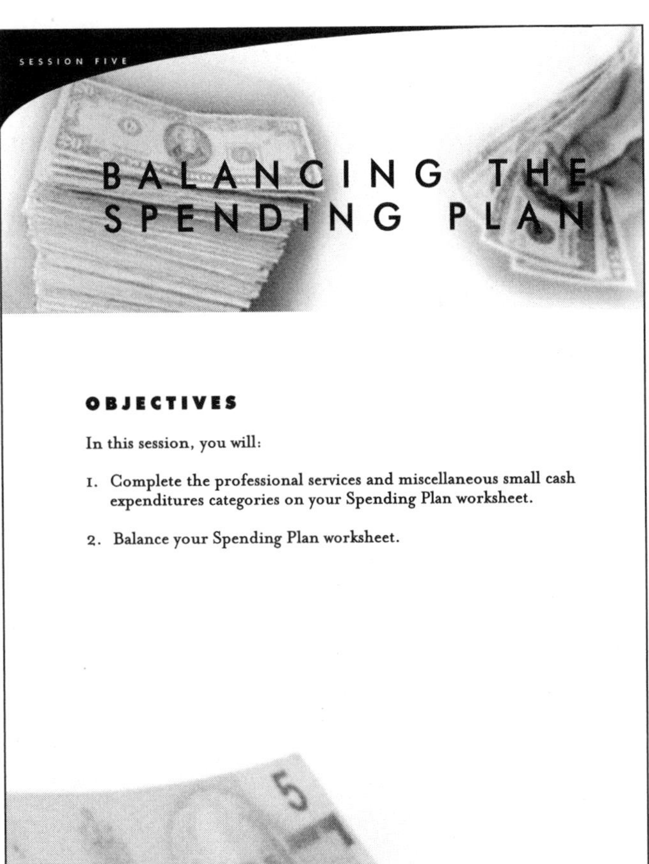

OBJECTIVES

In this session, you will:

1. Complete the professional services and miscellaneous small cash expenditures categories on your Spending Plan worksheet.
2. Balance your Spending Plan worksheet.

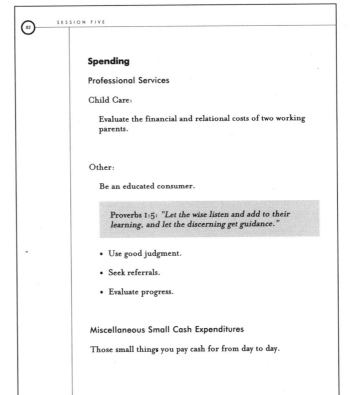

Spending

Professional Services

Child Care:

Evaluate the financial and relational costs of two working parents.

Other:

Be an educated consumer.

> Proverbs 1:5: *"Let the wise listen and add to their learning, and let the discerning get guidance."*

- Use good judgment.
- Seek referrals.
- Evaluate progress.

Miscellaneous Small Cash Expenditures

Those small things you pay cash for from day to day.

We're not advocating anything less than the best child care you can afford. Obviously, working single parents must utilize some form of child care.

But, we suggest married couples carefully evaluate both the financial and relational costs of two working parents.

Financially, the spendable income from the second salary may not warrant the sacrifices made after subtracting extra costs like taxes, gas, transportation, clothing, and more meals out. Relationally, the costs include things like less time together, added stress, and fatigue.

Note that there's an excellent book listed in the Recommended Resources section of the Appendix titled *Two Incomes and Still Broke* that speaks to this issue.

When considering your need for other professional services such as lawyers or counselors, be an educated consumer.

Proverbs 1:5 says, "Let the wise listen and add to their learning, and let the discerning get guidance."

If you feel like your attorney is billing a lot of hours but not getting the job done, or if you have been seeing a counselor for years and feel that the relationship is moving you toward continued dependence rather than independence, raise questions. It's important to be a wise consumer of professional services.

Here's some advice:

- Use good judgment.
- Seek referrals.
- Evaluate progress.

NOTES

Spending

Professional Services

Child Care:

Evaluate the financial and relational costs of two working parents.

Other:

Be an educated consumer.

> Proverbs 1:5: *"Let the wise listen and add to their learning, and let the discerning get guidance."*

- Use good judgment.
- Seek referrals.
- Evaluate progress.

Miscellaneous Small Cash Expenditures

Those small things you pay cash for from day to day.

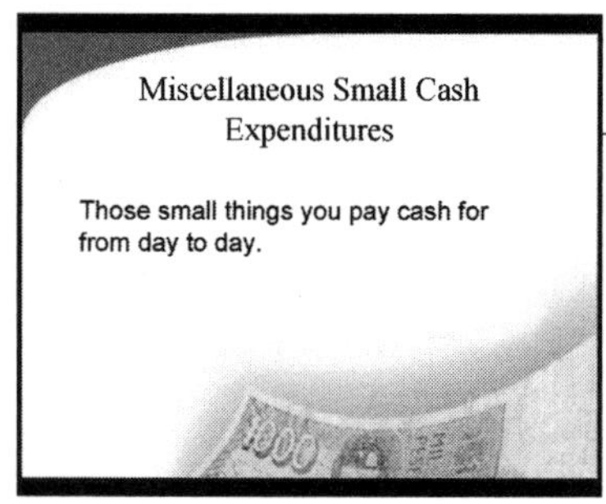

Miscellaneous Small Cash Expenditures

There is one final category on your Spending Plan worksheet—miscellaneous small cash expenditures. This category is set up for those small things you pay cash for from day to day, that often don't have receipts.

You can choose what you will put here, but typical examples include newspapers, soft drinks, coffee, etc. We will talk further about the value of this category when we get to record keeping, but I want to be sure we account for this category on our Spending Plan worksheets.

18 minutes

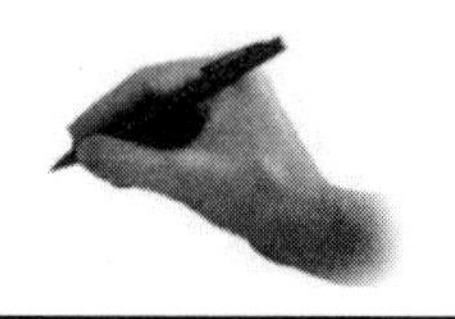

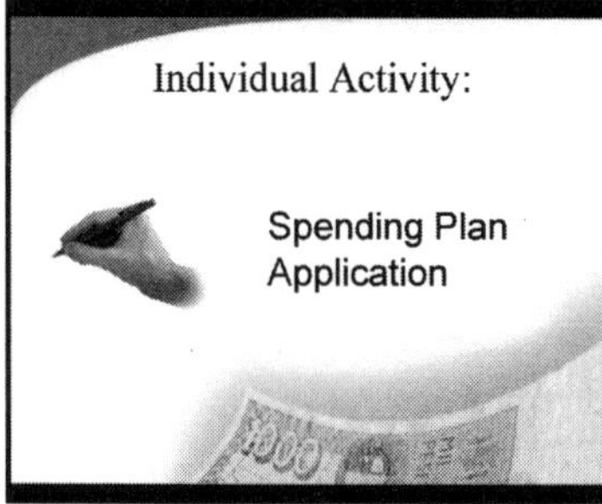

Individual Activity: *Spending Plan Application*

Participant's Guide, page 83.

Objective
For participants to set short-term goals for the professional services, entertainment, and miscellaneous small cash expenditures categories on their Spending Plan worksheets.

Directions

1. Look at your pre-work sheet for what you currently spend for professional services and miscellaneous small cash expenditures.

   If you didn't complete the pre-work, use your best estimate of these expenses. The percentage guidelines on the Spending Plan worksheet can help you.

2. Consider some of the ideas discussed for these categories. Write down at least one action step you plan to take.

3. Set short-term goals for professional services and miscellaneous small cash expenditures, and fill in these categories on your Spending Plan worksheet.

4. Review your entire Spending Plan worksheet. If there are any categories that you did not have time to complete, do so now.

NOTES

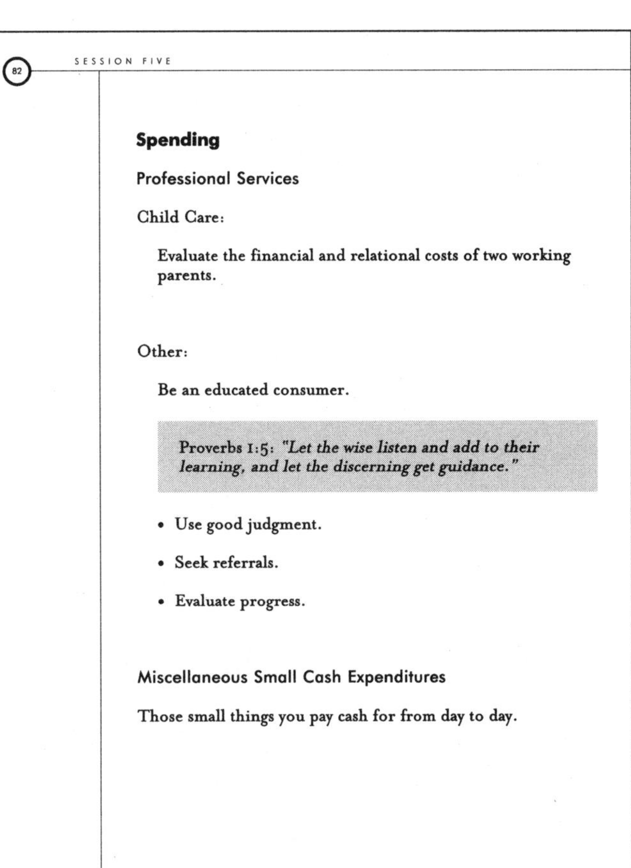

82 SESSION FIVE

Spending

Professional Services

Child Care:

Evaluate the financial and relational costs of two working parents.

Other:

Be an educated consumer.

> Proverbs 1:5: *"Let the wise listen and add to their learning, and let the discerning get guidance."*

- Use good judgment.
- Seek referrals.
- Evaluate progress.

Miscellaneous Small Cash Expenditures

Those small things you pay cash for from day to day.

SESSION FIVE 83

Individual Activity: *Spending Plan Application*

1. Look at your pre-work sheet for what you currently spend for professional services and miscellaneous small cash expenditures.

   If you didn't complete the pre-work, use your best estimate of these expenses. The percentage guidelines on the Spending Plan worksheet can help you.

2. Consider some of the ideas discussed for these categories. Write down at least one action step you plan to take.

   Action Step:

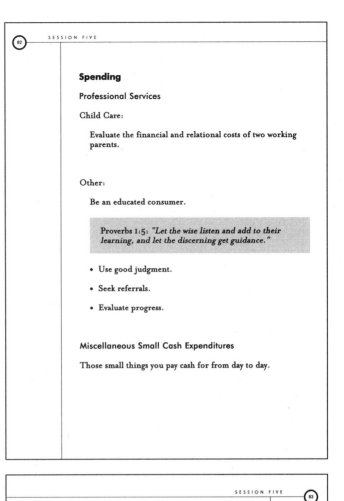

3. Set short-term goals for professional services and miscellaneous small cash expenditures, and fill in these categories on your Spending Plan worksheet.

4. Review your entire Spending Plan worksheet. If there are any categories that you did not have time to complete, do so now.

5. Add up all the expenses on your Spending Plan worksheet. **Complete the box in the lower right-hand corner of the worksheet.**

5. Add up all the expenses on your Spending Plan worksheet. Complete the box in the lower right hand corner of the worksheet.

You have 17 minutes to do this.

Call the group back together after 17 minutes.

If time allows, you may want to give participants more time to work.

Turn to page 84.

3 minutes

Adjusting the Spending Plan

Participant's Guide, page 84.

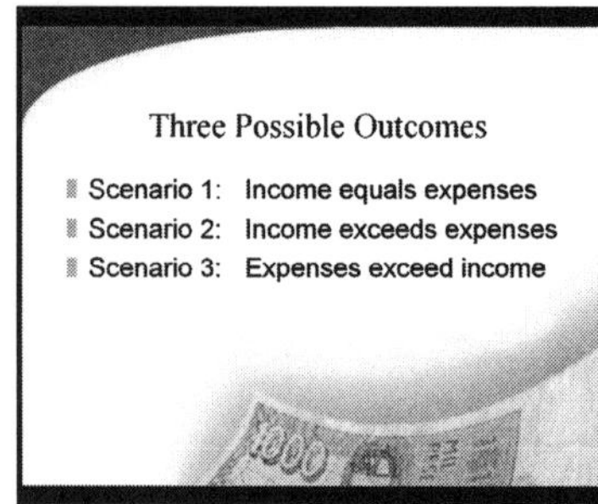

There are three possible outcomes of this activity:

Scenario one is that your income equals your expenses. This is a balanced plan.

Scenario two is that your income exceeds your expenses.

Scenario three is that your expenses exceed your income. This may be the case for many of us.

If you fall within scenario one or two, you are to be congratulated, but you still have some work to do.

If you fall within scenario three, take a deep breath. Realize that God is in control. Call on him to help you as you make additional adjustments to your plan. Remember, you can do it!

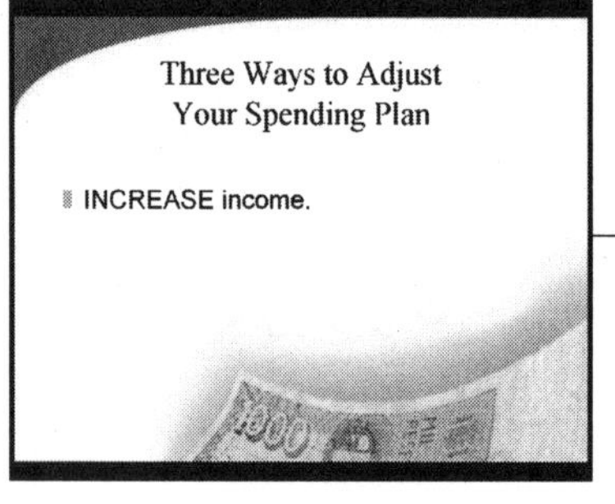

There are three ways to adjust your Spending Plan if your expenses exceed your income.

First, you can INCREASE income.

NOTES

Individual Activity: *Spending Plan Application*

1. Look at your pre-work sheet for what you currently spend for professional services and miscellaneous small cash expenditures.

   If you didn't complete the pre-work, use your best estimate of these expenses. The percentage guidelines on the Spending Plan worksheet can help you.

2. Consider some of the ideas discussed for these categories. Write down at least one action step you plan to take.

   Action Step:

3. Set short-term goals for professional services and miscellaneous small cash expenditures, and fill in these categories on your Spending Plan worksheet.

4. Review your entire Spending Plan worksheet. If there are any categories that you did not have time to complete, do so now.

5. Add up all the expenses on your Spending Plan worksheet. **Complete the box in the lower right-hand corner of the worksheet.**

Adjusting the Spending Plan

Three Possible Outcomes:

- Scenario 1: Income equals expenses
- Scenario 2: Income exceeds expenses
- Scenario 3: Expenses exceed income

Three ways to adjust your Spending Plan if your expenses exceed your income:

1. ________________ income.

   Simply increasing income does not deal with the root issue.

2. Sell assets to pay off some debt.

3. ___________ expenses.

   - Do I have optional expenses I can eliminate?
   - Do I have variable expenses I can further control and reduce?
   - Can I eliminate any assumptions about my "__________" expenses?

Key Question: How serious are you?

Under most circumstances, this isn't the recommended approach. Taking on a second job or asking another family member to begin working may provide some extra money in the short term. But it might also add stress and fatigue to an already tense situation. In addition, you would have to make a relatively large amount with that second salary to have a little net income after taxes and additional expenses.

➔ Most importantly, simply increasing income does not, in most cases, deal with the root issue of why spending is exceeding income.

Until that issue has been addressed, having more income will probably only lead to more spending and not solve the problem.

➔ The second way to adjust your Spending Plan is to sell assets to pay off some debt.

It's a short-term approach that can give you a jump-start toward balancing your budget and may be a very wise thing to do. But it's not a long-term solution because it doesn't get to the root problem of why spending is exceeding income. If that doesn't change, then debt will soon build back up.

➔ The final way—our recommended approach—is to REDUCE expenses.

The key is to live within existing income. To do this, look very carefully once again at each expense category on your Spending Plan worksheet, and ask yourself the following questions:

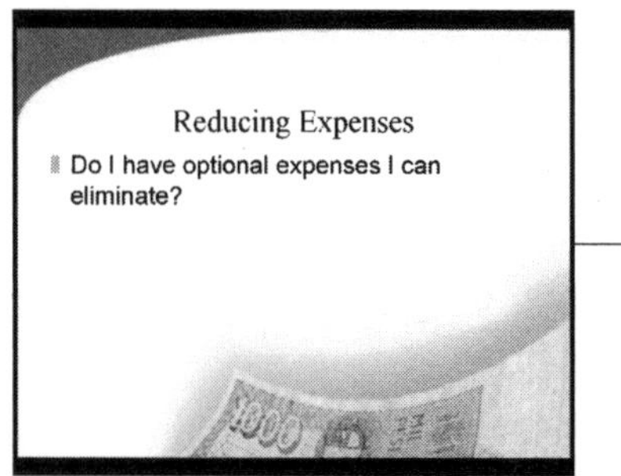
Reducing Expenses
Do I have optional expenses I can eliminate?

➔ Do I have optional expenses I can eliminate?

Good places to look for these are in the household, professional services, and entertainment categories.

➔ Do I have variable expenses I can further control and reduce?

NOTES

Adjusting the Spending Plan

Three Possible Outcomes:

- Scenario 1: Income equals expenses
- Scenario 2: Income exceeds expenses
- Scenario 3: Expenses exceed income

Three ways to adjust your Spending Plan if your expenses exceed your income:

1. ____________________ income.

   Simply increasing income does not deal with the root issue.

2. Sell assets to pay off some debt.

3. ____________ expenses.

   - Do I have optional expenses I can eliminate?
   - Do I have variable expenses I can further control and reduce?
   - Can I eliminate any assumptions about my "____________" expenses?

Key Question: How serious are you?

Look at utilities, groceries, clothing, and other household items.

Can I eliminate any assumptions about my "FIXED" expenses?

Costs such as mortgage or rent and car payments are "fixed" only if we continue to live where we are and drive what we do. We may need to consider downsizing our living situation or renting out a room. Is there a way to eliminate the "fixed" cost of two cars by finding a creative way to get by with one?

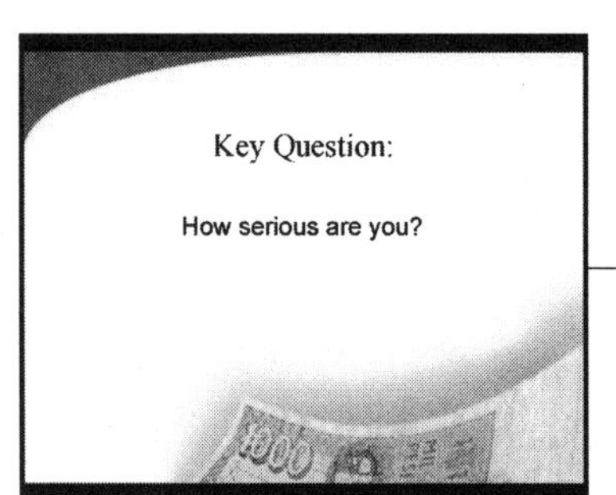

The key question is, How serious are you?

How much pain are you willing to bear for how long before you bring expenses in line with income? If the perceived sacrifices seem too great, perhaps you're underestimating the long-term pain and consequences of not getting your financial house in order now!

Trust God and follow his principles. It's amazing how often he takes what we consider a sacrifice and turns it into a blessing.

> If you have a personal story or know of someone whose experience demonstrates how God can turn sacrifice into blessing, you may wish to replace the story below with your own story.

Here is a true story that illustrates this:

As a result of meeting with a Good $ense counselor, Denise realized she was in serious financial difficulty and couldn't afford her expensive apartment unless she took in a roommate. Coming to this conclusion was very difficult because she greatly valued her privacy and enjoyed living by herself. However, she also loved her apartment and didn't want to live in a less expensive one.

NOTES

Adjusting the Spending Plan

Three Possible Outcomes:

- Scenario 1: Income equals expenses
- Scenario 2: Income exceeds expenses
- Scenario 3: Expenses exceed income

Three ways to adjust your Spending Plan if your expenses exceed your income:

1. ____________________ income.

   Simply increasing income does not deal with the root issue.

2. Sell assets to pay off some debt.

3. _____________ expenses.

   - Do I have optional expenses I can eliminate?
   - Do I have variable expenses I can further control and reduce?
   - Can I eliminate any assumptions about my "____________" expenses?

Key Question: How serious are you?

Reluctantly, Denise took in a roommate. And in a short period of time, a deep friendship developed between the two. The roommate was a mature Christian and had a strong influence on Denise's faith. When Denise was married a few years later, the roommate was her maid of honor. As a result of their deep friendship and its impact on her spiritual growth, Denise looks on her perceived sacrifice as one of God's richest blessings in her life.

Let's take some time now to adjust our Spending Plan worksheets. Those of you whose income equals or exceeds expenses should work on Part A of the Spending Plan Application, and those whose expenses exceed income should work on Part B.

27 minutes

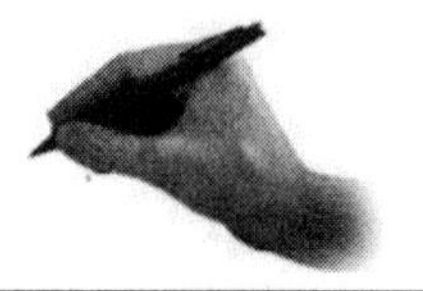

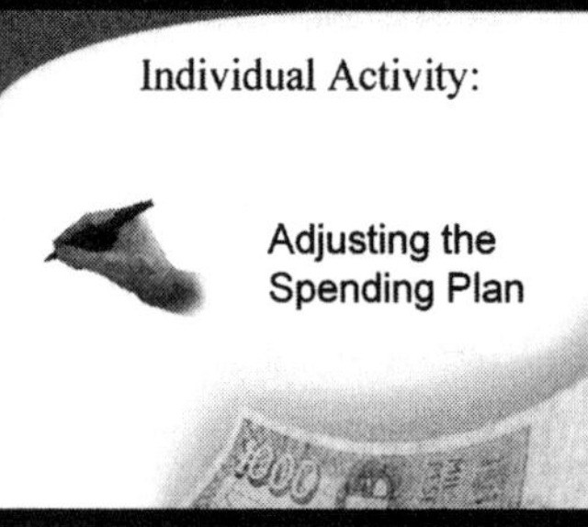
Individual Activity:
Adjusting the Spending Plan

Individual Activity: *Adjusting the Spending Plan*

Participant's Guide, page 85.

Objectives
A) For participants whose income equals or exceeds their expenses to review their Spending Plan to see if the margin can be increased further, decide how to use the margin, and adjust their Spending Plan accordingly.

B) To have those participants whose expenses exceed their income to reduce expenses and balance their Spending Plan.

Directions

A) If income equals or exceeds expenses, prayerfully and carefully review all categories to see if the margin can be increased further, and then reflect on how that margin can best be used to further your goals. Write down at least one action step you plan to take, and make any adjustments to your Spending Plan worksheet.

NOTES

Individual Activity: *Adjusting the Spending Plan*

A. If income equals or exceeds expenses, prayerfully and carefully review all categories to see if the margin can be increased further, and then reflect on how that margin can best be used to further your goals.

Write down at least one action step you plan to take, and make any adjustments to your Spending Plan worksheet.

Action Step:

B. If your expenses exceed your income, prayerfully and carefully review all the categories to reduce expenses.

Write down at least one action step you plan to take to adjust your Spending Plan. Then, adjust the plan and bring it into balance as best you can.

Action Step:

B) If your expenses exceed your income, prayerfully and carefully review all the categories to reduce expenses. Write down at least one action step you plan to take to adjust your Spending Plan. Then, adjust the plan and bring it into balance as best you can.

Now, I recognize that some of you may need to check with your spouse or gather further information before you can finalize your plan. I want to encourage you to still use this time to put down some tentative numbers and next steps to take.

You have 27 minutes to do this.

Call the group back together after 27 minutes.

Some of you weren't able to balance your Spending Plan for a variety of reasons. Keep working on it after today's session. If you still have difficulty, please seek assistance.

Briefly mention here the ministries, counselors, or other assistance your church provides to help participants. You may want to mention the Consumer Credit Counseling Service (800)388-2227.

For those of you who now have a balanced Spending Plan, congratulations!

SESSION SUMMARY

We have now completed work on the Spending Plan. The Spending Plan is the first and fundamental step in budgeting, but there is another important aspect to budgeting. It is record keeping.

NOTES

SESSION FIVE

Individual Activity: *Adjusting the Spending Plan*

A. If income equals or exceeds expenses, prayerfully and carefully review all categories to see if the margin can be increased further, and then reflect on how that margin can best be used to further your goals.

Write down at least one action step you plan to take, and make any adjustments to your Spending Plan worksheet.

Action Step:

B. If your expenses exceed your income, prayerfully and carefully review all the categories to reduce expenses.

Write down at least one action step you plan to take to adjust your Spending Plan. Then, adjust the plan and bring it into balance as best you can.

Action Step:

In the next session, we will discuss three different record-keeping systems you can use to keep track of how much you spend. You'll have the opportunity to select and set up the system you plan to use. And here's the good news—the record-keeping systems we're going to learn are quick and easy to use.

Break.

Session Six

RECORD KEEPING AND COMMITMENT

SESSION SNAPSHOT

OBJECTIVES

In this session, participants will:

1. Choose and set up a record-keeping system.
2. Consider the obstacles they may encounter implementing their Spending Plan and record-keeping system.
3. Commit to implementing and keeping records for their Spending Plan.

OUTLINE

I. Introduction

II. Discovery

A. Record Keeping
1. Benefits of Record Keeping
2. Envelope System
3. Written Record System
4. Individual Activity: *Spending Record*
5. Electronic System
6. Individual Activity: *Setting up Your Record-Keeping System*
7. Implementation Issues
8. Individual Activity: *Obstacles*

B. Review and Commitment
1. Video: *Financial Freedom*
2. Individual Activity: *Becoming Financially Faithful, Financially Free*
3. Keeping Your Commitment

III. Summary: God Is Able

RECORD KEEPING AND COMMITMENT

TIME & MEDIA	CONTENTS

INTRODUCTION

The Good $ense Budget Course
Session 6
Record Keeping and Commitment

Participant's Guide, page 87.

In the previous session, you completed your Spending Plan. In this session we'll discuss three record-keeping systems that you could use. You'll also have the opportunity to consider any obstacles you might encounter while implementing your Spending Plan. And finally, there will be a time for you to think through the commitment it will take to implement your Spending Plan.

Turn to page 88.

DISCOVERY (45 minutes)

3 minutes

Record Keeping

Participant's Guide, page 88.

We have completed the crucial and necessary first step in the budgeting process, which is the Spending Plan, but our job isn't finished. To implement our Spending Plan, we need a means to determine whether the plan is working—a record-keeping system.

What is a record-keeping system?

NOTES

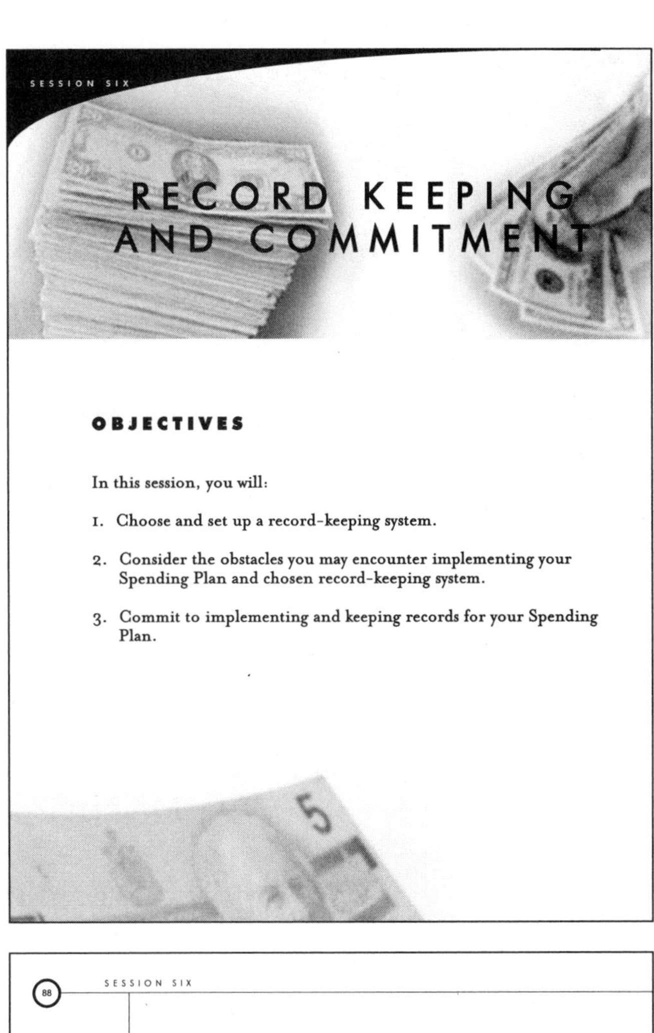

SESSION SIX
RECORD KEEPING AND COMMITMENT
OBJECTIVES
In this session, you will:
1. Choose and set up a record-keeping system.
2. Consider the obstacles you may encounter implementing your Spending Plan and chosen record-keeping system.
3. Commit to implementing and keeping records for your Spending Plan.

Record Keeping

A record-keeping system is:

A way to keep track of how much you spend.

Benefits of record keeping:

- Gives accurate data.
- Improves ______________________.
- Allows for mid-course corrections.
- Provides ______________________.

The truth about record keeping:

- It's simpler than it seems.
- It takes less time than you think.
- It does not require a Ph.D. in math.

Three Systems:

- Envelope
- Written record
- Electronic

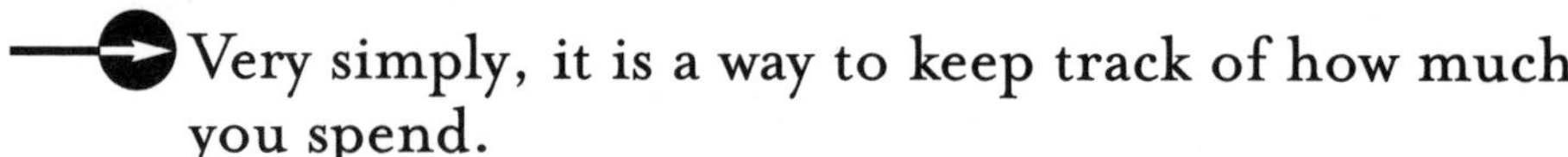

Very simply, it is a way to keep track of how much you spend.

It checks the Spending Plan against what we actually spend.

Why do we need a record-keeping system?

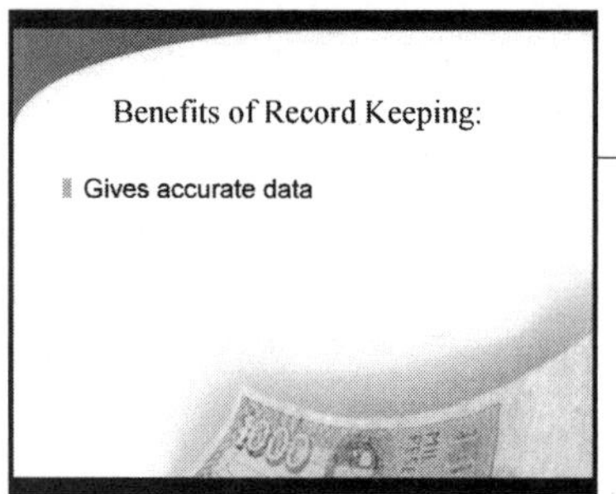

Benefits of Record Keeping

First, record keeping gives us accurate data.

Right now, we have a theoretical plan. Some of the numbers are what we really spend, others are what we think we spend, and some are simply goals. We need accurate information on what *really* takes place.

Second, record keeping improves COMMUNICATION.

For example, early in their marriage, before they kept track of their expenses, Dick—an author of this course—argued with his generous wife about how much they spent on gifts. He was sure it was one amount. She was equally certain it was another much lower amount. When they finally kept track they discovered the actual amount was in between the two. Having the facts then allowed them to base their discussions on actual information versus emotional accusations. With the facts in hand they were able to agree together on an appropriate amount to spend.

Third, record-keeping allows for mid-course corrections.

If our actual expenses are higher or lower than we estimated in some categories, we have the information to make adjustments to our plan.

Finally, keeping records provides a form of ACCOUNTABILITY.

NOTES

Record Keeping

A record-keeping system is:

A way to keep track of how much you spend.

Benefits of record keeping:

- Gives accurate data.
- Improves ________________________.
- Allows for mid-course corrections.
- Provides ________________________.

The truth about record keeping:

- It's simpler than it seems.
- It takes less time than you think.
- It does not require a Ph.D. in math.

Three Systems:

- Envelope
- Written record
- Electronic

The simple act of record keeping will dramatically impact our spending behavior because it's a daily reminder of our goals and commitment and how well we're doing.

I realize that record keeping has been the stumbling block in the budgeting process for many people. Either past failure or the perceived difficulty of even trying makes record keeping a very scary and overwhelming prospect.

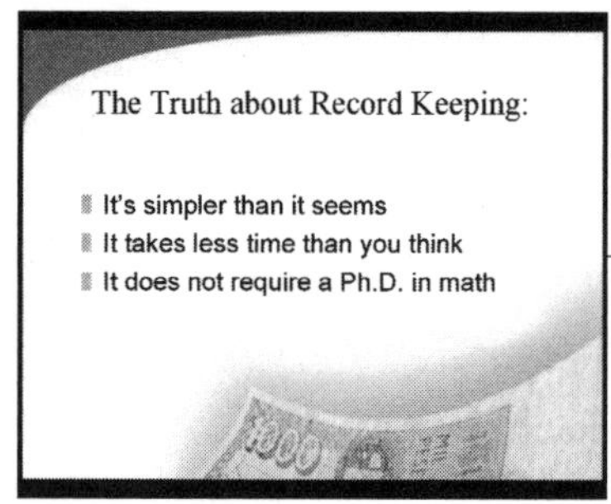

Our goal is to introduce you to several approaches to record keeping that will convince you of the truth that:

- It's simpler than it seems.
- It takes less time than you think.
- It does not require a Ph.D. in math.

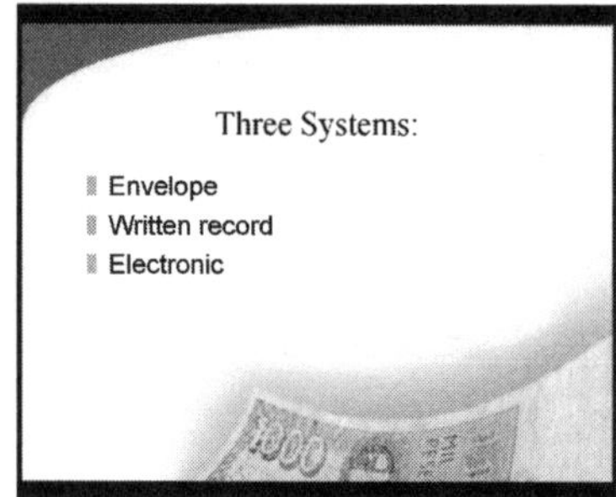

There are three record-keeping systems we will discuss:

- Envelope
- Written record
- Electronic

Before the course is over, I'd like for you to make a decision on which one you'll use to track your Spending Plan.

3 minutes

Envelope System

Participant's Guide, page 89.

Let's start with the envelope system. A form of this system was used by many of our great-grandparents. They had a variety of containers—a coffee tin here and a sugar bowl there—in which money was placed. One container held money for groceries, one for clothes, and another for a rainy day. When a purchase was considered, they looked into the appropriate container and determined what could or could not be spent based on how much money was in it.

NOTES

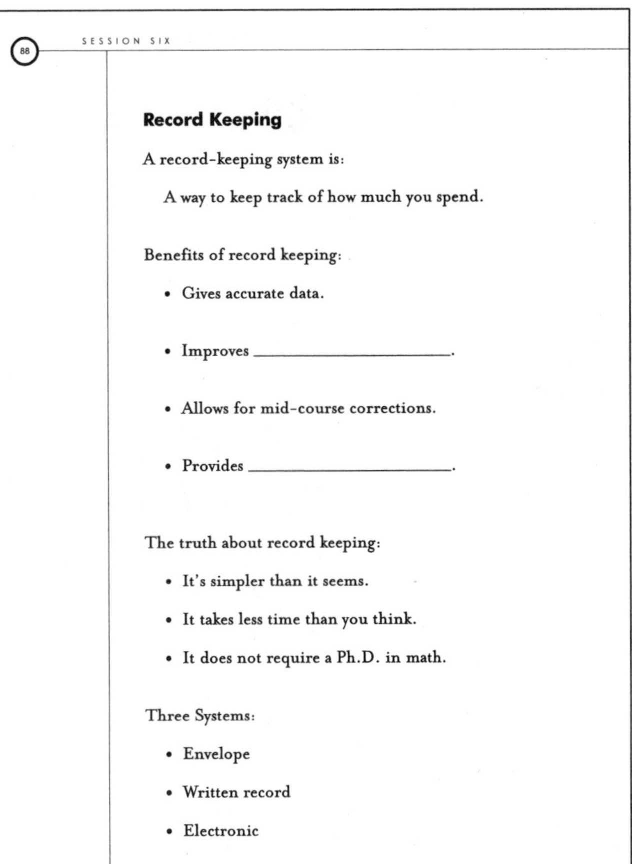

Record Keeping

A record-keeping system is:

A way to keep track of how much you spend.

Benefits of record keeping:

- Gives accurate data.
- Improves ______________________.
- Allows for mid-course corrections.
- Provides ______________________.

The truth about record keeping:

- It's simpler than it seems.
- It takes less time than you think.
- It does not require a Ph.D. in math.

Three Systems:

- Envelope
- Written record
- Electronic

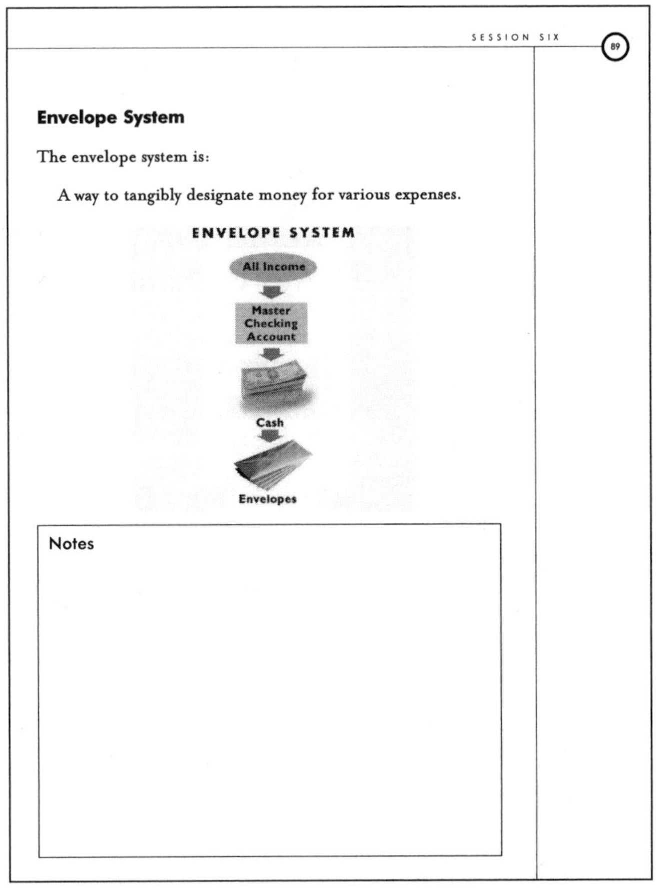

Envelope System

The envelope system is:

A way to tangibly designate money for various expenses.

Notes

The envelope system is based on the same principles.

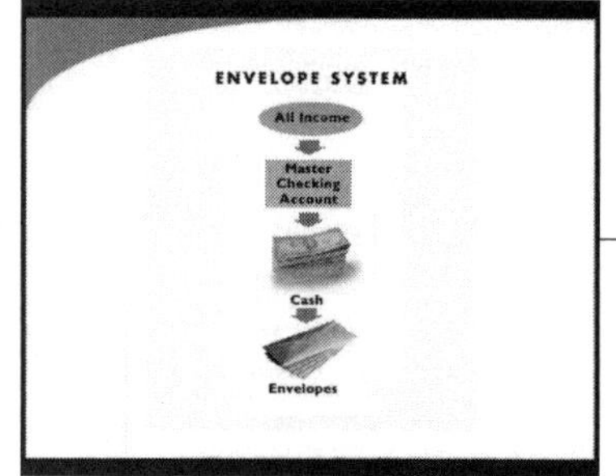

➔ It's a way to tangibly designate money for various expenses.

Here is how it works.

Basically, you deposit all your income into a master checking account. Then, each pay period, you withdraw and distribute the cash among labeled envelopes.

In its purest form this system would have an envelope for each of the different expense categories like giving, savings, mortgage, utilities, car payment, groceries, clothes, gifts, and household items. The monthly amount from the Spending Plan worksheet is written on each envelope and that amount of cash is placed in each one. When it is time to make a purchase, you look in the appropriate envelope, see how much money is available, and then use the cash to make your purchase.

Obviously, it would not be practical or wise to have an envelope for every category on the Spending Plan worksheet—for example, having an envelope for mortgage or rent. You probably don't want that kind of cash sitting around, and you probably wouldn't find it very convenient to pay your mortgage with cash. Therefore, the way we handle certain categories is by writing a check.

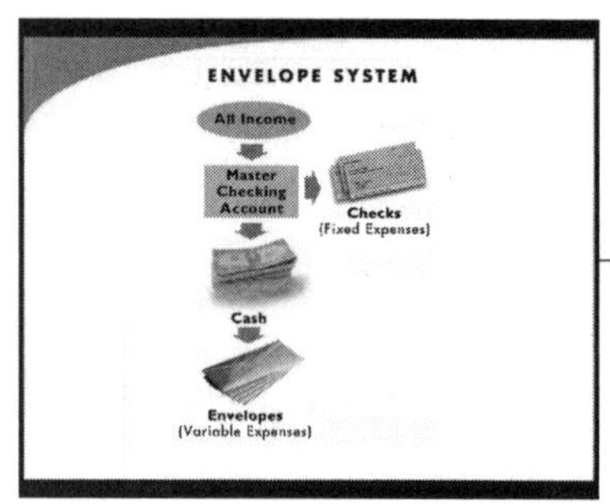

Let's expand our diagram of the envelope system to reflect these types of payments.

Turn to page 90.

Participant's Guide, page 90.

NOTES

Envelope System

The envelope system is:

A way to tangibly designate money for various expenses.

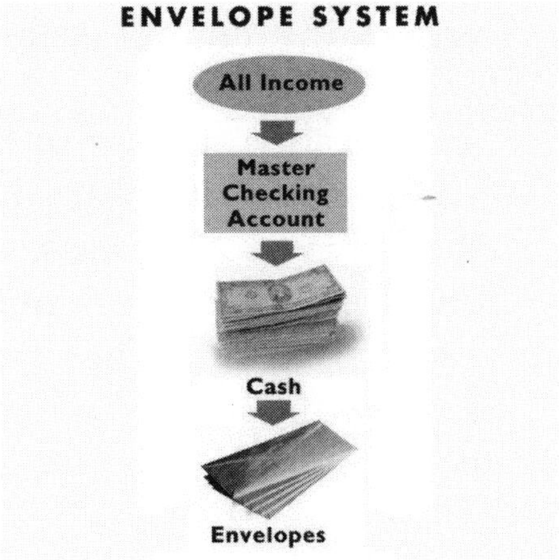

ENVELOPE SYSTEM

All Income

Master Checking Account

Cash

Envelopes

Notes

You still deposit all income into a master checking account. But now, you don't have envelopes for those categories that you write monthly checks for. This would include your mortgage, utilities, car payment, etc. Note that these expenses are often fixed monthly amounts, and controlling them is not a problem. You don't overspend on your rent payments! For the other variable categories, which are more difficult to control—food, clothes, entertainment, household, etc.—you have envelopes.

This is all you need to know to get started with the envelope system. An advantage of this system is that you don't have to bother keeping written records. The envelopes and your checkbook become your record-keeping system. Each pay period you put the budgeted amount of cash into each envelope. What's left at the end of the month tells you how much you spent.

Another huge advantage is that each time you go to an envelope to get cash, it is a tangible reminder of how much you have to spend. That consistent feedback provides a powerful check-and-balance on your spending. Just putting the system in place will reduce spending.

If you have never budgeted before, or if you have tried and didn't succeed, this system may be the best one for you. I want to point out, however, that it's not just for beginners. Many who have tried other systems and have budgeted for many years prefer this system because of its simplicity and because it works.

Now, let's look at the second means of record keeping, which is the written record system.

8 minutes

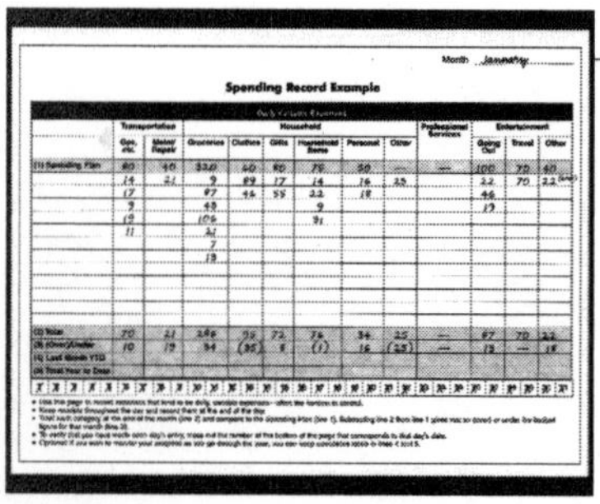

Written Record System

Get out your Spending Plan worksheet and then turn to page 91 and look at the sheet titled "Spending Record Example."

Participant's Guide, page 91.

NOTES

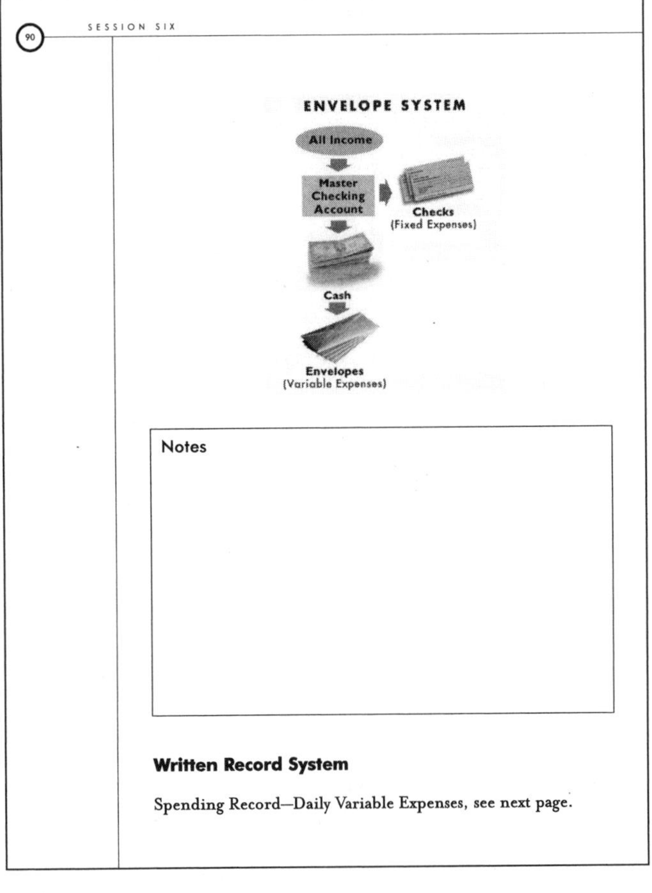

90 SESSION SIX

ENVELOPE SYSTEM

Notes

Written Record System

Spending Record—Daily Variable Expenses, see next page.

Month *January*

Spending Record Example

Daily Variable Expenses													
	Transportation		Household						Professional Services	Entertainment		
	Gas, etc.	Maint/ Repair	Groceries	Clothes	Gifts	Household Items	Personal	Other		Going Out	Travel	Other
(1) Spending Plan	80	40	320	60	80	75	50	—	—	100	70	40
	14	21	9	89	17	14	16	25		22	70	22 (sitter)
	17		87	6	55	22	18			46		
	9		43			9				19		
	19		106			31						
	11		21									
			7									
			13									
(2) Total	70	21	286	95	72	76	34	25	—	87	70	22
(3) (Over)/Under	10	19	34	(35)	8	(1)	16	(25)	—	13	—	18
(4) Last Month YTD												
(5) Total Year to Date												

~~1~~ ~~2~~ ~~3~~ ~~4~~ ~~5~~ ~~6~~ ~~7~~ ~~8~~ ~~9~~ ~~10~~ ~~11~~ ~~12~~ ~~13~~ ~~14~~ ~~15~~ ~~16~~ ~~17~~ ~~18~~ ~~19~~ ~~20~~ ~~21~~ ~~22~~ ~~23~~ ~~24~~ ~~24~~ ~~26~~ ~~27~~ ~~28~~ ~~29~~ ~~30~~ ~~31~~

- Use this page to record expenses that tend to be daily, variable expenses—often the hardest to control.
- Keep receipts throughout the day and record them at the end of the day.
- Total each category at the end of the month (line 2) and compare to the Spending Plan (line 1). Subtracting line 2 from line 1 gives you an (over) or under the budget figure for that month (line 3).
- To verify that you have made each day's entry, cross out the number at the bottom of the page that corresponds to that day's date.
- Optional: If you wish to monitor your progress as you go through the year, you can keep cumulative totals in lines 4 and 5.

SESSION SIX 91

At the top of this sheet are the categories you would have cash envelopes for if you were using the envelope system. These are the categories that vary each month, have multiple transactions, and are generally the hardest to control.

Let's walk through an example of how to fill this form out.

On line 1 where it says "Spending Plan" you fill in the amounts your Spending Plan worksheet calls for.

The categories in the columns across the sheet represent the expenses that are in capital letters on your Spending Plan worksheet. A couple of the sub-categories have been combined. For example, under entertainment, going out includes meals, movies and events, and babysitting. This was done to reduce the number of columns so that the plan would fit on one sheet.

In this example, you can see that the monthly Spending Plan calls for $80 for gas/etc., $40 for maintenance/repair, $320 for groceries, $60 for clothes, $80 for gifts, $75 for household items, $50 for personal, $100 for going out, $70 for travel, and $40 for other, which is under entertainment.

The blank lines in the middle of the form are to record what is spent. In order to fill them in, you simply save each of your receipts as you make daily expenditures. Save them in an accessible, consistent place. This may be your pants pocket or a certain section of your purse, or even a special envelope you label "receipts."

Then, when you come home at the end of the day, write the amount of each receipt under the proper column.

Over the course of the month, the family in this example recorded five expenditures for gas, one for auto maintenance, seven for groceries, etc.

NOTES

Month *January*

Spending Record Example

Daily Variable Expenses												
	Transportation		Household						Professional Services	Entertainment		
	Gas, etc.	Maint/ Repair	Groceries	Clothes	Gifts	Household Items	Personal	Other		Going Out	Travel	Other
(1) Spending Plan	80	40	320	60	80	75	50	—	—	100	70	40
	14	21	9	89	17	14	16	25		22	70	22 (sitter)
	17		87	6	55	22	18			46		
	9		43			9				19		
	19		106			31						
	11		21									
			7									
			13									
(2) Total	70	21	286	95	72	76	34	25	—	87	70	22
(3) (Over)/Under	10	19	34	(35)	8	(1)	16	(25)	—	13	—	18
(4) Last Month YTD												
(5) Total Year to Date												

1	2	3	4	5	6	7	8	9	10	11	12	13	14	15	16	17	18	19	20	21	22	23	24	24	26	27	28	29	30	31

- Use this page to record expenses that tend to be daily, variable expenses—often the hardest to control.
- Keep receipts throughout the day and record them at the end of the day.
- Total each category at the end of the month (line 2) and compare to the Spending Plan (line 1). Subtracting line 2 from line 1 gives you an (over) or under the budget figure for that month (line 3).
- To verify that you have made each day's entry, cross out the number at the bottom of the page that corresponds to that day's date.
- Optional: If you wish to monitor your progress as you go through the year, you can keep cumulative totals in lines 4 and 5.

SESSION SIX

91

At the bottom of the sheet are numbers from 1 to 31. When you finish recording your daily expenses, cross out the number corresponding to the date, so you'll know that you didn't forget a day.

Toward the bottom of the sheet, there's a line marked "(2) Total." At the end of the month, total what you spent in each category and record it on this line.

What is the total for groceries in the example?

Pause briefly for participants' responses

Yes, $286.

How about the total for household items?

Pause briefly for participants' responses.

The amount is $76.

The line below, "(3) (Over)/Under," then shows how much you're over or under for the month—the difference between lines 1 and 2. It's not necessarily bad if you overspend in a category in a given month. The Spending Plan worksheet is set up to reflect an average month. And since there's no such thing as an "average" month, some categories may be a little higher or lower than the plan in a given month.

For example, this family spent $95 for clothes versus the $60 their Spending Plan called for, so they could take advantage of after-Christmas sales. Line 3 shows that they are $35 over budget in this category for the month. That's okay, if they're committed to underspending in the next few months. The key is to fall within the safe limits of the Spending Plan over a series of months.

NOTES

Month *January*

Spending Record Example

Daily Variable Expenses	Transportation		Household						Professional Services	Entertainment		
	Gas, etc.	Maint/ Repair	Groceries	Clothes	Gifts	Household Items	Personal	Other		Going Out	Travel	Other
(1) Spending Plan	80	40	320	60	80	75	50	—	—	100	70	40
	14	21	9	89	17	14	16	25		22	70	22 (sitter)
	17		87	6	55	22	18			46		
	9		43			9				19		
	19		106			31						
	11		21									
			7									
			13									
(2) Total	70	21	286	95	72	76	34	25	—	87	70	22
(3) (Over)/Under	10	19	34	(35)	8	(1)	16	(25)	—	13	—	18
(4) Last Month YTD												
(5) Total Year to Date												

~~1~~ ~~2~~ ~~3~~ ~~4~~ ~~5~~ ~~6~~ ~~7~~ ~~8~~ ~~9~~ ~~10~~ ~~11~~ ~~12~~ ~~13~~ ~~14~~ ~~15~~ ~~16~~ ~~17~~ ~~18~~ ~~19~~ ~~20~~ ~~21~~ ~~22~~ ~~23~~ ~~24~~ ~~25~~ ~~26~~ ~~27~~ ~~28~~ ~~29~~ ~~30~~ ~~31~~

- Use this page to record expenses that tend to be daily, variable expenses—often the hardest to control.
- Keep receipts throughout the day and record them at the end of the day.
- Total each category at the end of the month (line 2) and compare to the Spending Plan (line 1). Subtracting line 2 from line 1 gives you an (over) or under the budget figure for that month (line 3).
- To verify that you have made each day's entry, cross out the number at the bottom of the page that corresponds to that day's date.
- Optional: If you wish to monitor your progress as you go through the year, you can keep cumulative totals in lines 4 and 5.

There are two optional rows at the bottom of your sheet—lines 4 and 5. These are year-to-date (Y-T-D) totals you can use to keep track of your progress through the year. It would enable you to see not only how you did that month, but also how you are doing so far that year.

These rows are not completed in your example because keeping year-to-date totals is another level of sophistication in record keeping. And for some of you, it may initially seem pretty confusing. If so, I'd recommend holding off on this for the first few months. When you're comfortable with the monthly process, you can then begin to determine your year-to-date figures. There is an explanation in the Appendix of how to do this or you can ask someone to help you.

Turn to page 92 in your Participant's Guide.

Participant's Guide, page 92.

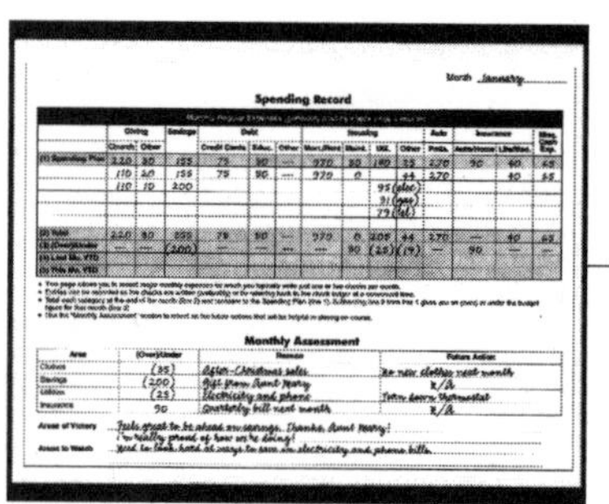
Spending Record

Monthly Assessment

Now look at the back side of the Spending Record form. This side of the form tracks regular monthly expenses. These are the ones in the envelope system you would write a check for. Take a look at the categories across the top of the sheet. They include giving, savings, debt, housing, auto, insurance, and miscellaneous cash expenses. These are the kinds of things that you normally pay once per month. An exception might be giving, which may have weekly checks. Preferably, these entries are recorded as you write the checks.

At the very bottom of the sheet, notice that there's a section for a monthly assessment. Take a couple moments each month and make a note of any unusual occurances that impacted the plan. Record the areas you need to watch more carefully and note the areas where you had victories. This could be very helpful to you. I'll give you a minute to look this over.

Pause briefly to let participants read this section.

NOTES

Month *January*

Spending Record Example

Daily Variable Expenses	Transportation		Household						Professional Services	Entertainment		
	Gas, etc.	Maint/ Repair	Groceries	Clothes	Gifts	Household Items	Personal	Other		Going Out	Travel	Other
(1) Spending Plan	80	40	320	60	80	75	50	—	—	100	70	40
	14	21	9	89	17	14	16	25		22	70	22 (sitter)
	17		87	6	55	22	18			46		
	9		43			9				19		
	19		106			31						
	11		21									
			7									
			13									
(2) Total	70	21	286	95	72	76	34	25	—	87	70	22
(3) (Over)/Under	10	19	34	(35)	8	(1)	16	(25)	—	13	—	18
(4) Last Month YTD												
(5) Total Year to Date												

~~1~~ ~~2~~ ~~3~~ ~~4~~ ~~5~~ ~~6~~ ~~7~~ ~~8~~ ~~9~~ ~~10~~ ~~11~~ ~~12~~ ~~13~~ ~~14~~ ~~15~~ ~~16~~ ~~17~~ ~~18~~ ~~19~~ ~~20~~ ~~21~~ ~~22~~ ~~23~~ ~~24~~ ~~25~~ ~~26~~ ~~27~~ ~~28~~ ~~29~~ ~~30~~ ~~31~~

- Use this page to record expenses that tend to be daily, variable expenses—often the hardest to control.
- Keep receipts throughout the day and record them at the end of the day.
- Total each category at the end of the month (line 2) and compare to the Spending Plan (line 1). Subtracting line 2 from line 1 gives you an (over) or under the budget figure for that month (line 3).
- To verify that you have made each day's entry, cross out the number at the bottom of the page that corresponds to that day's date.
- Optional: If you wish to monitor your progress as you go through the year, you can keep cumulative totals in lines 4 and 5.

SESSION SIX 91

92 SESSION SIX

Month *January*

Spending Record

Monthly Regular Expenses (generally paid by check once a month)	Giving		Savings	Debt			Housing				Auto	Insurance		Misc. Cash Exp.
	Church	Other		Credit Cards	Educ.	Other	Mort./Rent	Maint.	Util.	Other	Pmts.	Auto/Home	Life/Med.	
(1) Spending Plan	220	30	155	75	50	—	970	30	180	25	270	90	40	65
	110	20	155	75	50	—	970	0		44	270		40	65
	110	10	200						95 (elec)					
									31 (gas)					
									79 (tel)					
(2) Total	220	30	355	75	50	—	970	0	205	44	270	—	40	65
(3) (Over)/Under	—	—	(200)	—	—	—	—	30	(25)	(19)	—	90	—	—
(4) Last Mo. YTD														
(5) This Mo. YTD														

- This page allows you to record major monthly expenses for which you typically write just one or two checks per month.
- Entries can be recorded as the checks are written (preferably) or by referring back to the check ledger at a convenient time.
- Total each category at the end of the month (line 2) and compare to the Spending Plan (line 1). Subtracting line 2 from line 1 gives you an (over) or under the budget figure for that month (line 3).
- Use the "Monthly Assessment" section to reflect on the future actions that will be helpful in staying on course.

Monthly Assessment

Area	(Over)/Under	Reason	Future Action
Clothes	(35)	After-Christmas sales	No new clothes next month
Savings	(200)	Gift from Aunt Mary	N/A
Utilities	(25)	Electricity and phone	Turn down thermostat
Insurance	90	Quarterly bill next month	N/A

Areas of Victory *Feels great to be ahead on savings. Thanks, Aunt Mary! I'm really proud of how we're doing!*

Areas to Watch *Need to look hard at ways to save on electricity and phone bills.*

Participant's Guide, page 93.

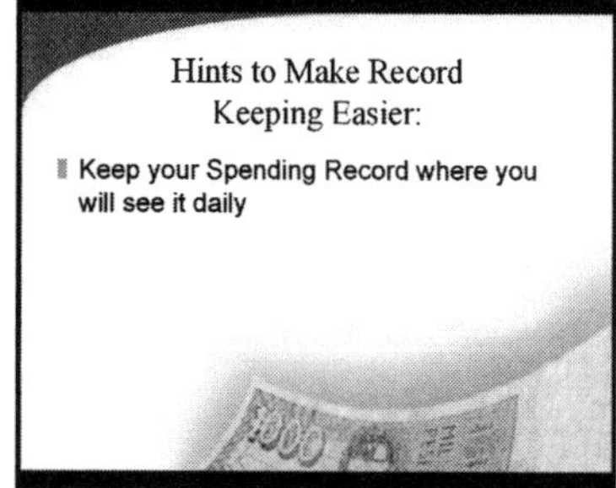
Hints to Make Record
Keeping Easier:
Keep your Spending Record where you will see it daily

In keeping with my statement that record keeping can be simpler than you think, here are some hints to make the written record-keeping system easier to use.

Number one, keep your Spending Record form where you will see it daily—don't tuck it away in a drawer.

If you are married, you might want to place it on your dresser where you and your spouse can fill it out before going to bed each night.

Number two, ROUND OFF to the nearest dollar.

A receipt for $12.88 becomes $13 so at the end of the month you are adding a lot fewer digits.

Number three, combine categories where feasible.

As I mentioned, several categories on the Spending Plan worksheet were combined to develop this form. Feel free to further combine categories if it is easier for you.

Fourth hint, use "EVEN billing" where possible.

Check to see if you can get your semi-annual insurance payment on a monthly basis so that every month the same amount is deducted. Check with your utility companies to see if you can have even billing. It just makes budgeting a little simpler than having high months and low months.

This last item is key: Have a miscellaneous cash envelope.

NOTES

Hints to Make Record Keeping Easier:

- Keep your Spending Record form where you will see it daily.
- ______________________ to the nearest dollar.
- Combine categories.
- Use "____________ billing."
- Have a miscellaneous cash envelope.

Individual Activity: *Spending Record*

Assume it's the end of the day and you've made some purchases. Using the receipts shown on the next page, fill out the Spending Record form on page 95.

Many of you may have been thinking, "This is all nice in theory, but writing down every time I buy a newspaper, purchase a soft drink, or spend 99 cents here or there is going to be a real hassle!" I agree with you!

Let's eliminate recording all those small expenses by first estimating what they add up to each month and combining them under miscellaneous small cash expenses.

Then get cash for that amount, put it in a separate place in your wallet or purse, and use it for those small purchases. If these purchases total $40 per month and average 75 cents each, you'd eliminate over fifty entries on your Spending Record!

There's one caution here. If you decide that forty dollars a month in your Spending Plan would cover these little cash items, but after ten days, you've spent almost the entire envelope, what does that mean? Miscellaneous small cash expenditures are adding up to a whole lot more than you thought. It's not $40 a month; it's more like $120.

You have a decision to make at that point. You can either increase your small cash expenses to $120 per month or find out what you're spending it on and make an effort to cut back. For example, you may start drinking water rather than buying cans of soda—two sodas a day at 75 cents a can would be $45 per month! You could also bring your own coffee to work, or start catching the news on the radio rather than buying a newspaper.

Combine these actions with packing a lunch a few days a week and you'll find the $100 per month to accelerate debt repayment we discussed in Session 3.

Now, let's take a moment to practice using the Spending Record form.

NOTES

Hints to Make Record Keeping Easier:

- Keep your Spending Record form where you will see it daily.
- ______________________ to the nearest dollar.
- Combine categories.
- Use "____________ billing."
- Have a miscellaneous cash envelope.

Individual Activity: *Spending Record*

Assume it's the end of the day and you've made some purchases. Using the receipts shown on the next page, fill out the Spending Record form on page 95.

6 minutes

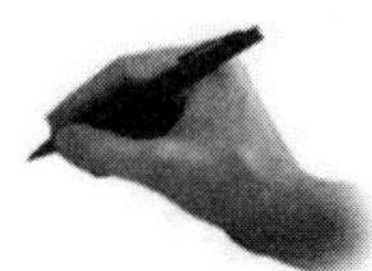

Individual Activity: *Spending Record*

Objective
For participants to practice the written record system.

Directions
Let's assume it's the end of the day and you've made some purchases. Using the receipts shown on the next page, take a couple of minutes to fill out the Spending Record form on page 95.

Call the group back together after about 2 minutes. Be sure to keep track of how long it actually takes them to complete the exercise because you will refer to it in a moment. Write that time here: ________.

Wrap-up (4 minutes)
Let's take a look at the answers.

Where did you put Main Street Gas?

Pause briefly for participants' responses.

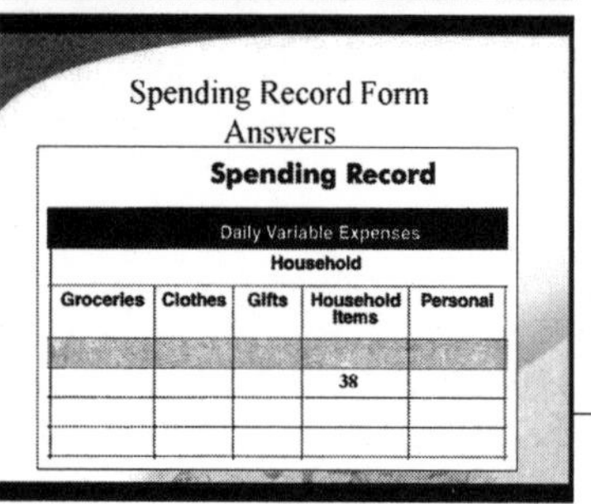

Transportation/gas—$18.

What about the paint store receipt?

Pause briefly for participants' responses.

Spending Record Form
Answers
Spending Record
Daily Variable Expenses
Household
Groceries | Clothes | Gifts | Household Items | Personal
38

Household items. It can be rounded to $38.

The Neighborhood Foods total obviously goes into "groceries," and you round the amount to $17.

Where did you put the department store receipt?

Pause briefly for participants' responses.

NOTES

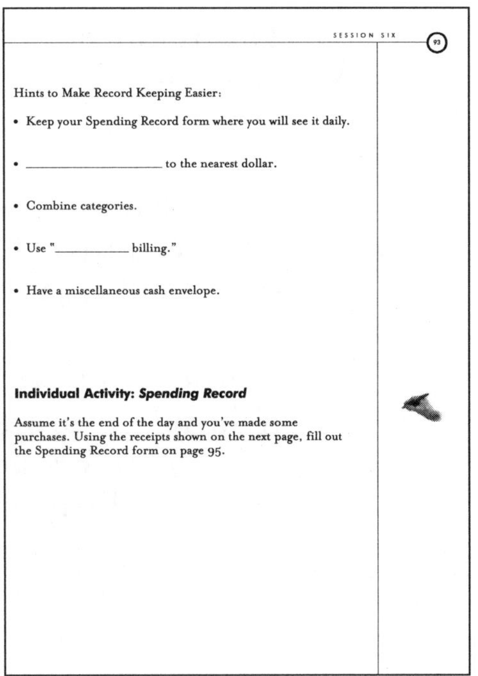

Hints to Make Record Keeping Easier:

- Keep your Spending Record form where you will see it daily.
- ____________________ to the nearest dollar.
- Combine categories.
- Use "___________ billing."
- Have a miscellaneous cash envelope.

Individual Activity: *Spending Record*

Assume it's the end of the day and you've made some purchases. Using the receipts shown on the next page, fill out the Spending Record form on page 95.

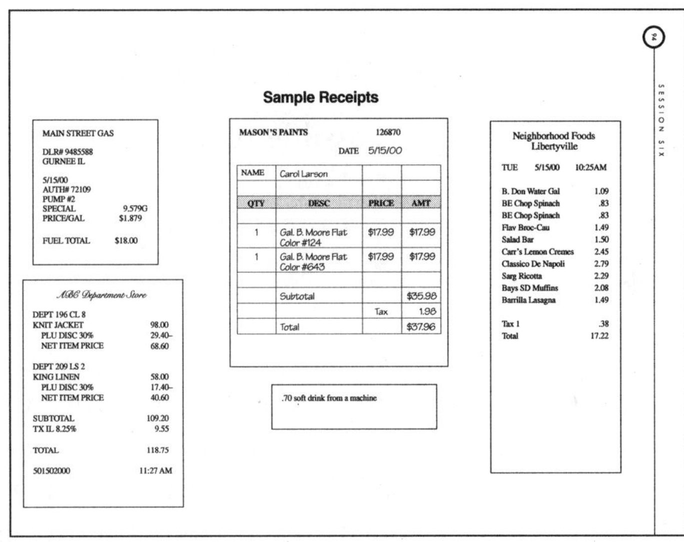

Sample Receipts

MAIN STREET GAS

DLR# 9485588
GURNEE IL

5/15/00
AUTH# 72109
PUMP #2
SPECIAL 9.579G
PRICE/GAL $1.879

FUEL TOTAL $18.00

ABC Department Store

DEPT 196 CL 8
KNIT JACKET 98.00
PLU DISC 30% 29.40–
NET ITEM PRICE 68.60

DEPT 209 LS 2
KING LINEN 58.00
PLU DISC 30% 17.40–
NET ITEM PRICE 40.60

SUBTOTAL 109.20
TX IL 8.25% 9.55

TOTAL 118.75

501502000 11:27 AM

MASON'S PAINTS 126870

DATE 5/15/00

NAME	Carol Larson		
QTY	**DESC**	**PRICE**	**AMT**
1	Gal. B. Moore Flat Color #124	$17.99	$17.99
1	Gal. B. Moore Flat Color #643	$17.99	$17.99
	Subtotal		$35.98
		Tax	1.98
	Total		$37.96

.70 soft drink from a machine

Neighborhood Foods
Libertyville

TUE 5/15/00 10:25AM

B. Don Water Gal 1.09
BE Chop Spinach .83
BE Chop Spinach .83
Flav Broc-Cau 1.49
Salad Bar 1.50
Carr's Lemon Cremes 2.45
Classico De Napoli 2.79
Sarg Ricotta 2.29
Bays SD Muffins 2.08
Barrilla Lasagna 1.49

Tax 1 .38
Total 17.22

Month ________________

Spending Record

Daily Variable Expenses												
	Transportation		Household						Professional Services	Entertainment		
	Gas, etc.	Maint/ Repair	Groceries	Clothes	Gifts	Household Items	Personal	Other		Going Out	Travel	Other
(1) Spending Plan												
(2) Total												
(3) (Over)/Under												
(4) Last Month YTD												
(5) Total Year–to–Date												

1 | 2 | 3 | 4 | 5 | 6 | 7 | 8 | 9 | 10 | 11 | 12 | 13 | 14 | 15 | 16 | 17 | 18 | 19 | 20 | 21 | 22 | 23 | 24 | 24 | 26 | 27 | 28 | 29 | 30 | 31

- Use this page to record expenses that tend to be daily, variable expenses—often the hardest to control.
- Keep receipts throughout the day and record them at the end of the day.
- Total each category at the end of the month (line 2) and compare to the Spending Plan (line 1). Subtracting line 2 from line 1 gives you an (over) or under the budget figure for that month (line 3).
- To verify that you have made each day's entry, cross out the number at the bottom of the page that corresponds to that day's date.
- Optional: If you wish to monitor your progress as you go through the year, you can keep cumulative totals in lines 4 and 5.

This is our most complicated receipt because it has two items that go under different categories, and it has nearly $10 in sales tax.

So, we handle that by putting the items under their categories first. Knit jacket, clothes, $69. King linen, household, $41.

Now let's deal with the sales tax, rounded up to $10. We'll split it proportionally between our two purchases—let's say $6 for the $69 purchase, and $4 for the $41 purchase. Estimating is fine. Then we put those additional amounts—$6 and $4—under clothes and household respectively.

Finally, where did you record the soft drink?

Pause briefly for participants' responses.

Possible responses:
- Food
- Entertainment
- Other

Actually, we don't put the soft drink on the form at all since it's a miscellaneous cash expenditure—and that monthly amount is already recorded on your form. You would get the money for the soft drink from your monthly miscellaneous cash envelope.

Let me now call your attention to a very important point. I noted the time it took you to make those entries, and it was only ____ minutes.

Use the time you kept track of on page 246 in the blank above.

And if you didn't finish it, I'm sure it would only be a matter of your practicing a time or two until you could complete this daily task in less than two minutes.

NOTES

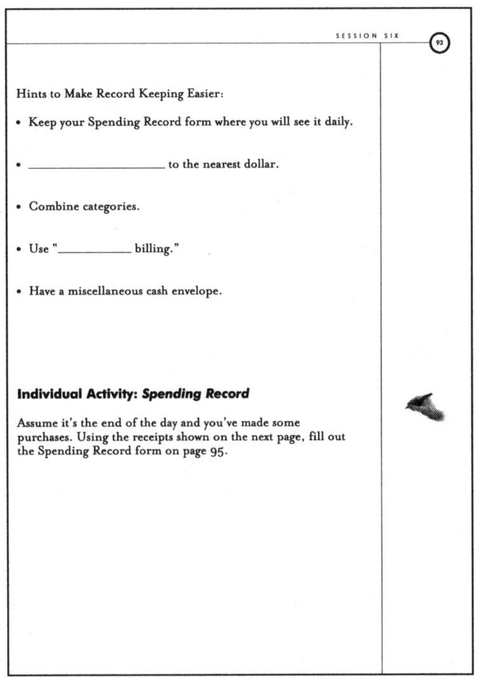

Hints to Make Record Keeping Easier:

- Keep your Spending Record form where you will see it daily.
- ____________________ to the nearest dollar.
- Combine categories.
- Use "___________ billing."
- Have a miscellaneous cash envelope.

Individual Activity: *Spending Record*

Assume it's the end of the day and you've made some purchases. Using the receipts shown on the next page, fill out the Spending Record form on page 95.

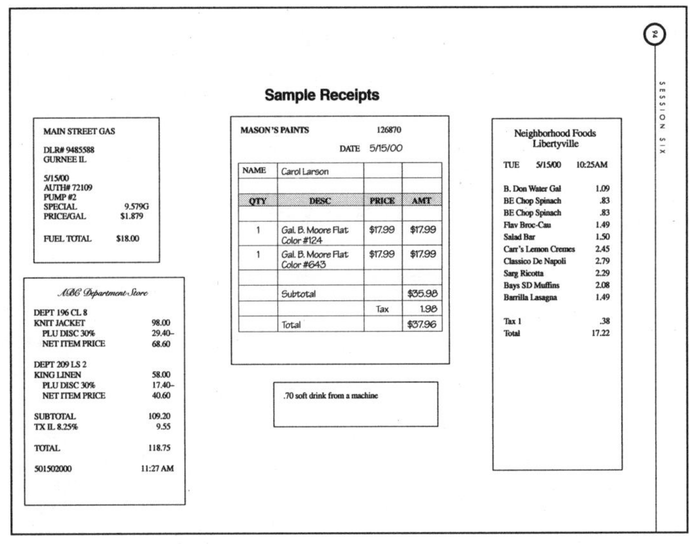

Sample Receipts

MAIN STREET GAS

DLR# 9485588
GURNEE IL

5/15/00
AUTH# 72109
PUMP #2
SPECIAL 9.579G
PRICE/GAL $1.879

FUEL TOTAL $18.00

ABC Department Store

DEPT 196 CL 8
KNIT JACKET 98.00
PLU DISC 30% 29.40–
NET ITEM PRICE 68.60

DEPT 209 LS 2
KING LINEN 58.00
PLU DISC 30% 17.40–
NET ITEM PRICE 40.60

SUBTOTAL 109.20
TX IL 8.25% 9.55

TOTAL 118.75

501502000 11:27 AM

MASON'S PAINTS 126870

DATE 5/15/00

NAME	Carol Larson		
QTY	**DESC**	**PRICE**	**AMT**
1	Gal. B. Moore Flat Color #124	$17.99	$17.99
1	Gal. B. Moore Flat Color #643	$17.99	$17.99
	Subtotal		$35.98
		Tax	1.98
	Total		$37.96

.70 soft drink from a machine

Neighborhood Foods
Libertyville

TUE 5/15/00 10:25AM

B. Don Water Gal 1.09
BE Chop Spinach .83
BE Chop Spinach .83
Flav Broc-Cau 1.49
Salad Bar 1.50
Carr's Lemon Cremes 2.45
Classico De Napoli 2.79
Sarg Ricotta 2.29
Bays SD Muffins 2.08
Barrilla Lasagna 1.49

Tax 1 .38
Total 17.22

Month ________________

Spending Record

Daily Variable Expenses												
	Transportation		Household						Professional Services	Entertainment		
	Gas, etc.	Maint/ Repair	Groceries	Clothes	Gifts	Household Items	Personal	Other		Going Out	Travel	Other
(1) Spending Plan												
(2) Total												
(3) (Over)/Under												
(4) Last Month YTD												
(5) Total Year-to-Date												

1 2 3 4 5 6 7 8 9 10 11 12 13 14 15 16 17 18 19 20 21 22 23 24 24 26 27 28 29 30 31

- Use this page to record expenses that tend to be daily, variable expenses—often the hardest to control.
- Keep receipts throughout the day and record them at the end of the day.
- Total each category at the end of the month (line 2) and compare to the Spending Plan (line 1). Subtracting line 2 from line 1 gives you an (over) or under the budget figure for that month (line 3).
- To verify that you have made each day's entry, cross out the number at the bottom of the page that corresponds to that day's date.
- Optional: If you wish to monitor your progress as you go through the year, you can keep cumulative totals in lines 4 and 5.

Turn to page 96.

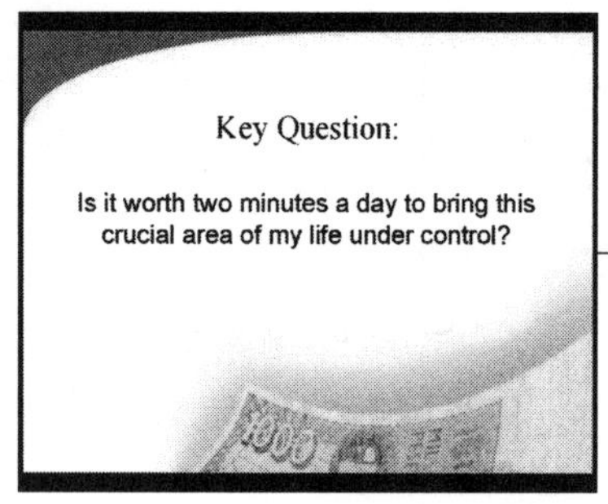

Participant's Guide, page 96.

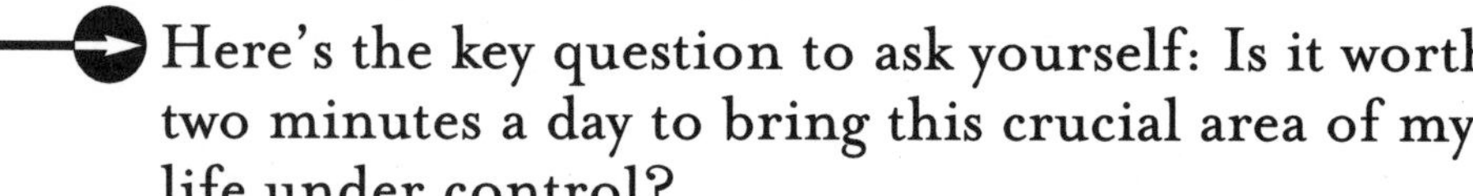

Here's the key question to ask yourself: Is it worth two minutes a day to bring this crucial area of my life under control?

Pause.

This is a key question. Be sure to give people time to reflect on the fact that written record keeping can be accomplished in just a few minutes a day.

Not only will these couple minutes ensure that you have the data you need for future wise decisions, but the simple act of recording expenses will have a strong influence on your spending behavior. You will be giving yourself daily feedback on what is actually taking place, and that will be a strong source of encouragement and correction.

Hopefully, you're becoming convinced that record keeping is simpler than it seems, takes less time than you think, and doesn't require a Ph.D. in math!

Electronic System

Some of you are probably thinking, "Why are you messing around with these archaic methods of envelopes and writing things down when there's great budgeting software out there that does it all? It adds and subtracts for you, does charts and graphs, prints out spreadsheets, and provides all kinds of helpful reports."

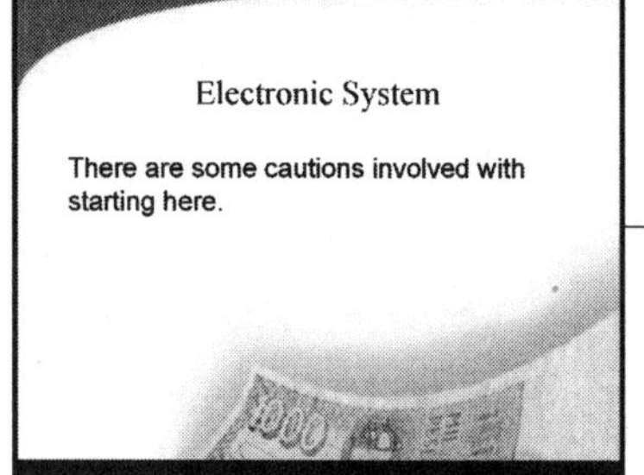

It's true, there are very real advantages to electronic systems, but if you've had difficulty with budgeting in the past or have never tried doing so, there are some cautions involved with starting here.

NOTES

Key Question: Is it worth two minutes a day to bring this crucial area of my life under control?

Electronic System

There are some cautions involved with starting here.

Individual Activity: *Setting Up Your Record-Keeping System*

1. Select which record-keeping system you plan to use to implement your Spending Plan: envelope, written record, or electronic.

2. If you plan on using the written or electronic systems, transfer the numbers from your Spending Plan worksheet to the first lines of the Spending Record form on pages 147 and 148.

   If you plan on using the envelope system, fill in each box under the Envelopes section on page 141, showing the category and dollar amounts. Under the Checks section, write in any expenses you plan to pay with a check.

A potential problem is that the computer may not be readily accessible. It may be off in a corner of the house or down in the basement. You may also forget to go to it each day or find you don't have time to get into the program on a daily basis. Pretty soon, a week goes by and you can't find the receipts. Incomplete records won't give you the data and feedback you need.

My suggestion is that if you are new to budgeting or have found it difficult to do in the past, start with the envelope or written record system. When tracking expenses becomes a habit, when you begin to experience the benefits of doing so, and when you are confident you will continue to follow through, then explore electronic programs. Again, just be careful of starting here.

We're now going to give you some time to set up your record-keeping system.

Individual Activity:
Setting Up Your Record-Keeping System

Individual Activity: *Setting Up Your Record-Keeping System*

5 minutes

> Objective
> For participants to select and set up their record-keeping system.

Directions

1. Select which record-keeping system you plan to use to implement your Spending Plan: envelope, written record, or electronic.
2. If you plan on using the written or electronic systems, transfer the numbers from your Spending Plan worksheet to the first lines of the Spending Record form on pages 147 and 148.

   If you plan on using the envelope system, fill in each box under the Envelopes section on page 141, showing the category and dollar amounts. Under the Checks section, write in any expenses that you plan to pay with a check.

You will have 5 minutes to do this.

NOTES

Key Question: Is it worth two minutes a day to bring this crucial area of my life under control?

Electronic System

There are some cautions involved with starting here.

Individual Activity: *Setting Up Your Record-Keeping System*

1. Select which record-keeping system you plan to use to implement your Spending Plan: envelope, written record, or electronic.

2. If you plan on using the written or electronic systems, transfer the numbers from your Spending Plan worksheet to the first lines of the Spending Record form on pages 147 and 148.

   If you plan on using the envelope system, fill in each box under the Envelopes section on page 141, showing the category and dollar amounts. Under the Checks section, write in any expenses you plan to pay with a check.

Call participants back together after 5 minutes.

2 minutes

Implementation Issues

Participant's Guide, page 97.

I want to alert you to a couple issues you may encounter as you begin implementing your Spending Plan and record-keeping system.

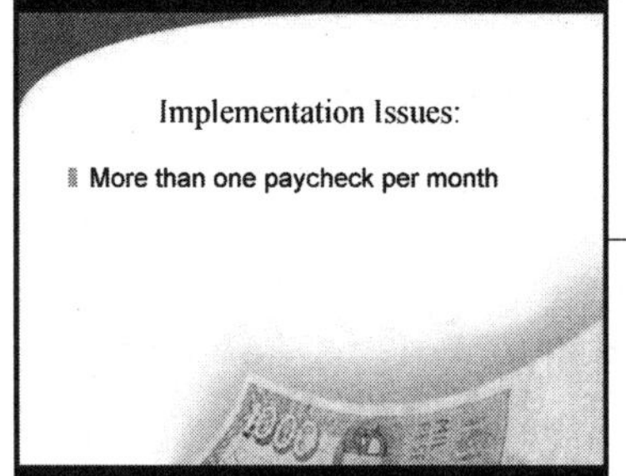

More Than One Paycheck Per Month

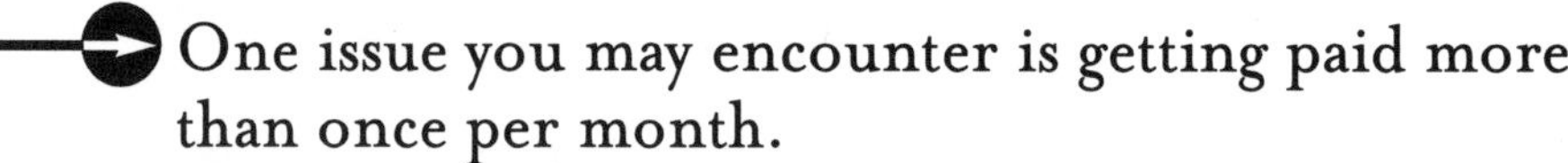

One issue you may encounter is getting paid more than once per month.

The solution is to write up a plan for the expenses you want each of your paychecks to cover. While it may take a little time initially to set up this plan, once it's set up, it will eliminate all the questions, anxiety, and uncertainty about where your paycheck goes each time you receive it. A fuller explanation and an example of how to do this are on page 126 in the Appendix.

Money Building Up in Accounts

The second issue you'll encounter is money building up in accounts.

If you use the envelope system, you'll find that cash will build up in some of the envelopes. For example, if you take one big vacation a year, for eleven months before the vacation, money will build up in that envelope. That creates two concerns: one, you could be tempted to borrow the funds for other things; two, having a large amount of cash on hand could be a security risk. Similarly, if you use the written record–keeping system, a balance would build up in the checking account, potentially giving the impression that you have extra money to spend.

NOTES

Implementation Issues

- More than one paycheck per month

- Money building up in accounts

Individual Activity: *Obstacles*

Write down the biggest obstacles you expect to encounter as you implement your Spending Plan and record-keeping system.

Notes

To avoid these situations, money for these kinds of accounts should be deposited in a short-term savings account; preferably by direct deposit and probably into the same account used for emergency savings. A further explanation of this process, and a simple form to track the various amounts in the savings account are found on pages 128–130 of the Appendix.

Obstacles
We've just identified a couple of issues you'll encounter when you begin implementing your Spending Plan and record-keeping system. Now we're going to give you a couple minutes to think through the obstacles you'll encounter that might keep you from implementing them.

Individual Activity:
Obstacles

Individual Activity: *Obstacles*

Objective
For participants to consider the obstacles they may encounter in implementing their Spending Plan and record-keeping system.

Directions
Write down the biggest obstacles you expect to encounter as you implement your Spending Plan and record-keeping system.

You will have a few minutes to do this.

Call the group back together after 3 minutes.

Wrap-up (2 minutes)
What were some of the obstacles you discussed?

NOTES

Implementation Issues

- More than one paycheck per month
- Money building up in accounts

Individual Activity: *Obstacles*

Write down the biggest obstacles you expect to encounter as you implement your Spending Plan and record-keeping system.

Notes

Solicit three or four comments from the group. Be sure to repeat their answers so everyone hears the response.

Possible responses:
- Lack of discipline
- Getting spouse to buy in
- Discouragement—especially when something unexpected comes up

We'll talk about keeping your commitment at the end of this session. Before we do, let me share with you one of the biggest obstacles first-time budgeters face. It's failing to have a short-term savings account and, specifically, not having emergency savings to draw on.

For example, let's say you put aside $60 per month—$720 for the year—for auto repair. And let's say that that amount is, in fact, precisely the amount that you'll wind up spending over the course of the year. Unfortunately, the second month of your budgeting process rolls around and you get hit with a brake job that costs $400.

Let me tell you what to do and what not to do in this situation. What not to do is say, "I give up. This system just doesn't work. I can't drive my car without brakes, and I can't get to work without a car. I only have $60 set aside from last month, and $60 budgeted this month so, clearly, I have to use my credit card to get the brakes fixed." *Don't do it.* You've made a commitment, and it includes incurring no new debt.

So what is the alternative? Look at every other area of your Spending Plan for that month, and say, "All right, it's come down to a short-term, very spartan lifestyle. I am going to temporarily cut way back on entertainment, I am not going to buy any clothes this month, and I am going to save every penny I can on food."

NOTES

Implementation Issues

- More than one paycheck per month

- Money building up in accounts

Individual Activity: *Obstacles*

Write down the biggest obstacles you expect to encounter as you implement your Spending Plan and record-keeping system.

Notes

Look for any opportunity to hold down expenses that month and apply those dollars to the brake job. If, after doing that, you still don't have enough, then continue to think creatively. "Okay, I can't drive the car without brakes, but what do I really need? I need a way to get back and forth to work. Does that mean I have to get the car repaired now? No, maybe that means I need to carpool, or ride a bus, or find some other way to get to work for a while. Maybe it means borrowing a car from a friend or letting the body of Christ know that I have a temporary need."

The point is, think creatively, make sacrifices where necessary, and stick to your commitment to freeze the debt. Let God and others know of your need. Do not use the credit card.

Turn to page 98.

1 minute

Review and Commitment

Participant's Guide, page 98.

We are almost through with the course. Let's take a few minutes to look back at what we've covered.

First, we became aware of the dilemma we face between following the Pull of the Culture or seeking the Mind and Heart of God. We talked about the daily decisions we make that lead us to either foolishly follow the culture or faithfully move toward God.

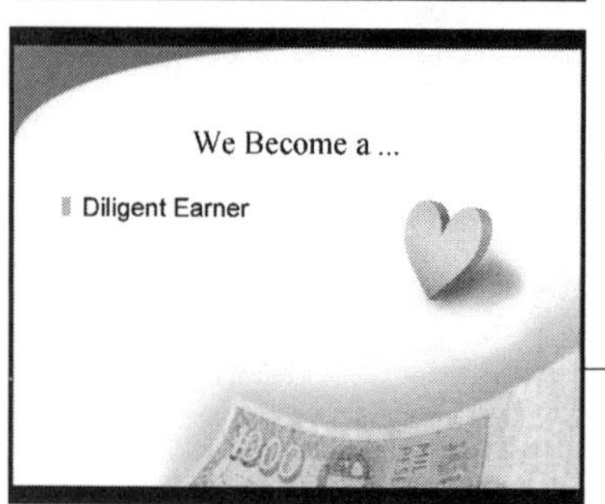

We also learned that when you faithfully move toward God, you increasingly become:

a Diligent Earner,

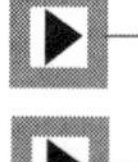

Generous Giver,

Wise Saver,

Cautious Debtor,

and a Prudent Consumer.

NOTES

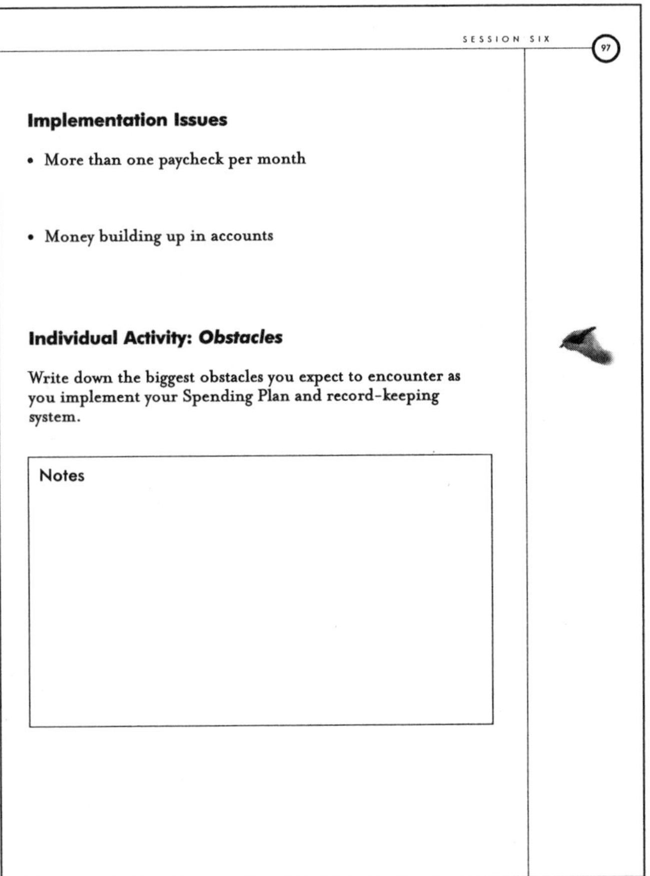

SESSION SIX 97
Implementation Issues
• More than one paycheck per month
• Money building up in accounts
Individual Activity: Obstacles
Write down the biggest obstacles you expect to encounter as you implement your Spending Plan and record-keeping system.
Notes

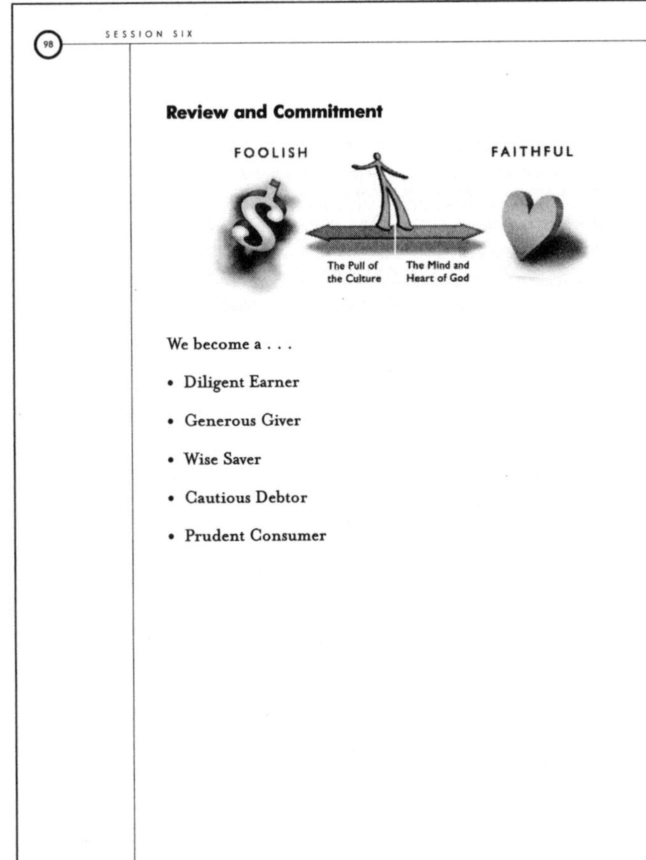

98 SESSION SIX
Review and Commitment
FOOLISH
FAITHFUL
The Pull of the Culture
The Mind and Heart of God
We become a . . .
• Diligent Earner
• Generous Giver
• Wise Saver
• Cautious Debtor
• Prudent Consumer

It's then that you experience a growing sense of financial freedom. Genuine financial freedom is the contentment you experience as you faithfully manage your financial resources according to God's principles and purposes. The more you become financially faithful, the more you'll experience financial freedom.

5 minutes

Video: *Financial Freedom* (5 minutes)

Now, we're going to watch a video that tells the stories of some people who have made this lifestyle change.

View video: *Financial Freedom.*

Let's take a minute to reflect on this.

4 minutes

Individual Activity: *Becoming Financially Faithful, Financially Free*

Individual Activity:

Becoming Financially Faithful, Financially Free

Participant's Guide, page 99.

Objective
For participants to picture what it would feel like to live a financially faithful and financially free lifestyle.

Directions
Write your answer to the following question: "If you could become financially faithful and experience real financial freedom, what would your life be like?"

I'll give you 3 minutes to complete this.

Call participants back together after 3 minutes.

Wrap-up (1 minute)
What are some of the answers you wrote down?

NOTES

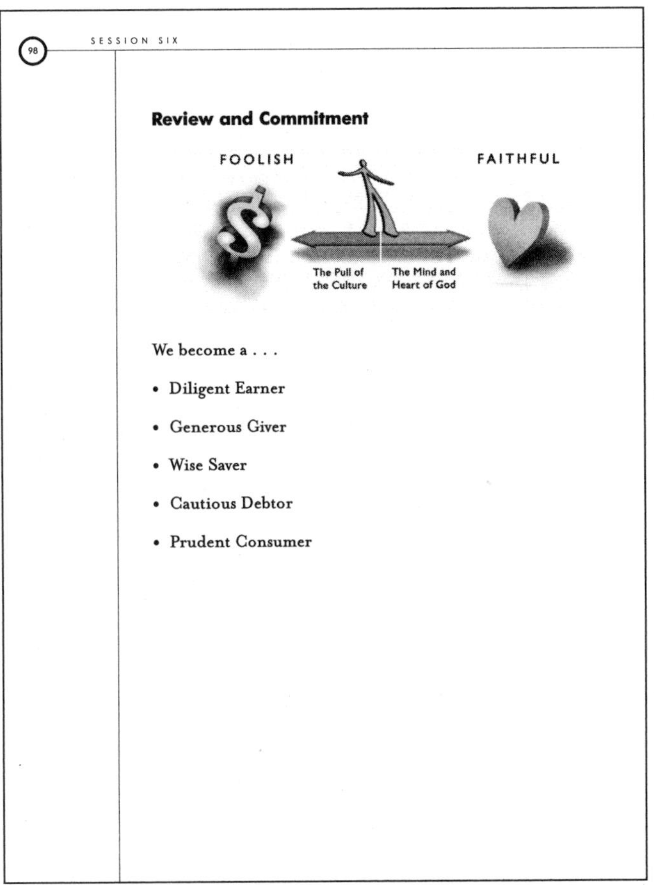
98
SESSION SIX
Review and Commitment
FOOLISH
FAITHFUL
The Pull of the Culture
The Mind and Heart of God
We become a . . .
• Diligent Earner
• Generous Giver
• Wise Saver
• Cautious Debtor
• Prudent Consumer

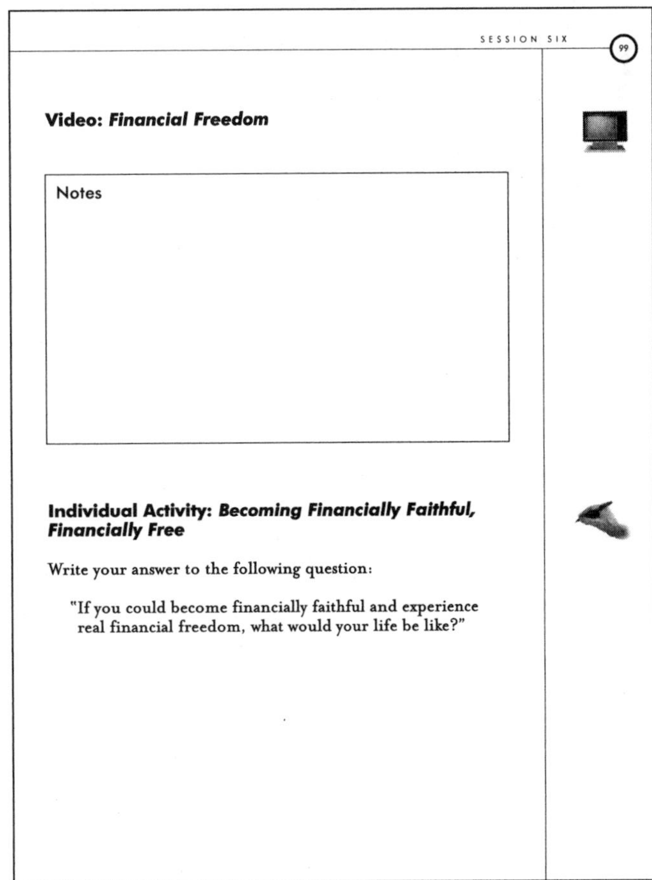
SESSION SIX
99
Video: Financial Freedom
Notes
Individual Activity: Becoming Financially Faithful, Financially Free
Write your answer to the following question:
"If you could become financially faithful and experience real financial freedom, what would your life be like?"

Solicit three or four comments from the group. Be sure to repeat their answers so everyone hears the response.

Possible responses:

- I would have less anxiety/stress in my life because I wouldn't have any more debt.
- I would have a more peaceful home because we wouldn't be arguing as much.

You now have a vision for what you can become by following the principles in this workshop. In addition, you have a Spending Plan in hand and a record-keeping system to track your progress.

Turn to page 100.

2 minutes

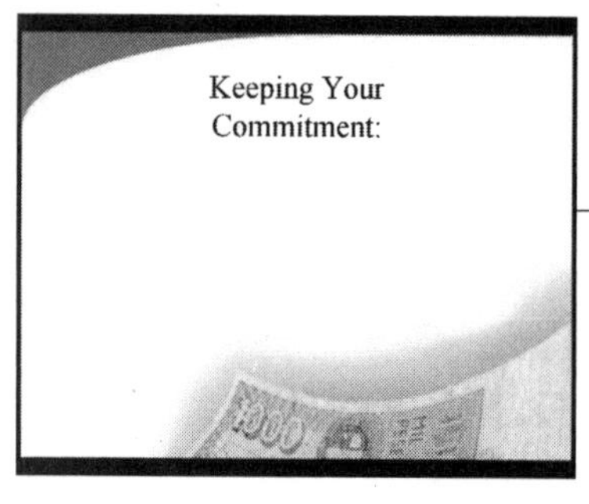
Keeping Your
Commitment:

Keeping Your Commitment

Participant's Guide, page 100.

Now, it's commitment time. Completing this Commitment Plan—and carrying it out—will play a key role in helping you overcome the obstacles you identified a few minutes ago.

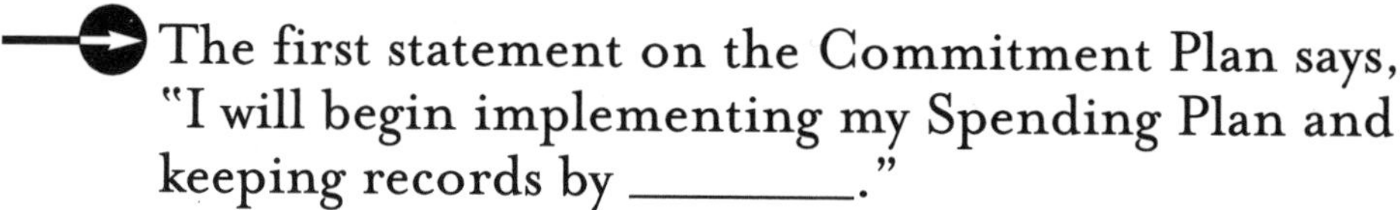

The first statement on the Commitment Plan says, "I will begin implementing my Spending Plan and keeping records by ________."

Take a moment and fill in a date here.

Pause.

The next statement says, "My accountability partner will be ________.

I will give you a moment to write down the name of someone who will hold you accountable."

Pause.

NOTES

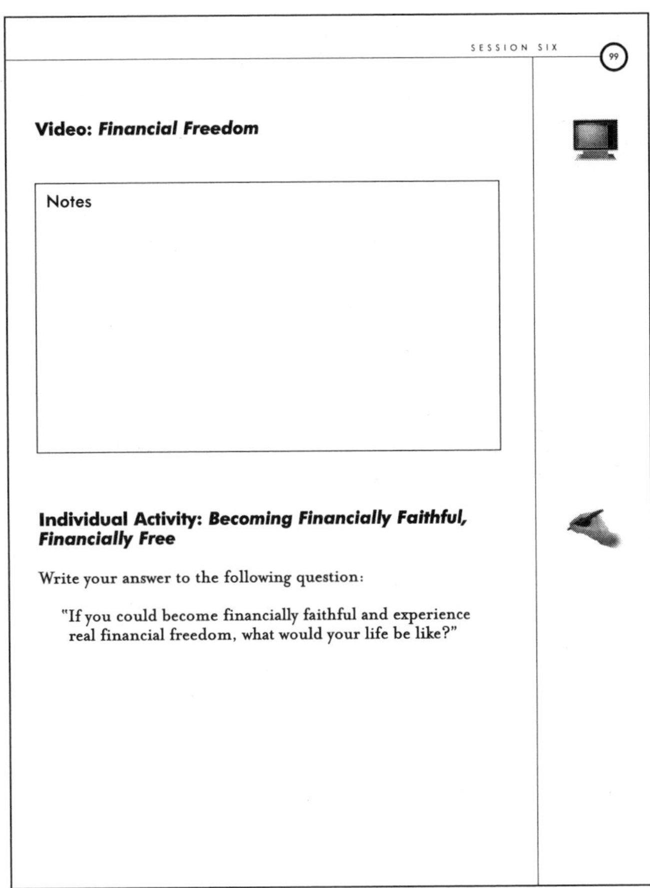

Video: *Financial Freedom*

Notes

Individual Activity: *Becoming Financially Faithful, Financially Free*

Write your answer to the following question:

> "If you could become financially faithful and experience real financial freedom, what would your life be like?"

Commitment Plan

- I will begin implementing my Spending Plan and keeping records by ________________.
- My accountability partner will be ________________________.
- I will pray daily for God's guidance and help.

Keeping Your Commitment:

- Commit to using your Spending Plan and record-keeping system for ninety days.
- Do not become discouraged.
- Seek assistance, if needed.
- Pray daily for God's guidance and wisdom.

Summary: God Is Able

He is able, more than able to
Accomplish what concerns me today
Handle anything that comes my way
Do much more than I could ever dream
To make me what he wants me to be.

You can do it!

Finally, notice the last statement, "I will pray daily for God's guidance and help."

We said at the beginning of the course that making some of the changes required to get our financial lives in order will take the power of the Holy Spirit. Your daily prayers will open the door for the Spirit to work within you.

Keeping this in mind, here are some tips for keeping your commitment.

Commit to using your Spending Plan and record-keeping system for ninety days.

This will give you enough time to develop new habits and to begin to see the first fruits of your efforts.

Do not become discouraged after the first month.

This initial data may only show whether or not the estimates on your Spending Plan worksheet were realistic. It could take three or four months to determine accurate figures for some of your categories. Some of the data you obtain may be good news, especially if you discover that your efforts have resulted in lower expenses than you initially projected.

Once you determine actual figures, you may need to adjust your Spending Plan. Several adjustments may be necessary before your plan is final and reflects your actual situation. This is normal. Remember, one month is not definitive. You're looking for patterns that emerge over several months.

> You may wish to have a celebration for participants ninety days after the course is completed. If you plan such a gathering, this is a good time to tell participants when and where the celebration will be.

Seek assistance if needed.

NOTES

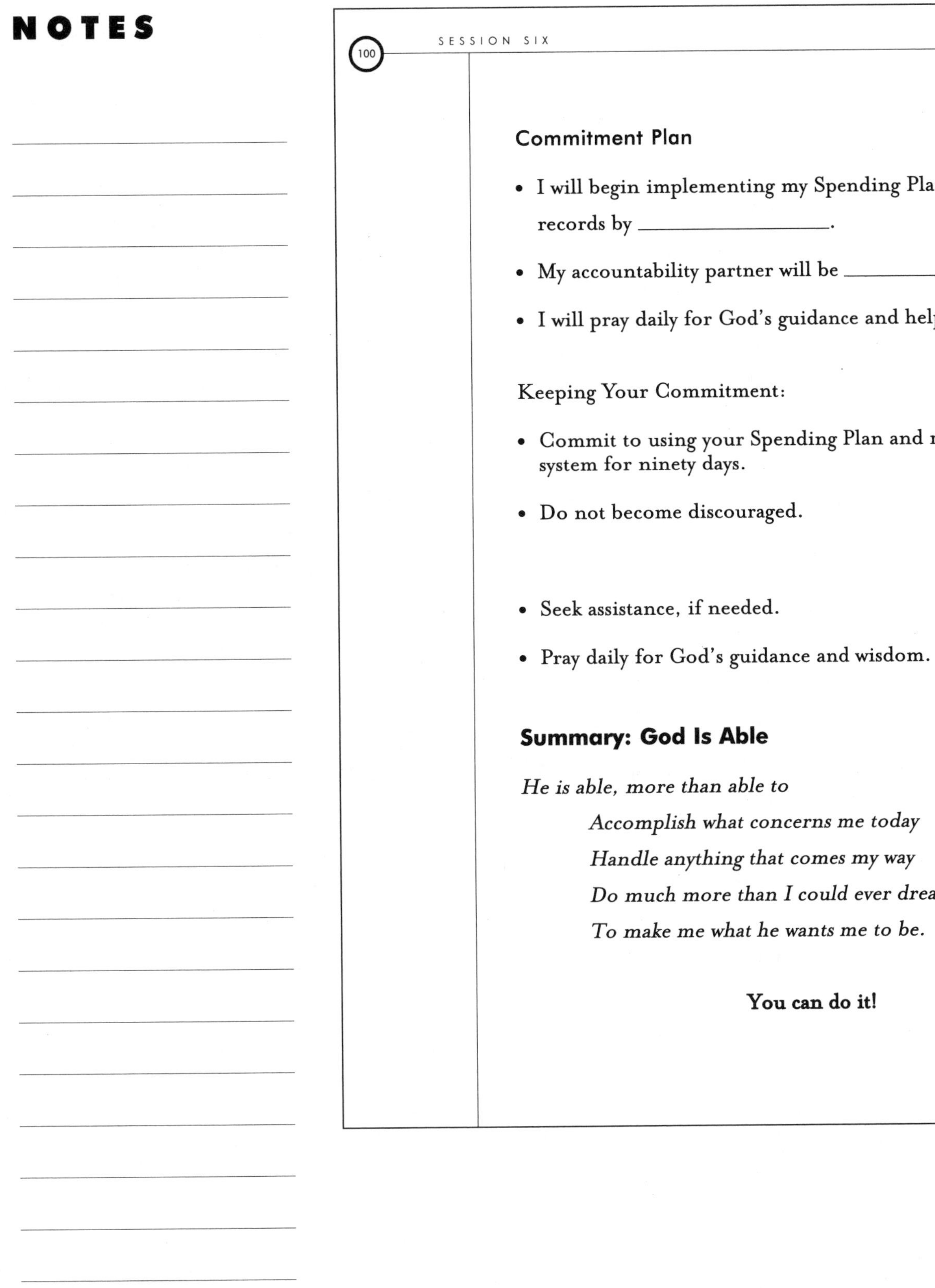

Commitment Plan

- I will begin implementing my Spending Plan and keeping records by ________________.
- My accountability partner will be ________________________.
- I will pray daily for God's guidance and help.

Keeping Your Commitment:

- Commit to using your Spending Plan and record-keeping system for ninety days.
- Do not become discouraged.

- Seek assistance, if needed.
- Pray daily for God's guidance and wisdom.

Summary: God Is Able

He is able, more than able to
Accomplish what concerns me today
Handle anything that comes my way
Do much more than I could ever dream
To make me what he wants me to be.

You can do it!

Briefly mention here the ministries, counselors, or other assistance your church provides to help participants.

Pray daily for God's guidance and wisdom.

There's hope for everyone, no matter what your situation is. One thing we haven't talked about is something we call "God's mathematics." It's amazing to see the number of ways God works when his principles are put into action. Often, it appears that it will take a person years and years to turn their financial life around, even by following all the principles we've talked about.

But time after time, things progress much more quickly than expected. At eighteen months, one man was far ahead of his plan because the old clunker he had been driving was still running miles beyond what he expected. In another situation, a woman received an unexpected check from a distant relative.

We can't predict how God will choose to act, but we do know that he will honor and be pleased by the fact that you commit to him and to following his principles.

5 minutes

SUMMARY: GOD IS ABLE

We began this course with the encouragement from Philippians 4:13 that you and I can do all things through Christ.

We've covered a lot of ground since then. Along with the hope and conviction you now have, you may also be feeling some apprehension and wonder whether this promise is really true for you.

I want to end our time by stating with complete confidence that, with God's help, you really can do this. You can manage your financial affairs according to Biblical Financial Principles and experience true financial freedom.

NOTES

Commitment Plan

- I will begin implementing my Spending Plan and keeping records by ____________.
- My accountability partner will be ____________.
- I will pray daily for God's guidance and help.

Keeping Your Commitment:

- Commit to using your Spending Plan and record-keeping system for ninety days.
- Do not become discouraged.
- Seek assistance, if needed.
- Pray daily for God's guidance and wisdom.

Summary: God Is Able

He is able, more than able to
Accomplish what concerns me today
Handle anything that comes my way
Do much more than I could ever dream
To make me what he wants me to be.

You can do it!

There is a song entitled "He Is Able" that affirms what God can do in our lives. It says:

He is able, more than able to
Accomplish what concerns me today
Handle anything that comes my way
Do much more than I could ever dream
To make me what he wants me to be.

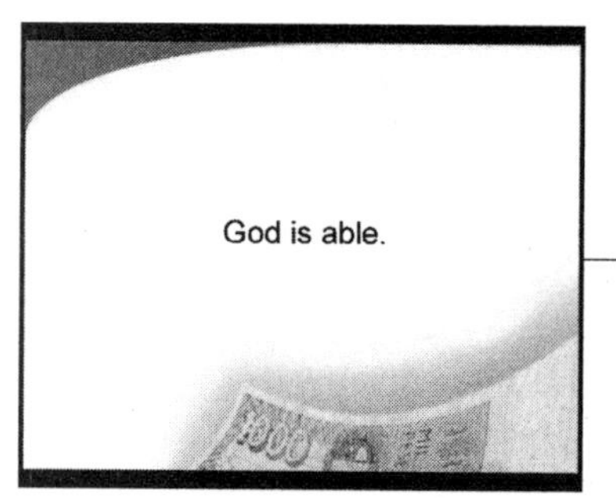

Based on the truth of Scripture, these words carry the hope of God's promise to you—that God is able, that he will be your strength, and that you really can do this with God's help. I encourage you to claim this promise as your own and to step out with courage and confidence, knowing God is with you.

Let's close our time with prayer.

Father God, we know that you have all the power in the world and are able to do incredible things in our lives, to change us from within, and to make each of us a new person. Help us to adopt a new way of thinking and a new way of living and to be good stewards of what you've entrusted to us. Empower us to live humbly and walk with you. We yearn to hear your words, "Well done, good and faithful servant . . . good and faithful trustee." In Christ we pray, amen.

APPENDIX

APPENDIX CONTENTS

Good $ense Budget Course Pre-work 275

Earning

Determining an Average Month for Variable Income 291
What Happens to Your Raises 292

Saving

The Cumulative Effect of Little Things Over an Extended Period . .293

Debt

Establishing a Debt Repayment Plan 296
Sample Debt Reduction Plan 298

Spending

When Is Enough, Enough? 299
Nothing Down, Nothing a Month 300
A Big Difference in a Short Time 301
Unplugging from the Consumptive Society 304

Record Keeping

Keeping Month-to-Date and Year-to-Date Totals on the Spending Record 307
Spending Record Example 309

Implementation Issues

More than One Paycheck per Month 310
Money Building Up in Accounts 312
Wendy and Dan's Money Market Fund for Short-term Savings 314

Recommended Resources 315

Forms

Debt Reduction Plan 321
Form for Tracking Short-term Savings 323
Envelope Record-Keeping Worksheet 325
Biblical Financial Principles 327
Spending Plan 329
Spending Records 331

PRE-WORK FOR

THE GOOD $ENSE BUDGET COURSE

IMPORTANT

Please read and complete all pre-work prior to attending the course.

Dear Good $ense Budget Course Participant,

We're glad you're registered for the *Good $ense Budget Course*! Regardless of your financial situation, a budget—what we call a "Spending Plan"—is the necessary and fundamental tool that enables you to control your money rather than having your money control you. Contrary to popular thought, a Spending Plan is not restrictive; rather, it is freeing. We believe the *Good $ense Budget Course* will prove this truth to you.

Course Goal

The goal of the *Good $ense Budget Course* is for you to commit to and begin developing a biblically-based Spending Plan. By the end of the course, you will have a Spending Plan in your hand, the knowledge in your head to implement it, and a commitment in your heart to follow through on it. The commitment of the Good $ense Ministry is to provide you with the principles, practical steps, and individual assistance to help make that happen.

Pre-work

In order for the course to be as valuable and productive as possible, it is very important to complete the pre-work prior to attending the course. Completing the forms may take several hours so it is advisable to begin as soon as your receive these materials. The information you are asked to collect is confidential and no one else will see it. Throughout the course, you will use your pre-work information to establish your personal Spending Plan.

Supplies

In addition to your completed pre-work, please bring to the course two or three pencils, an eraser, and a pocket calculator.

Prayer

Pray that this experience will be a valuable one for you and the others in attendance, and that we will all grow in our understanding of Biblical Financial Principles and our ability to put them into practice.

Looking forward to seeing you there!

The Good $ense Ministry

PRE-WORK INSTRUCTIONS

Six forms are included in the pre-work to help you prepare for the *Good $ense Budget Course.* Please allow plenty of time prior to attending the course to gather the information and to complete each form. Instructions to help you complete each form are listed below.

Goals to Achieve this Year

Make it a priority to reflect on your financial goals. If you are married, make time to discuss financial goals with your spouse. These goals will become the basis for shaping your Spending Plan, and they will provide motivation for following through on your decisions in the months ahead.

What I Owe

As you fill out the second column (Amount) of this section, use the total balance due on each item.

What I Own

These sections are optional, but we encourage you to fill them out so you can calculate a simplified version of your "net worth." Consider that the value of things you own should be the amount you would expect to get if you sold the items.

Gift List

Here's an often overlooked or underestimated part of spending. Write the names of individuals you will be purchasing gifts for in the coming year. Remember to include cards, postage at Christmas, parties, etc. You may wish to include some money for as yet unannounced weddings, etc.

What I Spend

Gather as much information as you can to determine a monthly average for expenses in each category. Going through your checkbook and your credit card bills for the past year will probably be helpful. Be sure to include periodic expense items such as auto insurance, taxes, etc., that may not be paid on a monthly basis. If you have not kept records in the past, some of the categories may be difficult to estimate. Give it your best shot, recognizing that if you don't have records showing how much you're spending in a particular area, the amount is probably more than you think it is!

The Income figures at the top of the page should be your take-home pay after taxes and other deductions. Make a note of any deductions (such as medical insurance, retirement, etc.). Where those items occur under expenses, enter the notation "payroll deduction." If your income varies from month to month, use a conservative monthly estimate based on the last two or three years' earnings. Referring back to your income tax records could be helpful in making this determination. Remember, you are looking for after-tax, take-home income.

Money Motivation Quiz

This is an optional exercise that will provide insightful information on your behavior regarding money. If you are married, two copies of the quiz are provided so you and your spouse can both take the quiz. Answers are included on the back of the quiz. No fair peeking before you answer the questions!

GOALS TO ACHIEVE THIS YEAR

Please allow adequate time to give serious consideration to your goals. Carefully considered, realistic goals—that flow out of what's really important to you—are powerful motivators. That motivation will be very helpful to you in following through on the steps necessary to achieve your goals.

OVERALL GOAL

My overall goal in attending this course is:

____

____

SPECIFIC GOALS TO ACHIEVE

Check the appropriate boxes and write in any details on the lines to the right of each item.

- ❑ Pay off debt: ______________
- ❑ Save for a major purchase (home, car, other): ______________
- ❑ Save for a dream vacation: ______________
- ❑ Save for emergencies: ______________
- ❑ Save to replace items that may wear out (major appliances, home repairs, car): ______________
- ❑ Save for college expenses: ______________
- ❑ Save for retirement: ______________
- ❑ Increase my giving to the church: ______________
- ❑ Increase other giving: ______________
- ❑ Other: ______________
- ❑ Other: ______________
- ❑ Other: ______________

What I Owe			
I Owe (liabilities)	**Amount**	**Minimum Monthly Payment**	**Interest Percentage**
Mortgage (current balance)			
Home Equity Loans			
Credit Cards			
Car Loans			
Education Loans			
Family/Friends			
Other			
Total of All I Owe			

What I Own (optional)	
I Own (assets)	**Amount**
Checking Account	
Savings Account	
Other Savings	
Insurance (cash value)	
Retirement	
Home (market value)	
Auto (market value)	
Second Auto (market value)	
Other Possessions (estimate)	
Money Owed to Me	
Other	
Other	
Total of All I Own	

Net Worth (optional)

(Total of All I Own – Total of All I owe = Net Worth (in earthly terms, not God's!)*

____________ – ____________ = ____________

*Never confuse your self-worth with your net worth. In God's eyes each one of us is of infinite worth.

GIFT LIST

List the names of those you for whom you buy gifts and the amounts you typically spend on each occasion.*

Name	Birthday	Christmas	Anniversary	Other
1.				
2.				
3.				
4.				
5.				
6.				
7.				
8.				
9.				
10.				
11.				
12.				
13.				
14.				
15.				
16.				
17.				
18.				
19.				
20.				
Total				

GRAND TOTAL $____________ MONTHLY AVERAGE (Total ÷ 12) = $____________
(of all columns)

*You may wish to also include the cost of holiday decorations, entertaining, etc.

SPENDING PLAN

EARNINGS/INCOME PER MONTH		TOTALS
Salary #1 (net take-home)	________	
Salary #2 (net take-home)	________	
Other (less taxes)	________	
TOTAL MONTHLY INCOME		$________

	% GUIDE	
1. GIVING		$________
Church	________	
OTHER CONTRIBUTIONS	________	
2. SAVING	**5–10%**	$________
EMERGENCY	________	
REPLACEMENT	________	
LONG TERM	________	
3. DEBT	**0–10%**	$________
CREDIT CARDS:		
VISA	________	
Master Card	________	
Discover	________	
American Express	________	
Gas Cards	________	
Department Stores	________	
EDUCATION LOANS	________	
OTHER LOANS:		
Bank Loans	________	
Credit Union	________	
Family/Friends	________	
OTHER	________	
4. HOUSING	**25–38%**	$________
MORTGAGE/TAXES/RENT	________	
MAINTENANCE/REPAIRS	________	
UTILITIES:		
Electric	________	
Gas	________	
Water	________	
Trash	________	
Telephone/Internet	________	
Cable TV	________	
OTHER	________	
5. AUTO/TRANSP.	**12–15%**	$________
CAR PAYMENTS/LICENSE	________	
GAS & BUS/TRAIN/PARKING	________	
OIL/LUBE/MAINTENANCE	________	

* This is a % of total monthly income. These are guidelines only and may be different for individual situations. However, there should be good rationale for a significant variance.

6. INSURANCE (Paid by you)	**5%**	$________
AUTO	________	
HOMEOWNERS	________	
LIFE	________	
MEDICAL/DENTAL	________	
Other	________	
7. HOUSEHOLD/PERSONAL	**15–25%**	$________
GROCERIES	________	
CLOTHES/DRY CLEANING	________	
GIFTS	________	
HOUSEHOLD ITEMS	________	
PERSONAL:		
Liquor/Tobacco	________	
Cosmetics	________	
Barber/Beauty	________	
OTHER:		
Books/Magazines	________	
Allowances	________	
Music Lessons	________	
Personal Technology	________	
Education	________	
Miscellaneous	________	
8. ENTERTAINMENT	**5–10%**	$________
GOING OUT:		
Meals	________	
Movies/Events	________	
Baby-sitting	________	
TRAVEL (VACATION/TRIPS)	________	
OTHER:		
Fitness/Sports	________	
Hobbies	________	
Media Rental	________	
OTHER	________	
9. PROF. SERVICES	**5–15%**	$________
CHILD CARE	________	
MEDICAL/DENTAL/PRESC.	________	
OTHER		
Legal	________	
Counseling	________	
Professional Dues	________	
10. MISC. SMALL CASH EXPENDITURES	**2–3%**	$________
TOTAL EXPENSES		$________

TOTAL MONTHLY INCOME	$________
LESS TOTAL EXPENSES	$________
INCOME OVER/(UNDER) EXPENSES	$________

MONEY MOTIVATION QUIZ

Directions

For each of the fourteen questions below, circle the letter that best describes your response.

1. Money is important because it allows me to . . .
   a. Do what I want to do.
   b. Feel secure.
   c. Get ahead in life.
   d. Buy things for others.

2. I feel that money . . .
   a. Frees up my time.
   b. Can solve my problems.
   c. Is a means to an end.
   d. Helps make relationships smoother.

3. When it comes to saving money, I . . .
   a. Don't have a plan and rarely save.
   b. Have a plan and stick to it.
   c. Don't have a plan but manage to save anyway.
   d. Don't make enough money to save.

4. If someone asks about my personal finances, I . . .
   a. Feel defensive.
   b. Realize I need more education and information.
   c. Feel comfortable and competent.
   d. Would rather talk about something else.

5. When I make a major purchase, I . . .
   a. Go with what my intuition tells me.
   b. Research a great deal before buying.
   c. Feel I'm in charge—it's my/our money.
   d. Ask friends/family first.

6. If I have money left over at the end of the month, I . . .
   a. Go out and have a good time.
   b. Put the money into savings.
   c. Look for a good investment.
   d. Buy a gift for someone.

7. If I discover I paid more for something than a friend did I . . .
   a. Couldn't care less.
   b. Feel it's okay because I also find bargains at times.
   c. Assume they spent more time shopping, and time is money.
   d. Feel upset and angry at myself.

8. When paying bills, I . . .
   a. Put it off and sometimes forget.
   b. Pay them when due, but no sooner.
   c. Pay when I get to it, but don't want to be hassled.
   d. Worry that my credit will suffer if I miss a payment.

9. When it comes to borrowing money I . . .
   a. Simply won't/don't like to feel indebted.
   b. Only borrow as a last resort.
   c. Tend to borrow from banks or other business sources.
   d. Ask friends and family because they know I'll pay.

10. When eating out with friends I prefer to . . .
    a. Divide the bill proportionately.
    b. Ask for separate checks.
    c. Charge the bill to my bankcard and have others pay me.
    d. Pay the entire bill because I like to treat my friends.

11. When it comes to tipping I . . .
    a. Sometimes do and sometimes don't.
    b. Just call me Scrooge.
    c. Resent it, but always tip the right amount.
    d. Tip generously because I like to be well thought of.

12. If I suddenly came into a lot of money, I . . .
    a. Wouldn't have to work.
    b. Wouldn't have to worry about the future.
    c. Could really build up my business.
    d. Would spend a lot on family and friends and enjoy time with them more.

13. When indecisive about a purchase I often tell myself . . .
    a. It's only money.
    b. It's a bargain.
    c. It's a good investment.
    d. He/she will love it.

14. In our family . . .
    a. I do/will handle all the money and pay all the bills.
    b. My partner does/will take care of the finances.
    c. I do/will pay my bills and my partner will do the same.
    d. We do/will sit down together to pay bills.

15. Bonus question: Describe how money was handled in your family of origin. Who managed the family budget? Was that person a spender or a saver? Which are you?

Score: Tally your answers to questions one through fourteen by the letter of your answer:

a. __________ c. ____________
b. __________ d. ____________

To understand your results, see the explanation on the back of this page.

UNDERSTANDING THE RESULTS OF YOUR MONEY MOTIVATION QUIZ

Money means different things to different people based on a variety of factors such as temperament and life experiences. Often the meaning of money and the way it motivates us is subtle and something we are not always aware of.

This simple quiz is designed to give you an indication of how strongly you are influenced by the following money motivations: Freedom, Security, Power, and Love. None are inherently good or bad, although each certainly has its dark side.

The key to your money motivation is reflected in the relative number of a, b, c, or d answers.

"A" answers indicate that money relates to **Freedom**. To you money means having the freedom to do what you like.

"B" answers indicate that money relates to **Security**. You need to feel safe and secure and you desire the stability and protection that money supposedly provides.

"C" answers indicate that money relates to **Power**. Personal success and control are important to you, and you appreciate the power money sometimes provides.

"D" answers indicate that money relates to **Love**. You like to use money to express love and build relationships.

One of the keys to managing money wisely is to understand our relationship to it. We hope this exercise gives you some helpful insights. You may wish to share your scores with your spouse or a friend and discuss whether their perceptions of your money motivations are consistent with your scores.

MONEY MOTIVATION QUIZ

Directions

For each of the fourteen questions below, circle the letter that best describes your response.

1. Money is important because it allows me to . . .
   a. Do what I want to do.
   b. Feel secure.
   c. Get ahead in life.
   d. Buy things for others.

2. I feel that money . . .
   a. Frees up my time.
   b. Can solve my problems.
   c. Is a means to an end.
   d. Helps make relationships smoother.

3. When it comes to saving money, I . . .
   a. Don't have a plan and rarely save.
   b. Have a plan and stick to it.
   c. Don't have a plan but manage to save anyway.
   d. Don't make enough money to save.

4. If someone asks about my personal finances, I . . .
   a. Feel defensive.
   b. Realize I need more education and information.
   c. Feel comfortable and competent.
   d. Would rather talk about something else.

5. When I make a major purchase, I . . .
   a. Go with what my intuition tells me.
   b. Research a great deal before buying.
   c. Feel I'm in charge—it's my/our money.
   d. Ask friends/family first.

6. If I have money left over at the end of the month, I . . .
   a. Go out and have a good time.
   b. Put the money into savings.
   c. Look for a good investment.
   d. Buy a gift for someone.

7. If I discover I paid more for something than a friend did I . . .
   a. Couldn't care less.
   b. Feel it's okay because I also find bargains at times.
   c. Assume they spent more time shopping, and time is money.
   d. Feel upset and angry at myself.

8. When paying bills, I . . .
   a. Put it off and sometimes forget.
   b. Pay them when due, but no sooner.
   c. Pay when I get to it, but don't want to be hassled.
   d. Worry that my credit will suffer if I miss a payment.

9. When it comes to borrowing money I . . .
   a. Simply won't/don't like to feel indebted.
   b. Only borrow as a last resort.
   c. Tend to borrow from banks or other business sources.
   d. Ask friends and family because they know I'll pay.

10. When eating out with friends I prefer to . . .
    a. Divide the bill proportionately.
    b. Ask for separate checks.
    c. Charge the bill to my bankcard and have others pay me.
    d. Pay the entire bill because I like to treat my friends.

11. When it comes to tipping I . . .
    a. Sometimes do and sometimes don't.
    b. Just call me Scrooge.
    c. Resent it, but always tip the right amount.
    d. Tip generously because I like to be well thought of.

12. If I suddenly came into a lot of money, I . . .
    a. Wouldn't have to work.
    b. Wouldn't have to worry about the future.
    c. Could really build up my business.
    d. Would spend a lot on family and friends and enjoy time with them more.

13. When indecisive about a purchase I often tell myself . . .
    a. It's only money.
    b. It's a bargain.
    c. It's a good investment.
    d. He/she will love it.

14. In our family . . .
    a. I do/will handle all the money and pay all the bills.
    b. My partner does/will take care of the finances.
    c. I do/will pay my bills and my partner will do the same.
    d. We do/will sit down together to pay bills.

15. Bonus question: Describe how money was handled in your family of origin. Who managed the family budget? Was that person a spender or a saver? Which are you?

Score: Tally your answers to questions one through fourteen by the letter of your answer:

a. __________ c. __________
b. __________ d. __________

To understand your results, see the explanation on the back of this page.

UNDERSTANDING THE RESULTS OF YOUR MONEY MOTIVATION QUIZ

Money means different things to different people based on a variety of factors such as temperament and life experiences. Often the meaning of money and the way it motivates us is subtle and something we are not always aware of.

This simple quiz is designed to give you an indication of how strongly you are influenced by the following money motivations: Freedom, Security, Power, and Love. None are inherently good or bad, although each certainly has its dark side.

The key to your money motivation is reflected in the relative number of a, b, c, or d answers.

"A" answers indicate that money relates to **Freedom**. To you money means having the freedom to do what you like.

"B" answers indicate that money relates to **Security**. You need to feel safe and secure and you desire the stability and protection that money supposedly provides.

"C" answers indicate that money relates to **Power**. Personal success and control are important to you, and you appreciate the power money sometimes provides.

"D" answers indicate that money relates to **Love**. You like to use money to express love and build relationships.

One of the keys to managing money wisely is to understand our relationship to it. We hope this exercise gives you some helpful insights. You may wish to share your scores with your spouse or a friend and discuss whether their perceptions of your money motivations are consistent with your scores.

DETERMINING AN AVERAGE MONTH FOR VARIABLE INCOME

The key to determining a budget in the case of a variable income (due to sales commissions or being self-employed, etc.), is to make a conservative estimate of net income for the coming year. Where possible, this would be done on the basis of the past several years' income. Conservative means not allowing one really good year to unduly influence the estimate for the coming year.

For example, if the past three years' net income were $37,000, $40,000, and 54,000—a really good year!—a conservative estimate for the coming year would be in the range of $44,000, not $56,000. The assumption is that this year may not be the exceptionally good year last year was.

In this example, a monthly budget would be $44,000 divided by 12 or $3,667. In the months when income exceeds $3,667, the excess would be put in a short-term savings account to be drawn on in months when income is less than $3,667.

A wise approach to variable income also includes predetermining the best use of any additional funds, in the event God blesses and actual income exceeds estimated income for the year. Thoughtful consideration before the fact will prevent impulsive decisions if and when the money becomes available, avoiding regrets afterward that it had not been spent in some other, better way.

WHAT HAPPENS TO YOUR RAISES?

Most of the time, the extra money we earn in raises gets used up. A few months later, we're not quite sure where it went. Yet, even a modest raise on a modest salary can add up to a significant amount of additional income in just a few years.

A 4 percent Annual Raise on a $30,000 Salary

	Year 1	Year 2	Year 3
4% raise	$31,200	$32,448	$33,745
Base salary	$30,000	$30,000	$30,000
Additional $ income	$ 1,200	$ 2,448	$ 3,745
Total additional income in three years = $7,393			

Consider the example in the chart above: a $30,000 salary and a 4 percent raise over a three-year period.

- The first year there is a $1,200 increase (4 percent of $30,000).
- The second-year salary is then $32,448, an additional margin of $2,448 from the original salary of $30,000.
- The third-year salary increases to $33,745, producing an increase from the original $30,000 of $3,745.

The total additional income in that three-year period adds up to almost $7,400—nearly one-fourth of the original salary! And that's just a three-year period! Taxes obviously impact the amount not given to charitable causes, but even the after-tax amount accumulates to a significant figure.

Deciding ahead of time how to use raises can be a key part of the strategy for reaching your financial goals.

SAVING

THE CUMULATIVE EFFECT OF LITTLE THINGS OVER AN EXTENDED PERIOD

A faucet dripping once a second can release fifty gallons in one week. In the same way, a slow trickle of money can gradually fill financial reservoirs to overflowing or drain them dry. Since everything we have ultimately belongs to God, every financial splash we make can have eternal significance and consequence. To have the financial freedom God intends, we need to learn how to use—rather than be victimized by—the cumulative effect of little things over an extended period.

To get a clearer picture of this important principle—what the Bible has to say about it and how small financial decisions really do add up—consider the Scriptures and examples below.

What the Bible Says

Scripture is clear in its support of the cumulative effect of a little effort over an extended period.

- "Go to the ant, you sluggard; consider its ways and be wise! . . . it stores its provisions in summer and gathers its food at harvest" (Proverbs 6:6–8).
- "If you have not been trustworthy in handling worldly wealth, who will trust you with true riches?" (Luke 16:11).
- "Everyone who competes in the games goes into strict training. They do it to get a crown that will not last; but we do it to get a crown that will last forever" (1 Corinthians 9:25).

Just a Dollar a Day

The cumulative effect of a little money, just one dollar a day, can be tremendous over a forty-five-year career depending on whether it is saved or added to debt. The chart below compares saving the dollar in a piggy bank, or a tax-sheltered mutual fund with a 10 percent return, versus charging the dollar to a credit card and incurring a 20 percent interest charge.

Years	Piggy bank	Invested in a mutual fund with a 10 percent rate of return	Charged to a credit card with a 20 percent interest rate
5	$1,825	$2,329	–$2,957
10	$3,650	$6,080	–$10,316
15	$5,475	$12,121	–$28,626
20	$7,300	$21,849	–$74,190
25	$9,125	$37,518	–$187,566
30	$10,950	$62,752	–$469,681
35	$12,775	$103,391	–$1,171,674
40	$14,600	$168,842	–$2,918,457
45	$16,425	$274,250	–$7,265,012

Major Purchases

The cumulative effect has a great impact on every major purchase. A $20,000 item can cost as little as $17,700 or as much as $25,500 depending on whether we allow the cumulative effect to work for us by saving for it in advance, or against us by incurring debt to purchase now. Consider this example:

To accumulate $20,000
in five years
at 5 percent interest
monthly payments
to ourselves
will have to be $295
and the total
of the sixty payments
will be $17,700.

To borrow $20,000
for five years
at 10 percent interest
monthly payments
to the finance company
will have to be $425
and the total
of the sixty payments
will be $25,500.

Start Young

Although students and young adults may not feel they have much in the way of assets, the greatest asset they have is *time.*

Saving $100 a month
during the first fifteen years
of a career,
and then saving nothing more
for the next twenty-five years
with a 10 percent return,
results in savings of $431,702.

Saving nothing
during the first fifteen years
of a career,
and then saving $100 a month
for the next twenty-five years
with a 10 percent return,
results in savings of $123,332.

It's Never Too Late

It's never too late to start making a little extra effort. For example, a $100,000 home loan for thirty years at 7 percent interest would have a monthly payment of $665, and the final cost of the loan would be double what was borrowed. However, paying just a little extra every month could dramatically reduce the total cost of the loan.

Extra Payment	Out of Debt	Total Interest
$0/month	30 years	$139,511
$25/month	<27 years	$121,296
$50/month	<24 years	$107,856
$100/month	<21 years	$ 89,003

DEBT

ESTABLISHING A DEBT REPAYMENT PLAN

1. **Establish a Spending Plan based on a temporary, spartan lifestyle.** This frees up every possible dollar for the top priority of debt reduction.

2. **Determine whether any nonessential assets can be sold.** Cash from the sale of assets can be used to give the debt repayment process a kick-start and provide the initial buffer to ensure success.

3. **List your debts from smallest to largest.** Do not pay attention to the interest rate of the debt.

4. **Pay the minimum payment on all debts and the maximum additional possible on the smallest.** The goal is to pay off smaller debts quickly. This will give a sense of accomplishment as well as simplify the process as the number of creditors is reduced. Although one could argue that the greatest overall savings would occur by paying off the highest interest debt first, the psychological impact of getting some debts paid quickly far exceeds the downside of the few additional interest dollars it may cost. When only debts of relatively the same amount remain to be paid, apply extra payment to the one with the highest interest.

5. **As each debt is paid off, roll the total amount you were paying to the next largest debt.** Add that amount to the minimum payment you were making.

6. **Continue this strategy until all debts are paid.** Do not reduce the total amount going to debt repayment as some debts are paid off. It is the "snowball" effect of rolling the previous payment into the next largest debt that gives this system its power.

7. **Incur no new debt, period!**
   Discipline will be necessary in this regard. Obviously, you will not make progress if you are continuing to incur new debt as you are attempting to pay off the old. Be creative. Have someone hold you accountable. Ask for God's help. Know in your heart you are doing the right thing.

8. **Discard credit cards.**
   Get rid of them. If you must have a card for travel or emergency, have only one.

9. **Reward yourself occasionally but modestly.**
   As progress is made and milestones are reached, it is appropriate to reward yourself. For some, the progress itself may be reward enough.

The following page shows a sample Debt Reduction Plan and an explanation for each column. A blank Debt Reduction Plan is included in the Forms section on page 321.

Sample Debt Reduction Plan

Item	Amount Owed	Interest	Minimum Monthly Payment	Additional Payment $ 150	Payment Plan and Pay-off Dates				
					3 Months	6 Months	15 Months	22 Months	26 Months
Sears	$372	18.0	$15	$165	Paid!				
Doctor	$550	0	$20	$20	$185	Paid!			
Visa	$1980	19.0	$40	$40	$40	$225	Paid!		
Master	$2369	16.9	$50	$50	$50	$50	$275	Paid!	
Auto	$7200	6.9	$259	$259	$259	$259	$259	$534	Paid!
Total	$12,471		$384	$534	$534	$534	$534	$534	0

- The first and second columns list to whom the debt is owed and the amount owed. Debts are listed in the order of lowest to highest amount.
- The third and fourth columns list the interest rate and the minimum monthly payment for each debt.
- The fifth column indicates the amount of additional payment above the minimum that can be made and adds that amount to the minimum payment for the first (smallest) debt listed.
- The remaining columns show how, as each debt is paid, the payment for it is rolled down to the next debt. Pay-off dates can be calculated in advance or simply recorded as they are achieved.

SPENDING

WHEN IS ENOUGH, ENOUGH?

The Bible doesn't give absolute guidelines for deciding when enough is enough, but the following nine principles can provide guidance for making wise financial decisions or evaluating a desire to purchase something.

1. Start with the right attitude: everything you have was created by God, is owned by God, and is to be used for God's purposes.
2. If the desire seems reasonable to mature Christian brothers and sisters whose discernment you respect, it is usually wise.
3. If the desire arises from pain over the plight of the poor, the unfortunate, or the disenfranchised, it is likely to be Spirit led and honoring to God.
4. If the desire involves the well-being of children, it is often right.
5. If the desire is primarily one of wanting to improve your own living conditions or lifestyle, you should not automatically assume it is wrong.
6. Consider whether the desire springs from an incompleteness in your relationship with Christ. Are you trying to fill with purchases an empty place in your heart?
7. Consider whether the resources of God's creation would be adequate to provide for all of his children the thing you desire for yourself.
8. Evaluate how important your desire seems in the context of your own mortality. Ask, "How important will this purchase seem to me when I am on my deathbed?"
9. Ask, "What would Jesus do in my situation?"

Points two through six adapted from *Freedom of Simplicity,* Richard J. Foster (HarperCollins, San Francisco, 1981), pages 88-89.

NOTHING DOWN, NOTHING A MONTH

Dave Ramsey

One way products and services are sold is by offering consumers unbelievable financing. Have you ever heard of "ninety days same as cash" or "no finance charges until January" or "no-interest financing"? Did it ever occur to you that in a world driven by money markets, a company offering zero interest with no ulterior motive would soon go broke?

Here is how it really works. First, the product is priced higher to cover the expense of the zero-interest financing. So there is actually no savings to begin with. But the story just starts there. Most dealers then sell the financing contract to a finance company to buy. And why would a finance company buy a contract at zero interest? Because the dealer (a furniture store, department store, electronics store, etc.)—who marked the item up in the first place—sells the financing contract to the finance company at a discount. Everyone but the purchaser wins. The dealer got what they wanted—an immediate sale at a regular profit (after the discount to the finance company). And when the buyer pays off the finance company, the finance company makes a profit because they got the buyer's contract at a discount from the dealer.

Second, and more importantly, over 70 percent of the time *the buyer does not pay off the dealer within the stated period.* Then the finance company gladly begins to charge interest and initiates a longer payment plan. When this occurs, the buyer often pays over 24 percent interest (if that state allows it) and the contract is on prepaid interest or "rule of 78's," which means there is a huge prepayment penalty. Plus, the company will add interest for the original ninety days, which is only "free" if paid off within the ninety days. They also typically will sell overpriced life and disability insurance to pay off their overpriced loan should something happen to your overpriced self. I once met a man who had life insurance on a loan against a rototiller!

This brilliant zero-interest plan now has turned into one of the worst financial decisions ever made because of the total cost of that item. A $1,000 couch at 25 percent for three years with credit life and disability insurance can end up costing at least $1,900.

Adapted from *Financial Peace,* Dave Ramsey (Viking Press, New York, 1992, 1997), pages 39-40.

A BIG DIFFERENCE IN A SHORT TIME

Question: I'm determined to be a better steward of God's resources. It would be an encouragement to me if I could do something that would make a big difference in a short time. Do you have a suggestion?

Answer: Except for housing (an expense that is pretty hard to change), cars are the biggest drain on most budgets. The average price of a new car in the United States is $19,000. Although cars remain reliable for an average of ten years and 120,000 miles, Americans tend to keep cars an average of only four-and-half years and 41,000 miles. Hanging on to your present car—or buying a good used car instead of a new one—may be the "one big thing" you could do to free up a significant amount of money for higher purposes.

Here are some facts you might consider when you decide whether having an older car is appropriate for you:

- A car loses most of its trade-in value in the first four years. If you trade in a new car after four years or less, you're paying a tremendous price for less than half the useful life of the car. On the other hand, if you buy a good used vehicle, you can get more than half the useful life of the car at a relatively thrifty price.

- We typically assume that new cars are more reliable than used cars. However, according to *Consumer Reports,* cars less than one year old make as many trips to the repair shop as cars that are four or five years old. The most reliable years of a car's life are the second and third years.

- When you select a new car, you have to base your decision on the manufacturer's claims, but used cars have a track record you can check. Most libraries have the *Consumer Reports Annual Buying Guide,* which has a chapter called "Ratings of Cars as Used Cars," and a huge chart giving "Six-Year Repair Records" for most models. Also, the National Highway Traffic Safety Administration has a toll-free hotline you can use to check to see if a used car has ever been recalled: (800) 424-9393.

- As a car gets older, the costs for gas and oil increase, but the costs for collision and theft insurance decrease.

- New car dealers typically save the best trade-in cars to sell on their own used car lots. These cars are often thoroughly checked and backed by a used car warranty. In some cases, used car buyers may even inherit the remainder of the manufacturer's new car warranty.

- Recently, leasing has become a popular option and is pushed heavily by many auto dealers. No wonder—it's a good deal for them. The appeal to many unsuspecting folks is the lower monthly payment. Payments should be lower—at the end of the lease you don't own anything! The up side for used car buyers is that an increasing number of leased cars are being turned in at the end of the lease and then turn up on used car lots.

Bottom Line:

- A recent comparison of the cost differential of keeping a four-year-old car for another four years and spending more on gas, oil, tires, and maintenance versus buying a new car showed the savings in keeping the four-year-old car to be over $5,000...assuming the new car would be paid for in cash. Add a couple thousand more dollars if it would be financed.

- A comparison of buying a two-year-old used car and keeping it for eight years versus leasing a new car every three years over a "driving lifetime" of forty-eight years revealed a staggering (almost unbelievable) differential of over $400,000.

You might quibble over some of the assumed costs, and the equation might change by some thousands of dollars, but the point is clear—huge savings are possible in the area of automobiles.

When Jesus spoke about avoiding "treasures on earth, where moth and rust destroy and where thieves break in and steal," he could have been speaking of cars. Probably his advice to Christian families today would be, "Keep the heap," and "Store up for yourselves treasures in heaven, where moth and rust do not destroy and where thieves do not break in and steal. For where your treasure is, there your heart will be also" (Matthew 6:19-21).

Information on costs and savings taken from "A Big Difference in a Short Time," by Jon Kopke, *College Hill Presbyterian Church Belltower News* (November, 1996).

UNPLUGGING FROM THE CONSUMPTIVE SOCIETY

"There are two ways of getting enough; one is to continue to accumulate more of it, the other is to desire less." *

Here are ten tips on simplifying life and being a good steward.

1. **Know where your money goes—develop a budget.**
   If we make no more than $25,000 per year for forty-five working years, we will have been the stewards of $1,125,000! How dare we consider handling that amount of money without keeping records and knowing where it went! Also, treat the giving portion of your budget differently than your operating budget. The goal of the operating budget is to hold down expenditures, but the goal of giving is to increase expenditures.

2. **Actively reject the advertising industry's persuasive and pervasive attempt to squeeze you into its mold.**
   Greet with sarcastic laughter all the patently false claims of phony TV commercials. Have your family shout in unison, "Who do you think you're kidding?" The goal of advertising is to create a desire for products. This is often done by creating dissatisfaction with what you now have, even though it may be quite satisfactory. Avoid settings that subject you to these overt efforts to create a mindset that is antithetical to Christ's teachings. Don't watch ads on TV. Don't read mail-order catalogs. Don't window shop in malls. Look at advertisements only after you have carefully determined your need for a particular product, and then only to seek the best quality at the lowest price.

3. **When you do decide it is right to purchase an item, see if God will provide it without you having to buy it.**
   Pray about it for a week, then consider if you still need it. If God hasn't provided it and you do still need the item, go ahead and purchase it. This practice integrates our needs with the concept of God's provision and has the additional benefit of avoiding impulse buying.

* Source of quote unknown.

4. **Stress the quality of life above quantity of life.**
Refuse to be seduced into defining life in terms of having, rather than being. Learn the wonderful lesson that to increase the quality of life means to decrease material desire—not vice versa.

5. **Make recreation healthy, happy, and gadget free.**
Consider noncompetitive games—why must there always be a winner? Avoid "spectatoritis." Modern spectator sports programs are obscene in their waste of human and material resources. It is a joy to watch some games, but addiction to doing so is another thing altogether. Develop the habit of homemade celebrations. Read together, play games, tell stories, have skits, invite other families in (and don't kill yourself preparing for them).

6. **Learn to eat sensibly and sensitively.**
Eliminate prepackaged dinners. Plan menus ahead, and buy only to meet the menu. Eliminate nonnutritious snack foods. Be conscious of the bio food chain. Grain-fed animals that require ten pounds of grain to produce one pound of meat are a luxury that the bio food chain cannot sustain for the masses of humanity. Get in on the joy of gardening. Dwarf fruit trees can supply large quantities of fresh fruit. Explore food cooperatives. Eat out less and make it a celebration when you do. Go without food one day a month and give the money you save to the poor. Buy less food rather than diet pills!

7. **Learn the difference between significant travel versus self-indulgent travel.**
Give your travel purpose. Travel inexpensively. Become acquainted with people as well as places.

8. **Buy things for their usefulness, not their status.**
Clothes can be quite presentable but inexpensive. Furniture can be used, refinished. Significant amounts of money can be saved buying good used cars and less expensive models. Are you alone after having raised your family? Consider inviting extended family, a college student, or single young person to live with you.

9. **Learn to enjoy things without owning them.**
Possession is an obsession in our culture. If we own it, we feel we can control it, and if we control it, we feel it will give us more pleasure. This is an illusion. Enjoy the beauty of the beach without

the compulsion to buy a piece of it. Many things can be shared among neighbors and friends. Give some things away just for the freedom it brings.

10. **Teach your children by word and deed about the varied uses of money. Provide clear guidelines about what you consider reasonable and unreasonable expenditures.**
Culture trains children to desire everything in sight when they enter a store. You do them no favor when you give in to their incessant demands. Get them what they need, not what they want; and in time, they will come to want what they need. Provide children with the experience of a growing self-governance. At a young age, offer them an allowance to give them the experience of saving and giving away, and decide with them how to spend the rest. In time, as their allowances and earning abilities grow, go one-half with them on necessities. Eventually, let them pay for everything themselves. Consider the goal of handling all income and expenses except for food and housing by age sixteen and financial independence, except for college expenses, by age eighteen. Consider approaching the cost of college as the young adult's responsibility, with parents acting as a safety net, as opposed to the cost of college being the parents' responsibility, with the young adult chipping in what they can—a very significant difference in philosophy.

* Adapted from *Celebration of Discipline*, Richard J. Foster, (HarperCollins, San Francisco, 1978, 1988, 1998), pages 78-83.

RECORD KEEPING

KEEPING MONTH-TO-DATE AND YEAR-TO-DATE TOTALS ON THE SPENDING RECORD

Often it can be helpful to know how you are doing in various categories not just for the current month but from the beginning of the Spending Plan year.

Lines 4 and 5 on the Spending Record provide that information.

Line 4 carries forward the amount each category was over or under the Spending Record from the month before. If this is done each month, and that figure is added to the over or under figure for the current month, the resulting figure represents the status of that category up to this point in the current budget year. In some cases, it may be of little interest to track certain accounts because they never vary from budget, and discipline is exercised in that area. But consider three categories of variable expenses—groceries, clothes, and going out—that have been tracked in the example on page 309.

This current month groceries were $34 under Spending Plan. A total of $320 was allocated but only $286 was spent. In previous months, a total of $118 (line 4) less than what had been allocated was actually spent. That amount, added to the $34 under for this month, gives a Year-to-Date (YTD) total of $152 under the budget (line 5). The food category is in good shape for the year.

The clothing category is $35 over budget for this month and $142 over for the year at the end of last month. As a result, this category is now $177 over for the year to date.

The going out category is $13 under the allotment for this month but was $96 over the allotment prior to this month. That means this category is $83 over the budget for the year.

This cumulative data can be very helpful as the year progresses. In this situation, if the holiday season were approaching, money would be available in the grocery category to have guests over for some nice holiday meals and still stay within the food budget for the year.

On the other hand, since the clothing category is over budget, it might be a good idea to pass the hint to others that it would be nice to get clothing gifts for Christmas! Moderation in the "going out" category is also in order to bring that Spending Plan category back into budget.

Month *October*

Spending Record Example

Daily Variable Expenses												
	Transportation		Household						Professional Services	Entertainment		
	Gas, etc.	Maint/ Repair	Groceries	Clothes	Gifts	Household Items	Personal	Other		Going Out	Travel	Other
(1) Spending Plan	80	40	320	60	80	75	50	—	—	100	70	40
	14	21	9	89	17	14	16	25		22	70	22 (sitter)
	17		87	6	55	22	18			46		
	9		43			9				19		
	19		106			31						
	11		21									
			7									
			13									
(2) Total	70	21	286	95	72	76	34	25	—	87	70	22
(3) (Over)/Under	10	19	34	(35)	8	(1)	16	(25)	—	13	—	18
(4) Last Month YTD			118	(142)						(96)		
(5) Total Year to Date			152	(177)						(83)		

1	2	3	4	5	6	7	8	9	10	11	12	13	14	15	16	17	18	19	20	21	22	23	24	24	26	27	28	29	30	31

- Use this page to record expenses that tend to be daily, variable expenses—often the hardest to control.
- Keep receipts throughout the day and record them at the end of the day.
- Total each category at the end of the month (line 2) and compare to the Spending Plan (line 1). Subtracting line 2 from line 1 gives you an (over) or under the budget figure for that month (line 3).
- To verify that you have made each day's entry, cross out the number at the bottom of the page that corresponds to that day's date.
- Optional: If you wish to monitor your progress as you go through the year, you can keep cumulative totals in lines 4 and 5.

IMPLEMENTATION ISSUES

More Than One Paycheck per Month

Item	Spending Plan ($)	1st Paycheck ($)	2nd Paycheck ($)
✓ Giving	250	125	125
✓ Saving	155		155
✓ Mortgage	970	970	
✓ Utilities	180		180
✓ Telephone	55		55
✓ Auto Payment	270		270
✓ Debt Repayment	110		110
Clothes	60		60
Gifts	80		80
Gas	80	40	40
Food	320	160	160
Household Misc.	75	30	45
Entertainment	100	50	50
Misc. Small Exp.	45		45
Total	**2,750**	**1,375**	**1,375**

✓ = paid by check

Making a one-time plan for how each paycheck will be allocated and simply referring to it each payday can be a wonderful way to ease the anxiety over questions like, "Which bill do I pay now?" and "Do I have enough for food and gas?"

In the above example, the person receives net take-home pay of $2,750 per month and is paid twice a month ($1,375 per pay period). The first column represents the Spending Plan for this family. They give $250 per month, save $155, have a mortgage payment of $970, etc.

Out of the first paycheck, checks are written for half of the monthly giving and for the mortgage. The rest of the check is used for half of the allocation for gas, food, entertainment, and a portion of household/miscellaneous.

Out of the second paycheck, checks are written for the other half of giving, all short-term savings, utilities, telephone, auto payment, and debt repayment. The remainder of that check covers the other half of gas, food, household items, entertainment, and the total for the monthly miscellaneous cash expenditures category.

In developing such a plan, it may be necessary to adjust some payment dates to balance out payments from the two checks. Once the plan has been devised, a copy can be kept with your checkbook, and it will eliminate any question about how each paycheck is to be used.

MONEY BUILDING UP IN ACCOUNTS

Once you begin placing money for certain categories that tend to build up over time into a short-term savings account, the question arises, "I have this savings account, and it has an amount of money in it, but how do I tell how much is for what category?"

The ledger sheet on page 314 shows an example to help answer this question. It is a ledger for a money market fund that contains short-term savings that have accumulated for several budgeting categories.

At the top, there is a description of the four funds into which money is being deposited each payday. In this case, the money is for emergencies, vacations, gifts, and auto repair. Lines 1 through 6 on the form are explained below.

Line 1 is the balance brought forward ($3,500) from the previous year. Based on the activity of that year, $2,100 of that $3,500 belongs to the Emergency account, $500 belongs to the Vacation account, $300 belongs to the Gift account, and $600 belongs to the Auto Repair account.

Lines 2 through 6 show the activity in the fund for the most recent month. On January 8, Dan bought Wendy a birthday gift. He entered $40 in the total balance column with a parenthesis around it indicating that it is an amount they need to subtract from the balance because they just spent $40. The $40 was also shown as being spent from the Gift fund.

On January 15, Dan got paid. He deposited $235 to the fund, so $235 is shown under the Total Balance column. Of that $235, $100 was for the Emergency fund, $70 was for the Vacation fund, $30 was for the Gift fund, and $35 was for the Auto Repair fund. They show those four figures under each of those funds. Since this was money being added to the funds, the figures do not have parentheses around them.

On January 17, Joe's Transmission Shop hit them hard with a $500 transmission job. They paid that out of their Auto Repair fund.

On January 25, they bought Sam and Mary a wedding present and recorded a $50 deduction from the total column, and a $50 deduction from the gift column.

On January 30, another paycheck was again distributed among the four categories.

The last line shows end-of-the-month totals based on adding and subtracting the transactions. The fund now has a total of $3,380 distributed as shown.

On page 323 is a blank form on which you can set up your own ledger to track savings.

Month *January*

Wendy and Dan's Money Market Fund for Short-Term Savings

	Date	Description	Total Fund Balance	Fund #1 *Emergency*	Fund #2 *Vacation*	Fund #3 *Gift*	Fund #4 *Auto Repair*	Fund #5
1	12/31	previous year balance forward	3500	2100	500	300	600	
2	1/8	Wendy's birthday gift	(40)			(40)		
3	1/15	Paycheck	235	100	70	30	35	
4	1/17	Joe's transmission	(500)				(500)	
5	1/25	Sam and Mary's wedding	(50)			(50)		
6	1/30	Paycheck	235	100	70	30	35	
		End of month total	3380	2300	640	270	170	

RECOMMENDED RESOURCES

BOOKS

Randy Alcorn, *Money, Possessions and Eternity.* Tyndale House Publishers, 1989.
Excellent integration of biblical truths and practical ways to live them out. Very challenging.

Ron Blue, *Master Your Money.* Thomas Nelson, 1997.
Nuts and bolts information and forms presented in a biblical context.

Richard Foster, *Freedom of Simplicity.* HarperSanFrancisco, 1998.
First published in 1981, this book is classic. An excellent resource for the person seeking to understand biblical stewardship at a deeper level. Foster points the way to finding harmony in a complex world through understanding simplicity.

Mary Hunt, *Mary Hunt's Debt-Proof Your Kids.* Broadman and Holman Publishers, 1998.
An excellent, hard-hitting book with lots of straight talk and good ideas for debt-proofing kids. Hunt also publishes the *Cheapskate Monthly* newsletter, that can be ordered by calling 800-550-3502.

Linda Kelly, *Two Incomes and Still Broke?* Crown Publishing, 1998.
The author introduces "new math" to show that there are many hidden costs involved with second incomes. She also provides advice and worksheets that enable a family to accurately assess the financial pros and cons of two incomes.

Austin Pryor, *Sound Mind Investing, Revised Edition. Victor Books, 2000.*
Pryor does an excellent job of presenting thoroughly researched material on a complex topic in layperson's terms . . . and does it all from a Christian perspective. However, don't even think about reading this book until consumer debt is repaid and a savings plan is in place! Austin also

publishes a monthly newsletter that can be obtained from his web site: www.soundmindinvesting.com.

David Ramsey, *Financial Peace.* Viking Press, 1992, 1997.
Lots of practical advice on avoiding "stuffitis" and learning how present sacrifice can produce long-term peace.

Juliet Schor, *The Overspent American.* HarperCollins, 1998.
A secular commentary that examines why so many of us feel materially dissatisfied in the midst of plenty. This Harvard economist looks at the plight of the consumer in the midst of a culture in which spending has become the ultimate social act.

Dallas Willard, *The Spirit of the Disciplines.* HarperSanFrancisco, 1991.
Chapter ten, "Is Poverty Spiritual?" is a powerful commentary on how to look at one's financial state from a biblical perspective. As quoted by Willard, "We need to reject both glorified aestheticism and sanctified consumerism."

AUDIO TAPES

The following audio tapes may be obtained by calling (800)570-9812 or by logging on to www.willowcreek.com.

M0042	John Ortberg	*It All Goes Back in the Box*
C9516	John Ortberg	*What Jesus Really Taught about Greed*
C9819	John Ortberg	*A Reward Worth Living For*
M9402	Bill Hybels	*The Truth about Earthly Treasures*
C9122	Bill Hybels	*The Gift of Giving*
M9820	Bill Hybels	*Words to the Rich*
AM9603	Bill Hybels	Achieving Financial Freedom (four-part series)
M9902	Bill Hybels	*Money, Sex, and Power: Who Owns What*
M9903	Bill Hybels	*Money, Sex, and Power: The Financial Ten Commandments*

M9949	Bill Hybels	*Truths that Transform, Part 9: Learn to Be Content in All Circumstances*
DF9906	Bill Hybels/ Dick Towner	*Establishing Financial Good $ense*

WEB SITES

www.bankrate.com
Lists certificate-of-deposit rates paid by banks throughout the country.

www.moneynet.com
Lists the seven-day annualized yields of the largest money market mutual funds open to individuals.

www.kbb.com
Lists Kelly Blue Book car values.

www.ssa.gov/retire
Provides online retirement income calculations. New calculators are being developed almost weekly. Also check the web sites of large brokerage houses.

www.ambest.com
Insurance company ratings by one of the industry's top rating services.

www.debtfree.org
Features a debt calculator to help you figure the amount of time needed to pay off a debt.

www.debtorsanonymous.org
The official site of the Debtors Anonymous Organization.

ADDITIONAL RESOURCES

Consumer Credit Counseling Service
Provides low-cost debt counseling. Call (800)388-2227 for the nearest location. Web site: www.nfcc.org

Consumer Credit Handbook
Explains how to fix errors on credit reports and what to do if you are turned down for credit. Write to Consumer Information Center, Pueblo, CO 81002.

Debtors Anonymous
Nationwide network of twelve-step groups to help folks with debt and spending addictions. Web site: www.debtorsanonymous.org

National Center for Financial Education
Provides free brochures on how to live debt free. Send self-addressed stamped envelope to P.O. Box 34070, San Diego, CA 92163.

Credit Report
To get a copy of your credit report contact Ecquifax at (800)685-1111 or on their web site: www.equifax.com

FORMS

Included on the following pages are perforated forms you can pull out and use. These include the Debt Reduction Plan, Form for Tracking Short-term Savings, Envelope Record-Keeping Worksheet, an expanded version of the Biblical Financial Principles taught in the course, the Spending Plan, and three copies of the Spending Record.

If you decide to use the written record-keeping system, these forms can be used for the next two months. Feel free to make photocopies of a blank Spending Record to use for subsequent months.

The Biblical Financial Principles are perforated so you can keep them handy and easily refer to them for the Bible's wisdom concerning the use of money.

Debt Reduction Plan

Item	Amount Owed	Interest	Minimum Monthly Payment	Additional Payment $______	Payment Plan and Pay-off Dates				
Total									

- The first and second columns list to whom the debt is owed and the amount owed. Debts are listed in the order of lowest to highest amount.
- The third and fourth columns list the interest rate and the minimum monthly payment for each debt.
- The fifth column indicates the amount of additional payment above the minimum that can be made and adds that amount to the minimum payment for the first (smallest) debt listed.
- The remaining columns show how, as each debt is paid, the payment for it is rolled down to the next debt. Pay-off dates can be calculated in advance or simply recorded as they are achieved.

Month ____________________

Form for Tracking Short-Term Savings

	Date	Description	Total Fund Balance	Fund #1	Fund #2	Fund #3	Fund #4	Fund #5

ENVELOPE RECORD-KEEPING WORKSHEET

Envelopes

The boxes below represent envelopes in which you will place cash for variable expenses each month. For each category, write in the category name (clothing, food, etc.) and the budgeted amount.

Category: ____________ $ ________	Category: ____________ $ ________
Category: ____________ $ ________	Category: ____________ $ ________
Category: ____________ $ ________	Category: ____________ $ ________
Category: ____________ $ ________	Category: ____________ $ ________

Checks

Use the entries below to list the monthly regular expenses you will pay by check.

Category ____________ $ ____________	Category ____________ $ ____________
Category ____________ $ ____________	Category ____________ $ ____________
Category ____________ $ ____________	Category ____________ $ ____________
Category ____________ $ ____________	Category ____________ $ ____________

BIBLICAL FINANCIAL PRINCIPLES

FOUNDATION OF THE GOOD $ENSE MINISTRY
Cultivate a steward's mindset.

GOD CREATED EVERYTHING
In the beginning there was nothing, and God created (Genesis 1:1).

GOD OWNS EVERYTHING
"'The silver is mine and the gold is mine,' declares the LORD Almighty" (Haggai 2:8). "Every animal of the forest is mine, and the cattle on a thousand hills" (Psalm 50:10). "The earth is the Lord's, and everything in it. The world and all its people belong to him." Psalm 24:1 NLT).

Flowing out of the fact that God created and owns everything is the logical conclusion that whatever we possess is not really ours, but belongs to God; we are simply entrusted with our possessions. Therefore, we are trustees, not owners. Although 1 Corinthians 4 (quoted below) does not directly refer to material possessions, its counsel is applicable to this aspect of life as well.

WE ARE TRUSTEES
"A person who is put in charge as a manager must be faithful" (1 Corinthians 4:1–2 NLT).

WE CAN'T SERVE TWO MASTERS
"No one can serve two masters. For you will hate one and love the other, or be devoted to one and despise the other. You cannot serve both God and money" (Matthew 6:24 NLT).

USE RESOURCES WISELY
"His master replied, 'Well done, good and faithful servant! You have been faithful with a few things; I will put you in charge of many things. Come and share your master's happiness!'" (Matthew 25:21–28).

PURSUE BIBLICAL, FINANCIAL KNOWLEDGE
"Buy the truth and do not sell it; get wisdom, discipline and understanding" (Proverbs 23:23). "Plans fail for lack of counsel, but with many advisers they succeed" (Proverbs 15:22).

MEASURABLE GOALS AND REALISTIC PLANS
"Commit to the LORD whatever you do, and your plans will succeed" (Proverbs 16:3).

TRUSTWORTHINESS MATTERS
"Whoever can be trusted with very little can also be trusted with much, and whoever is dishonest with very little will also be dishonest with much. So if you have not been trustworthy in handling worldly wealth, who will trust you with true riches? And if you have not been trustworthy with someone else's property, who will give you property of your own?" (Luke 16:10–12).

EARNING
The Diligent Earner—One who produces with diligence and purpose and is content and grateful for what he or she has.

God established work while Adam and Eve were yet in the Garden of Eden. God invited them to join him in the ongoing act of caring for creation. Work before the fall of Adam and Eve is a blessing, not a curse. All work has dignity. Our work should be characterized by the following principles.

BE DILIGENT; SERVE GOD
"Whatever you do, work at it with all your heart, as working for the Lord" (Colossians 3:23).

PROVIDE FOR OURSELVES AND THOSE DEPENDENT ON US
"Those who won't care for their own relatives, especially those living in the same household, have denied what we believe. Such people are worse than unbelievers" (1 Timothy 5:8 NLT).

BE GRATEFUL; REMEMBER FROM WHOM INCOME REALLY COMES
"Remember the LORD your God, for it is he who gives you the ability to produce wealth" (Deuteronomy 8:18).

ENJOY YOUR WORK; BE CONTENT IN IT
"It is good for people to eat well, drink a good glass of wine, and enjoy their work—whatever they do under the sun—for however long God lets them live. And it is a good thing to receive wealth from God and the good health to enjoy it. To enjoy your work and accept your lot in life—that is indeed a gift from God" (Ecclesiastes 5:18-19 NLT).

BE TRANSFORMED WORKERS
"Slaves, obey your earthly masters with respect and fear, and with sincerity of heart, just as you would obey Christ. Obey them not only to win their favor when their eye is on you, but like slaves of Christ, doing the will of God from your heart" (Ephesians 6:5-6).

EARN POTENTIAL, SHARE EXCESS
"If you are a thief, stop stealing. Begin using your hands for honest work, and then give generously to others in need" (Ephesians 4:28 NLT).

GIVING
The Generous Giver—One who gives with an obedient will, a joyful attitude, and a compassionate heart.

WE ARE MADE TO GIVE
We are made in the image of God (Genesis 1:26-27). God is gracious and generous. We will lead a more satisfied and fulfilled life when we give to others.

GIVE AS A RESPONSE TO GOD'S GOODNESS
"Every good and perfect gift is from above" (James 1:17). Therefore, we give out of gratefulness for what we have received.

GIVE TO FOCUS ON GOD AS OUR SOURCE AND SECURITY
"But seek first his kingdom and his righteousness and all these things will be given to you as well" (Matthew 6:33).

GIVE TO HELP ACHIEVE ECONOMIC JUSTICE
"Our desire . . . is that there might be equality. At the present time your plenty will supply what they need" (2 Corinthians 8:13-14). Throughout Scripture, God expresses his concern for the poor and calls us to share with those less fortunate.

GIVE TO BLESS OTHERS
"I will make you into a great nation and I will bless you; I will make your name great, and you will be a blessing. And I will bless you, and make your name great; and so you shall be a blessing" (Genesis 12:2-3). If we are blessed with resources beyond our needs, it is not for the purpose of living more lavishly but to bless others. We are blessed to be a blessing.

BE WILLING TO SHARE
"Command them [the rich] to do good, to be rich in good deeds, and to be generous and willing to share" (I Timothy 6:18).

GIVE TO BREAK THE HOLD OF MONEY
Another reason to give is that doing so breaks the hold that money might otherwise have on us. While the Bible doesn't specifically say so, it is evident that persons who give freely and generously are not controlled by money but have freedom.

GIVE JOYFULLY, GENEROUSLY, IN A TIMELY MANNER
"Out of the most severe trial, their overflowing joy and their extreme poverty welled up in rich generosity. For I testify that they gave as much as they were able, and even beyond their ability. Entirely on their own, they urgently pleaded with us for the privilege of sharing in this service to the saints" (2 Corinthians 8:1-5).

GIVE WISELY
"We want to avoid any criticism of the way we administer this liberal gift" (2 Corinthians 8:20).

GIVE EXPECTANTLY AND CHEERFULLY
"The one who plants generously will get a generous crop. You must each make up your own mind as to how much you should give. Don't give reluctantly or in response to pressure. For God loves the person who gives cheerfully" (2 Corinthians 9:6-7 NLT; see also verses 10-14).

MOTIVES FOR GIVING ARE IMPORTANT
Unless our motives are right, we can give all we have—even our bodies as sacrifices—and it will be for naught (I Corinthians13). We can be scrupulous with tithing and still not have the right motives. Jesus rebuked the religious leaders of his day for this very thing: " You hypocrites! You give a tenth of your spices—mint, dill and cummin. But you have neglected the more important matters of the law—justice, mercy and faithfulness" (Matthew 23:23).

SAVING
The Wise Saver—One who builds, preserves, and invests with discernment.

IT IS WISE TO SAVE
"In the house of the wise are stores of choice food and oil, but [the] foolish . . . devour all [they have]" (Proverbs 21:20). "Go to the ant, you sluggard; consider its ways and be wise! It has no commander, no overseer or ruler, yet it stores its provisions in summer and gathers it food at harvest" (Proverbs 6:8).

IT IS SINFUL TO HOARD
And he gave them an illustration: "A rich man had a fertile farm that produced fine crops. In fact, his barns were full to overflowing. So he said, 'I know! I'll tear down my barns and build bigger ones. Then I'll have room enough to store everything. And I'll sit back and say to myself, My friend, you have enough stored away for years to come. Now take it easy! Eat, drink, and be merry!' But God said to him, 'You fool! You will die this very night. Then who will get it all?' Yes, a person is a fool to store up earthly wealth but not have a rich relationship with God" (Luke 12:16-21 NLT).

CALCULATE COST; PRIORITIZE
"But don't begin until you count the cost. For who would begin construction of a building without first getting estimates and then checking to see if there is enough money to pay the bills? Otherwise, you might complete only the foundation before running out of funds. And then how everyone would laugh at you! They would say, 'There's the person who started that building and ran out of money before it was finished!'" (Luke 14:28-30 NLT).

AVOID GET-RICH-QUICK SCHEMES
"The trustworthy will get a rich reward. But the person who wants to get rich quick will only get into trouble" (Proverbs 28:20 NLT).

SEEK WISE COUNSELORS
"Let the wise listen and add to their learning, and let the discerning get guidance" (Proverbs 1:5).

ESTABLISH A JOB BEFORE BUYING HOME
"Finish your outdoor work and get your fields ready; after that, build your house" (Proverbs 24:27).

DIVERSIFY YOUR HOLDINGS
"Give portions to seven, yes to eight, for you do not know what disaster will come upon the land" (Ecclesiastes 11:2).

DEBT
The Cautious Debtor—One who avoids entering into debt, is careful and strategic when incurring debt, and always repays debt.

REPAY DEBT AND DO SO PROMPTLY
"The wicked borrow and do not repay, but the righteous give generously" (Psalm 37:21). " Do not say to your neighbor, 'Come back later; I'll give it tomorrow'—when you now have it with you" (Proverbs 3:28).

AVOID THE BONDAGE OF DEBT
"The rich rule over the poor, and the borrower is servant to the lender" (Proverbs 22:7).

DEBT PRESUMES ON THE FUTURE
"Now listen, you who say, 'Today or tomorrow we will go to this or that city, spend a year there, carry on business and make money.' Why, you do not even know what will happen tomorrow. What is your life? You are a mist that appears for a little while and then vanishes" (James 4:13–14).

DEBT CAN DENY GOD THE OPPORTUNITY TO WORK IN OUR LIVES AND TEACH US VALUABLE LESSONS
God may wish to show us his love by providing us with something we desire but for which we have no resources. If we go into debt to get it anyway, we deny him that opportunity (see Luke 12:22–32). In the same way that parents refrain from giving a child everything the child wants because parents know it isn't in the child's best interest, incurring debt can rob God of the opportunity to teach us through denial. Ecclesiastes 7:14 reminds us: "When times are good, be happy; but when times are bad, consider: God has made the one as well as the other."

DEBT CAN FOSTER ENVY AND GREED
"Beware! Don't be greedy for what you don't have. Real life is not measured by how much we own" (Luke 12:15).

GIVE AND PAY WHAT YOU OWE
"Give everyone what you owe them: Pay your taxes and import duties, and give respect and honor to all to whom it is due" (Romans 13:7 NLT).

DON'T CO-SIGN
"Do not co-sign another person's note or put up a guarantee for someone else's loan. If you can't pay it, even your bed will be snatched from under you" (Proverbs 22:26–27 NLT).

DEBT CAN DISRUPT SPIRITUAL GROWTH
"The fruit of the Spirit is love, joy, peace, patience, kindness, goodness, faithfulness, gentleness and self-control. Against such things there is no law" (Galatians 5:22-23).

SPENDING
The Prudent Consumer—One who enjoys the fruits of their labor yet guards against materialism.

BEWARE OF IDOLS
"You shall not make yourself an idol in the form of anything in heaven above or on the earth beneath or in the waters below" (Deuteronomy 5:8). Materialism—which so saturates our culture—is nothing less than a competing theology in which matter (things) is of ultimate significance; that is, things become gods or idols. " They . . . worshipped and served created things rather than the Creator" (Romans 1:25).

GUARD AGAINST GREED; THINGS DO NOT BRING HAPPINESS
"Beware! Don't be greedy for what you don't have. Real life is not measured by how much we own" (Luke 12:15).

SEEK MODERATION
"Give me neither poverty nor riches, but give me only my daily bread. Otherwise, I may have too much and disown you and say, 'Who is the LORD?' Or I may become poor and steal, and so dishonor the name of my God" (Proverbs 30:8-9).

BE CONTENT
"I know what it is to be in need, and I know what it is to have plenty. I have learned the secret of being content in any and every situation, whether well fed or hungry, whether living in plenty or in want. I can do everything through him who gives me strength" (Philippians 4:12–13).

"Godliness with contentment is great gain. For we brought nothing into the world, and we can take nothing out of it. But if we have food and clothing, we will be content with that" (1 Timothy 6:6–8).

DON'T WASTE GOD'S RESOURCES
"When they had all had enough to eat, he said to his disciples, 'Gather the pieces that are left over. Let nothing be wasted'" (John 6:12).

ENJOY A PORTION OF GOD'S PROVISION
"Command those who are rich in this present world not to be arrogant nor to put their hope in wealth, which is so uncertain, but to put their hope in God, who richly provides us with everything for our enjoyment. Command them to do good, to be rich in good deeds, and to be generous and willing to share. In this way they will lay up treasure for themselves as a firm foundation for the coming age, so that they may take hold of the life that is truly life" (1 Timothy 6:17–19).

WATCH YOUR FINANCES (BUDGET)
"Be sure you know the condition of your flocks, give careful attention to your herds; for riches do not endure forever, and a crown is not secure for all generations" (Proverbs 27:23–24).

SPENDING PLAN

EARNINGS/INCOME PER MONTH		TOTALS
Salary #1 (net take-home)	______	
Salary #2 (net take-home)	______	
Other (less taxes)	______	
TOTAL MONTHLY INCOME		$______

	% GUIDE		
1. GIVING			$______
Church		______	
OTHER CONTRIBUTIONS		______	
2. SAVING	**5–10%**		$______
EMERGENCY		______	
REPLACEMENT		______	
LONG TERM		______	
3. DEBT	**0–10%**		$______
CREDIT CARDS:			
VISA		______	
Master Card		______	
Discover		______	
American Express		______	
Gas Cards		______	
Department Stores		______	
EDUCATION LOANS		______	
OTHER LOANS:			
Bank Loans		______	
Credit Union		______	
Family/Friends		______	
OTHER		______	
4. HOUSING	**25–38%**		$______
MORTGAGE/TAXES/RENT		______	
MAINTENANCE/REPAIRS		______	
UTILITIES:			
Electric		______	
Gas		______	
Water		______	
Trash		______	
Telephone/Internet		______	
Cable TV		______	
OTHER		______	
5. AUTO/TRANSP.	**12–15%**		$______
CAR PAYMENTS/LICENSE		______	
GAS & BUS/TRAIN/PARKING		______	
OIL/LUBE/MAINTENANCE		______	

* This is a % of total monthly income. These are guidelines only and may be different for individual situations. However, there should be good rationale for a significant variance.

6. INSURANCE (Paid by you)	**5%**		$______
AUTO		______	
HOMEOWNERS		______	
LIFE		______	
MEDICAL/DENTAL		______	
Other		______	
7. HOUSEHOLD/PERSONAL	**15–25%**		$______
GROCERIES		______	
CLOTHES/DRY CLEANING		______	
GIFTS		______	
HOUSEHOLD ITEMS		______	
PERSONAL:			
Liquor/Tobacco		______	
Cosmetics		______	
Barber/Beauty		______	
OTHER:			
Books/Magazines		______	
Allowances		______	
Music Lessons		______	
Personal Technology		______	
Education		______	
Miscellaneous		______	
8. ENTERTAINMENT	**5–10%**		$______
GOING OUT:			
Meals		______	
Movies/Events		______	
Baby-sitting		______	
TRAVEL (VACATION/TRIPS)		______	
OTHER:			
Fitness/Sports		______	
Hobbies		______	
Media Rental		______	
OTHER		______	
9. PROF. SERVICES	**5–15%**		$______
CHILD CARE		______	
MEDICAL/DENTAL/PRESC.		______	
OTHER			
Legal		______	
Counseling		______	
Professional Dues		______	
10. MISC. SMALL CASH EXPENDITURES	**2–3%**		$______
TOTAL EXPENSES			$______

TOTAL MONTHLY INCOME	$______
LESS TOTAL EXPENSES	$______
INCOME OVER/(UNDER) EXPENSES	$______

Month ______________

Spending Record

Daily Variable Expenses													
	Transportation		Household						Professional Services	Entertainment		
	Gas, etc.	Maint/ Repair	Groceries	Clothes	Gifts	Household Items	Personal	Other		Going Out	Travel	Other
(1) Spending Plan													
(2) Total													
(3) (Over)/Under													
(4) Last Month YTD													
(5) Total Year–to–Date													

1	2	3	4	5	6	7	8	9	10	11	12	13	14	15	16	17	18	19	20	21	22	23	24	24	26	27	28	29	30	31

- Use this page to record expenses that tend to be daily, variable expenses—often the hardest to control.
- Keep receipts throughout the day and record them at the end of the day.
- Total each category at the end of the month (line 2) and compare to the Spending Plan (line 1). Subtracting line 2 from line 1 gives you an (over) or under the budget figure for that month (line 3).
- To verify that you have made each day's entry, cross out the number at the bottom of the page that corresponds to that day's date.
- Optional: If you wish to monitor your progress as you go through the year, you can keep cumulative totals in lines 4 and 5.

Month ____________

Spending Record

Monthly Regular Expenses (generally paid by check once a month)														
	Giving		Savings	Debt			Housing				Auto	Insurance		Misc. Cash Exp.
	Church	Other		Credit Cards	Educ.	Other	Mort./Rent	Maint.	Util.	Other	Pmts.	Auto/Home	Life/Med.	
(1) Spending Plan														
(2) Total														
(3) (Over)/Under														
(4) Last Mo. YTD														
(5) This Mo. YTD														

- This page allows you to record major monthly expenses for which you typically write just one or two checks per month.
- Entries can be recorded as the checks are written (preferably) or by referring back to the check ledger at a convenient time.
- Total each category at the end of the month (line 2) and compare to the Spending Plan (line 1). Subtracting line 2 from line 1 gives you an (over) or under the budget figure for that month (line 3).
- Use the "Monthly Assessment" section to reflect on the future actions that will be helpful in staying on course.

Monthly Assessment

Area	(Over)/Under	Reason	Future Action

Areas of Victory ____________________

____

Areas to Watch ____________________

____

Month ______________

Spending Record

Daily Variable Expenses												
	Transportation		Household						Professional Services	Entertainment		
	Gas, etc.	Maint/ Repair	Groceries	Clothes	Gifts	Household Items	Personal	Other		Going Out	Travel	Other
(1) Spending Plan												
(2) Total												
(3) (Over)/Under												
(4) Last Month YTD												
(5) Total Year–to–Date												

1	2	3	4	5	6	7	8	9	10	11	12	13	14	15	16	17	18	19	20	21	22	23	24	24	26	27	28	29	30	31

- Use this page to record expenses that tend to be daily, variable expenses—often the hardest to control.
- Keep receipts throughout the day and record them at the end of the day.
- Total each category at the end of the month (line 2) and compare to the Spending Plan (line 1). Subtracting line 2 from line 1 gives you an (over) or under the budget figure for that month (line 3).
- To verify that you have made each day's entry, cross out the number at the bottom of the page that corresponds to that day's date.
- Optional: If you wish to monitor your progress as you go through the year, you can keep cumulative totals in lines 4 and 5.

Month ______________

Spending Record

Monthly Regular Expenses (generally paid by check once a month)														
	Giving		Savings	Debt			Housing				Auto	Insurance		Misc. Cash Exp.
	Church	Other		Credit Cards	Educ.	Other	Mort./Rent	Maint.	Util.	Other	Pmts.	Auto/Home	Life/Med.	
(1) Spending Plan														
(2) Total														
(3) (Over)/Under														
(4) Last Mo. YTD														
(5) This Mo. YTD														

- This page allows you to record major monthly expenses for which you typically write just one or two checks per month.
- Entries can be recorded as the checks are written (preferably) or by referring back to the check ledger at a convenient time.
- Total each category at the end of the month (line 2) and compare to the Spending Plan (line 1). Subtracting line 2 from line 1 gives you an (over) or under the budget figure for that month (line 3).
- Use the "Monthly Assessment" section to reflect on the future actions that will be helpful in staying on course.

Monthly Assessment

Area	(Over)/Under	Reason	Future Action

Areas of Victory ______________________________

____

Areas to Watch ______________________________

____

Month ____________

Spending Record

Daily Variable Expenses												
	Transportation		Household						Professional Services	Entertainment		
	Gas, etc.	Maint/ Repair	Groceries	Clothes	Gifts	Household Items	Personal	Other		Going Out	Travel	Other
(1) Spending Plan												
(2) Total												
(3) (Over)/Under												
(4) Last Month YTD												
(5) Total Year-to-Date												

1	2	3	4	5	6	7	8	9	10	11	12	13	14	15	16	17	18	19	20	21	22	23	24	24	26	27	28	29	30	31

- Use this page to record expenses that tend to be daily, variable expenses—often the hardest to control.
- Keep receipts throughout the day and record them at the end of the day.
- Total each category at the end of the month (line 2) and compare to the Spending Plan (line 1). Subtracting line 2 from line 1 gives you an (over) or under the budget figure for that month (line 3).
- To verify that you have made each day's entry, cross out the number at the bottom of the page that corresponds to that day's date.
- Optional: If you wish to monitor your progress as you go through the year, you can keep cumulative totals in lines 4 and 5.

Month ______________

Spending Record

Monthly Regular Expenses (generally paid by check once a month)														
	Giving		Savings	Debt			Housing				Auto	Insurance		Misc. Cash Exp.
	Church	Other		Credit Cards	Educ.	Other	Mort./Rent	Maint.	Util.	Other	Pmts.	Auto/Home	Life/Med.	
(1) Spending Plan														
(2) Total														
(3) (Over)/Under														
(4) Last Mo. YTD														
(5) This Mo. YTD														

- This page allows you to record major monthly expenses for which you typically write just one or two checks per month.
- Entries can be recorded as the checks are written (preferably) or by referring back to the check ledger at a convenient time.
- Total each category at the end of the month (line 2) and compare to the Spending Plan (line 1). Subtracting line 2 from line 1 gives you an (over) or under the budget figure for that month (line 3).
- Use the "Monthly Assessment" section to reflect on the future actions that will be helpful in staying on course.

Monthly Assessment

Area	(Over)/Under	Reason	Future Action

Areas of Victory ______________________________

____

Areas to Watch ______________________________

____

WILLOW CREEK ASSOCIATION

Vision, Training, Resources

for Prevailing Churches

This resource was created to serve you and to help you in building a local church that prevails!

Since 1992, the Willow Creek Association (WCA) has been linking like-minded, action-oriented churches with each other and with strategic vision, training, and resources. Now a worldwide network of over 7,000 churches from more than ninety denominations, the WCA works to equip Member Churches and others with the tools needed to build prevailing churches. Our desire is to inspire, equip, and encourage Christian leaders to build biblically functioning "Acts 2" churches that reach increasing numbers of unchurched people, not just with innovations from Willow Creek Community Church in South Barrington, Illinois, but from any church in the world that has experienced God-given breakthroughs.

Willow Creek Conferences

Each year, thousands of local church leaders, staff and volunteers—from WCA Member Churches and others—attend one of our conferences or training events. Conferences offered on the Willow Creek campus in South Barrington, Illinois, include:

- Prevailing Church Conference—Offered twice a year, it is the foundational, overarching, training conference for staff and volunteers working to build a prevailing local church.
- Select ministry workshops—A wide variety of strategic, day-long workshops covering seven topic areas that represent key characteristics of a prevailing church; offered multiple times throughout the year.
- Promiseland Conference—Children's ministries; infant through fifth grade.
- Student Ministries Conference—Junior and senior high ministries.
- Arts Conference—Vision and training for Christian artists using their gifts in the ministries of local churches.
- Leadership Summit—Envisioning and equipping Christians with leadership gifts and responsibilities; broadcast live via satellite to scores of cities across North America.
- Contagious Evangelism Conference—Encouragement and training for churches and church leaders who want to be strategic in reaching lost people for Christ.
- Small Groups Conference—Exploring how developing a church of small groups can play a vital role in developing authentic Christian community that leads to spiritual transformation.

To find out more about WCA conferences, visit our website at www.willowcreek.com.

Regional Conferences and Training Events

Each year the WCA team leads a variety of topical conferences and training events in select cities across the United States. Ministry and topic topic areas include leadership, next-generation ministries, small groups, arts and worship, evangelism, spiritual gifts, financial stewardship, and spiritual formation. These events make quality training more accessible and affordable to larger groups of staff and volunteers.

To find out more about upcoming events in your area, visit our website at www.willowcreek.com.

Willow Creek Resources®

Churches can look to Willow Creek Resources® for a trusted channel of ministry tools in areas of leadership, evangelism, spiritual gifts, small groups, drama, contemporary music, financial stewardship, spiritual transformation, and more. For ordering information, call (800) 570-9812 or visit our website at www.willowcreek.com.

WCA Membership

Membership in the Willow Creek Association as well as attendance at WCA Conferences is for churches, ministries, and leaders who hold to an historic, orthodox understanding of biblical Christianity. The annual church membership fee of $249 provides substantial discounts for your entire team on all conferences and Willow Creek Resources, networking opportunities with other outreach-oriented churches, a bimonthly newsletter, a subscription to the Defining Moments monthly audio journal for leaders, and more.

To find out more about WCA membership, visit our website at www.willowcreek.com.

WillowNet www.willowcreek.com

This Internet resource service provides access to hundreds of Willow Creek messages, drama scripts, songs, videos, and multimedia ideas. The system allows you to sort through these elements and download them for a fee.

Our website also provides detailed information on the Willow Creek Association, Willow Creek Community Church, WCA membership, conferences, training events, resources, and more.

WillowCharts.com www.WillowCharts.com

Designed for local church worship leaders and musicians, WillowCharts.com provides online access to hundreds of music charts and chart components, including choir, orchestral, and horn sections, as well as rehearsal tracks and video streaming of Willow Creek Community Church performances.

The NET http://studentministry.willowcreek.com

The NET is an online training and resource center designed by and for student ministry leaders. It provides an inside look at the structure, vision, and mission of prevailing student ministries from around the world. The NET gives leaders access to complete programming elements, including message outlines, dramas, small group questions, and more. An indispensable resource and networking tool for prevailing student ministry leaders!

Contact the Willow Creek Association

If you have comments or questions, or would like to find out more about WCA events or resources, please contact us:

Willow Creek Association
P.O. Box 3188
Barrington, IL 60011-3188
Phone: (800) 570-9812 or (847) 765-0070
Fax (888) 922-0035 or (847) 765-5046
Web: www.willowcreek.com

Resources You've Been Waiting For . . .

To Build the Church You've Been Dreaming About

Willow Creek Resources

What do you dream about for your church?

At the Willow Creek Association we have a dream for the church . . . one that envisions the local church—your church—as the focal point for individual and community transformation.

We want to partner with you to make this happen. We believe when authentic, life-changing resources become an integral part of everyday life at your church—and when they become an extension of how your ministries function—transformation is inevitable.

It then becomes normal for people to:

- identify their personal style of evangelism and use it to bring their unchurched friends to Christ
- grow in their ability to experience God's presence with them in each moment of the day
- feel a deep sense of community with others
- discover their spiritual gifts and put them to use in ministry
- use their resources in ways that honor God and care for others

If this is the kind of church you're dreaming about, keep reading. The following pages highlight just a few of the many Willow Creek Resources available to help you. Together, we can build a local church that transforms lives and transfigures communities. We can build a church that *prevails.*

Everything You Need to Launch and Lead a B

Good $ense

Transformational Stewardship for Today's Church

DICK TOWNER
with contributions from the Good $ense Ministry team of
Willow Creek Community Church

GRACE. JOY. FREEDOM.
Are these the first words that come to mind when you think of stewardship? They could be! Grace, joy, and freedom are words people most often use to describe Good $ense—a field-tested, proven resource for changing hearts and lives in the area of finances.

There is a tremendous need for churches to educate and assist people with managing their resources in God-honoring ways. Implementing a Good $ense Ministry in your church does that. It can relieve the crushing stress and anxiety caused by consumer debt, restore marriages torn by conflict over money, and heal the wounded self-esteem and shattered confidence resulting from poor financial decisions.

Most significantly, a Good $ense Ministry can be used by God to remove stumbling blocks to spiritual growth. This is *transformational stewardship*. The result is a congregation whose finances—and lives—are characterized by grace, joy, and freedom.

Complete Kit	0744137241
Casting a Vision for Good $ense video	0744137268
Implementation Guide	074413725X
Budget Course Leader's Guide	0744137276
Budget Course Participant's Guide	0744137284
Budget Course Video	0744137292
Budget Course PowerPoint CD-ROM	0744137306
Counselor Training Workshop Leader's Guide	0744137314
Counselor Training Workshop Participant's Guide	0744137322
Counselor Training Workshop Video	0744137330
Counselor Training Workshop PowerPoint CD-ROM	0744137349

al Stewardship Ministry that Transforms Lives

Based on over sixteen years of ministry at Willow Creek Community Church, Good $ense includes resources designed to train and equip: church leaders, volunteer counselors, and everyone in your church.

Envision Church Leaders and Implement the Ministry

Good $ense Implementation Guide
Casting a Vision for Good $ense Video

FOR: Senior church leaders.

PURPOSE: To envision and equip leaders to launch and lead a year-round stewardship ministry.

CONTENTS: The Implementation Guide provides a roadmap for implementing a Good $ense Ministry as well as the practical tools to do so. The video provides an inspiring tool to help leaders cast vision for a Good $ense Ministry.

Equip Volunteer Counselors

Good $ense Counselor Training Workshop

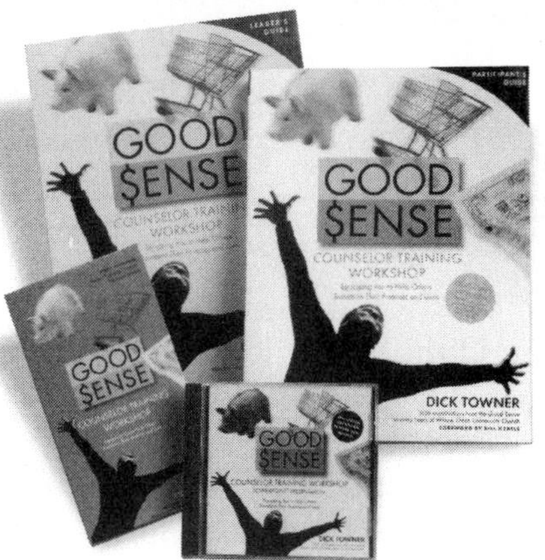

FOR: Volunteer counselors.

PURPOSE: To train and equip laypersons to provide free, biblically-based, confidential counsel to assist families and individuals in addressing financial questions or difficulties.

CONTENTS: This one-day, five-session workshop offers training for volunteers to become Good $ense budget counselors.

Train Everyone in Your Church

Good $ense Budget Course

FOR: Everyone in your church—not just those in financial difficulty.

PURPOSE: To train every believer to integrate Biblical Financial Principles into their lives—financially and spiritually.

CONTENTS: Contrasts the Pull of the Culture with the Mind and Heart of God in five areas—earning, giving, saving, spending, debt. Six, fifty-minute sessions can be taught in a variety of formats.

Experience the Reality of God's Presence Every Day

An Ordinary Day with Jesus

JOHN ORTBERG AND RUTH HALEY BARTON

An Ordinary Day with Jesus uses aspects of an ordinary day and illustrates how we can connect with Jesus in those moments. Participants will learn how to:

- wake up and go to sleep in Jesus' name
- review their day with God
- silence competing voices in order to hear God's leadings
- experience time alone with God as an opportunity not an obligation
- use their own unique spiritual pathway to connect with God
- eliminate hurry and simplify their pace of life
- and much more!

	WCA ISBNs	Zondervan ISBNs
Leader's Guide	0744137217	0310245850
Participant's Guide	0744137225	0310245869
Drama Vignettes Video	0744136652	0310245575
PowerPoint CD-ROM	0744137195	0310245885
Complete Kit	0744136555	0310245877

Train Believers to Share Christ Naturally

Becoming a Contagious Christian

Mark Mittelberg, Lee Strobel, Bill Hybels

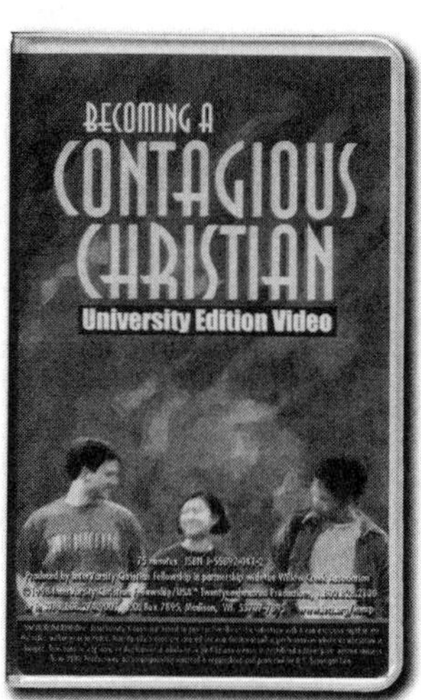

Over 500,000 believers have been trained to share their faith confidently and effectively with this proven curriculum. In eight, fifty-minute sessions, participants experience the joy of discovering their own unique evangelism style, learn how to transition conversations to spiritual topics, present gospel illustrations, and more.

Leader's Guide	0310500818
Participant's Guide	0310501016
Drama Vignettes Video	0310201691
Overhead Masters	0310500915
Complete Kit	0310501091

Also available—*Becoming a Contagious Christian* University Edition Video. Developed in partnership with InterVarsity Christian Fellowship, these drama vignettes feature college students building relationships with seekers. Designed to be used with the adult version of the curriculum.

Video	1558920412

Equip Students to Lead this Generation to Christ

Becoming a Contagious Christian Youth Edition

Mark Mittelberg, Lee Strobel, Bill Hybels

Revised and expanded for students by Bo Boshers

The award-winning *Becoming a Contagious Christian* curriculum has been revised and expanded to equip junior high and high school students to be contagious with their faith.

In eight, fifty-minute sessions, students learn how to:

- Develop relationships intentionally
- Transition an ordinary conversation to a spiritual conversation
- Tell their personal story of meeting Christ
- Share the gospel message using two different illustrations
- Answer ten common objections to Christianity
- Pray with a friend to receive Christ

Real stories of students who have led their friends to Christ make the material come alive as students see how God can work through them.

Leader's Guide	0310237718
Student's Guide	0310237734
Drama Vignettes Video	0310237742
Complete Kit	0310237696

Bestselling Books by John Ortberg

If You Want to Walk on Water, You've Got to Get Out of the Boat

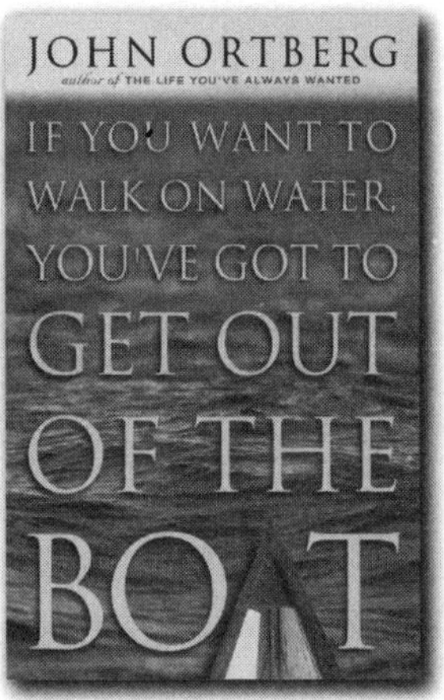

With engaging illustrations, humor, and relevant applications, John Ortberg explains how discerning God's call, rising above fear, and taking next steps can strengthen your faith.

Hardcover 0310228638

The Life You've Always Wanted

Gain a fresh perspective on the power of spiritual disciplines and how God can use them to deepen your relationship with him.

Hardcover 0310212146
Softcover 0310226996

Love Beyond Reason

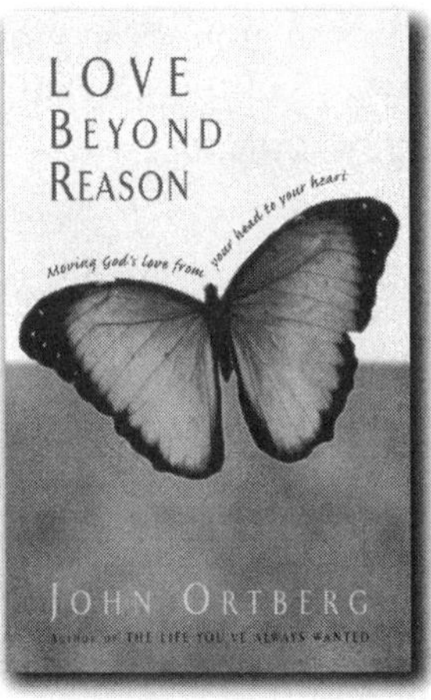

Filled with poignant illustrations, real-life applications, and humor, *Love Beyond Reason* describes the numerous facets of God's reason-defying, passionate love.

Hardcover 0310212154
Softcover 0310234492

Life-changing Small Group Resources

Pursuing Spiritual Transformation Series

John Ortberg, Laurie Pederson, Judson Poling

Explore fresh, biblically-based ways to think about and experience life with God through Willow Creek's Five Gs: Grace, Growth, Groups, Gifts, and Good Stewardship (Giving). Each study challenges the popular notion that merely "trying harder" will lead to Christlikeness. Instead, this series helps you identify the practices, experiences, and relationships God can use to help you become the person he longs for you to be.

Fully Devoted	0310220734
Grace	0310220742
Growth	0310220750
Groups	0310220769
Gifts	0310220777
Giving	0310220785

New Community Series

Bill Hybels, John Ortberg

New Community studies provide in-depth Bible study, thought-provoking questions, and community building exercises so groups can grow in faith together.

1 John: Love Each Other	0310227682
1 Peter: Stand Strong	0310227739
Acts: Build Community	0310227704
Colossians: Discover the New You	0310227690
Exodus: Journey Toward God	0310227712
James: Live Wisely	0310227674
Philippians: Run the Race	0310233143
Romans: Find Freedom	0310227658
Parables: Imagine Life God's Way	0310228816
Revelation: Experience God's Power	0310228824
Sermon on the Mount, part 1: Connect with God	0310228832
Sermon on the Mount, part 2: Connect with Others	0310228840

Bible 101 Series

Bill Donahue, Kathy Dice, Judson Poling, Michael Redding, Gerry Mathisen

Bible 101 provides a solid, foundational understanding of God's Word in a format uniquely designed for a small group setting.

Cover to Cover	0830820639
Foundations	0830820612
Great Themes	0830820671
Interpretation	0830820655
Parables and Prophecy	0830820663
Personal Devotion	083082068X
Study Methods	0830820647
Times and Places	0830820620

InterActions Series

Bill Hybels

InterActions studies encourage participants to share interests, experiences, values, and lifestyles, and uses this common ground to foster honest communication, deeper relationships, and growing intimacy with God.

Authenticity	031020674X
Community	0310206774
Lessons in Love	0310206804
Marriage	0310206758
The Real You	0310206820
Commitment	0310206839
Essential Christianity	0310224438
Evangelism	0310206782
Freedom	0310217172
Getting a Grip	0310224446
Parenthood	0310206766
Serving Lessons	0310224462
Overcoming	0310224454
Character	0310217164
Fruits of the Spirit	0310213150
Jesus	0310213169
Prayer	0310217148
Psalms	0310213185
Transparency	0310217156
Transformation	0310213177

Walking with God Series

Don Cousins, Judson Poling

Practical, interactive, and biblically based, this dynamic series follows a two-track approach. Series 1 plugs new believers into the transforming power of discipleship to Christ. Series 2 guides mature believers into a closer look at the church.

Series 1

"Follow Me"	0310591635
Friendship with God	0310591430
The Incomparable Jesus	0310591538
Leader's Guide	0310592038

Series 2

Building Your Church	031059183X
Discovering Your Church	0310591732
Impacting Your World	0310591937
Leader's Guide	0310592135

Tough Questions Series

Garry Poole, Judson Poling

Created for seeker small groups, this series guides participants through an exploration of key questions about and objections to Christianity.

How Does Anyone Know God Exists?	0310222257
Is Jesus the Only Way?	0310222311
How Reliable Is the Bible?	0310222265
How Could God Allow Suffering/Evil?	0310222273
Don't All Religions Lead to God?	031022229X
Do Science and the Bible Conflict?	031022232X
Why Become a Christian?	0310222281
Leader's Guide	0310222249

Build a Church Where Nobody Stands Alone

Building a Church of Small Groups

Bill Donahue, Russ Robinson

Experience the vision, values, and necessary initial steps to begin transitioning your church from a church *with* small groups to a church *of* small groups in this groundbreaking book.

Hardcover 0310240352

The Connecting Church

Randy Frazee

Pastor Randy Frazee explores the three essential elements of connecting churches: Common Purpose, Common Place, and Common Possessions. An excellent resource to help leaders create the kind of church where every member feels a deep sense of connection.

Hardcover 0310233089

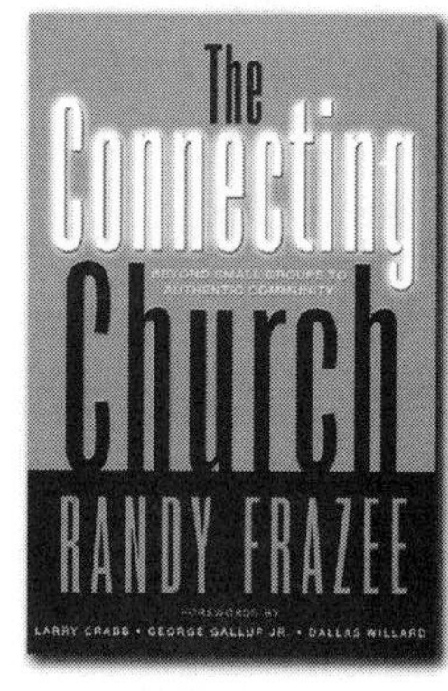

Leading Life-Changing Small Groups

Bill Donahue

Leading Life-Changing Small Groups covers everything from starting, structuring, leading, and directing an effective small group, to developing effective leaders.

Softcover 0310205956

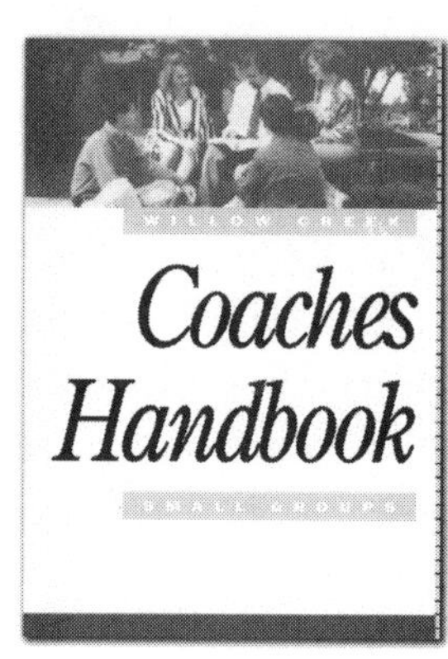

The Coaches Handbook

This comprehensive resource provides teaching and tools to those who coach small group leaders. An excellent resource for small group ministry leaders.

Softcover 0744106567

Evangelistic Resources—for Believers and Seekers

Building a Contagious Church

Mark Mittelberg with contributions from Bill Hybels

Building a Contagious Church offers a proven, six-stage process to help your church become evangelistically contagious.
Hardcover 0310221498

Becoming a Contagious Christian

Bill Hybels and Mark Mittelberg

This groundbreaking book offers practical insights and real-life applications on how to reach friends and family for Christ.
Softcover 0310210089
Hardcover 0310485002

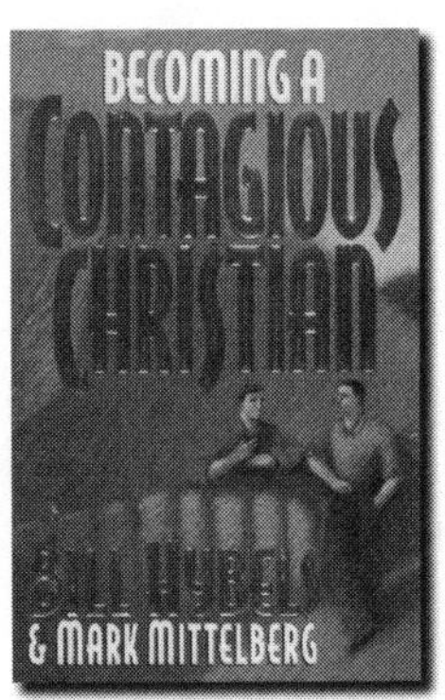

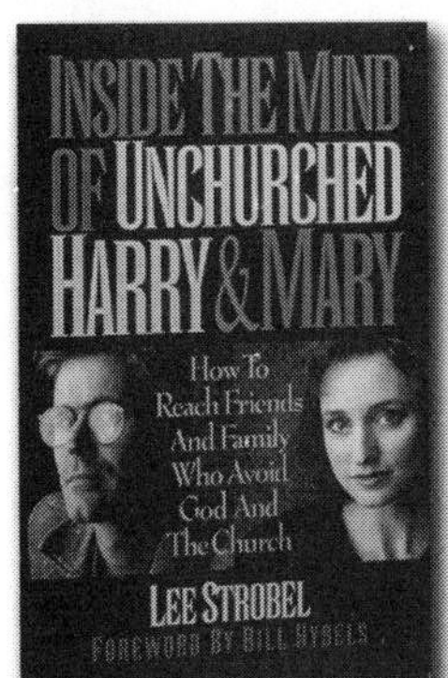

Inside the Mind of Unchurched Harry and Mary

Lee Strobel

Learn how to build relational bridges with friends and family who avoid God and the church.
Softcover 0310375614

The Case for Christ

Lee Strobel

Award-winning investigative reporter Lee Strobel puts the toughest questions about Christ to acclaimed psychology, law, medicine, and biblical studies experts.
Softcover 0310209307

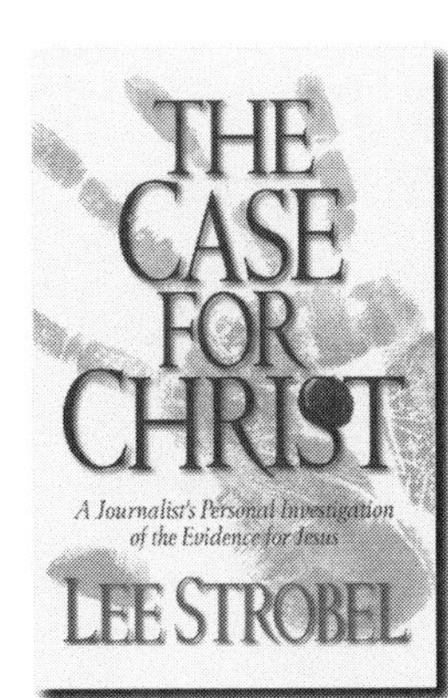

The Case for Christ Student Edition

Lee Strobel with Jane Vogel

Based on the best-selling book for adults, the student edition is a fast, fun, informative tour through the evidence for Christ designed especially for students.
Softcover 0310234840

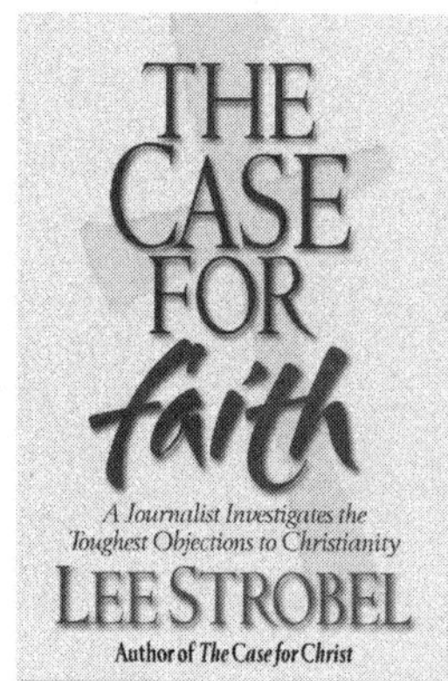

The Case for Faith

Lee Strobel

Tackles eight obstacles to faith, such as suffering, the doctrine of hell, evolution, and more.
Softcover 0310234697

The Journey

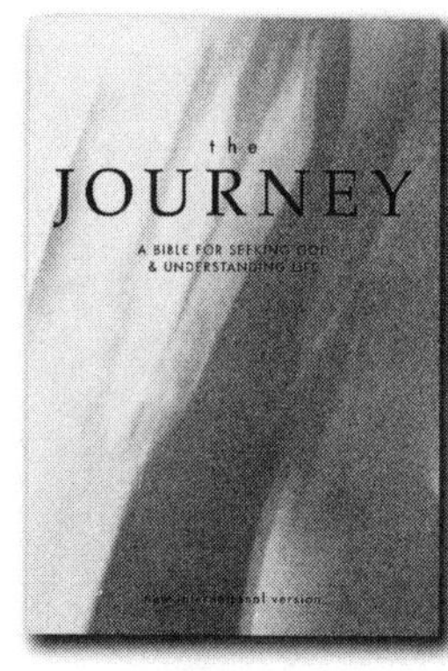

Uniquely designed to help spiritual seekers discover the relevance of Christianity.
Softcover 031092023X

Christianity 101

Gilbert Bilezikian

Explores eight core beliefs of the Christian faith. A great resource for both seekers and believers.
Softcover 0310577012

Proven Resources for Church Leaders

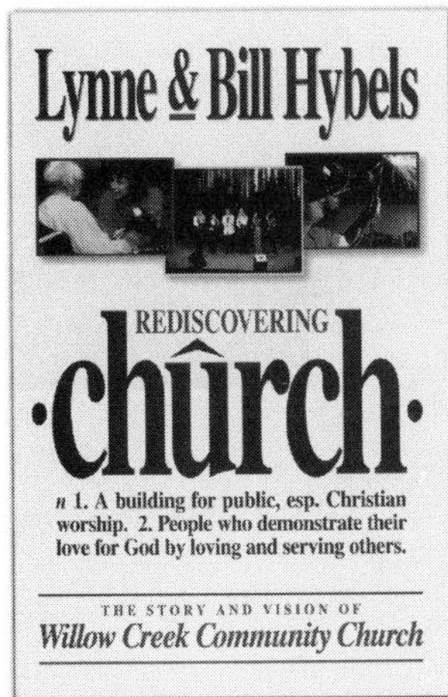

Rediscovering Church

Lynne and Bill Hybels

Rediscovering Church relates the beginnings of Willow Creek Community Church as well as its joys and struggles, and the philosophy and strategies behind its growth.

Softcover 0310219272

Leadership by the Book

Ken Blanchard, Bill Hybels, Phil Hodges

Filled with insights and simple strategies for becoming a successful leader, this best-selling book outlines the story of a professor and a pastor who mentor a young professional in management skills and ethics.

Hardcover 1578563089

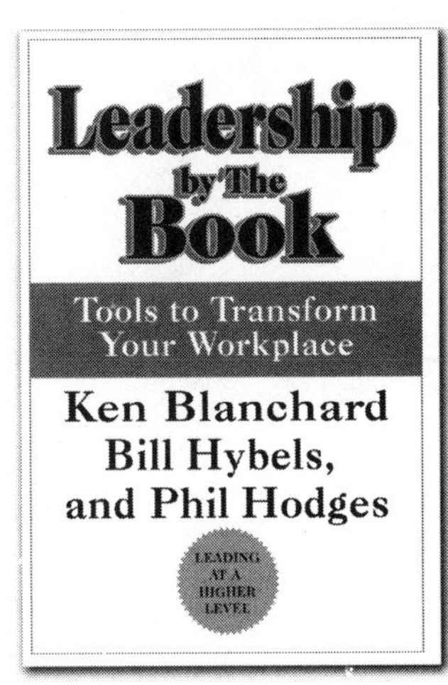

Casting a Courageous Vision

Bill Hybels, John Maxwell

In this inspiring video, Bill Hybels challenges those who attend Willow Creek to become active participants in fulfilling the mission God has for them. John Maxwell then shares principles to help you cast a compelling vision for your church.

Video 0310676045

An Inside Look at the Willow Creek Worship Service

Featuring John Ortberg

Experience Willow Creek's weekly worship service, New Community. Featured is a look at Willow Creek's worship style with patterns and ideas that can be integrated into your church's unique worship style.
Video 0310223571

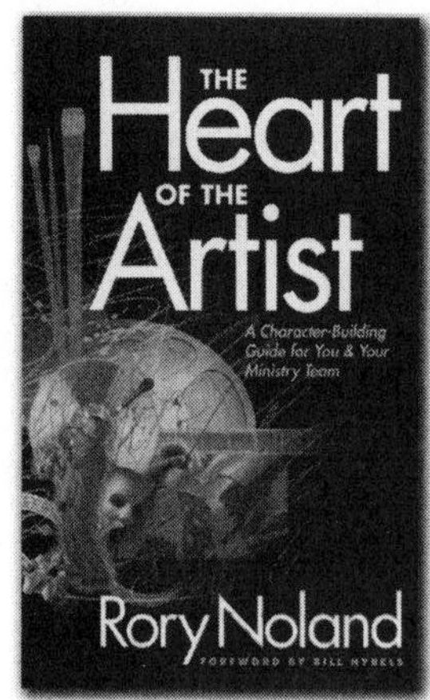

The Heart of the Artist

Rory Noland

Willow Creek's music director looks at the unique gifts and challenges artists bring to spiritual life.
Softcover 0310224713

Drama Ministry

Steve Pederson

A powerful and practical "how-to" book for drama directors from the director of Willow Creek's drama ministry.
Softcover 0310219450

The Source

Scott Dyer and Nancy Beach

Whatever the size of your church, this book will help you and your staff plan creative, impactful services.
Softcover 0310500214